Frost & Flame

Frost & Flame

Matthew Petchinsky

Frost & Flame: The Enchanted Yule Grimoire of 1000 Winter Spells

By: Matthew Petchinsky

Introduction
Yule and Its Significance

Yule, celebrated on the winter solstice, is one of the oldest known holidays, steeped in rich traditions that honor the cyclical nature of life, death, and rebirth. Its origins trace back to ancient pagan cultures, particularly the Germanic and Norse peoples, who viewed the solstice as a time of profound spiritual significance. Yule marks the longest night of the year, a moment when the darkness reaches its peak, and the promise of returning light is at its most poignant. The ancient peoples saw this as a turning point—a time when the sun, having withdrawn into the shadows, is reborn to begin its journey back to full strength.

Yule's celebration is rooted in the idea of the sun's rebirth and the promise of renewal. The dark, cold winter months provide a period of reflection, hibernation, and inner work, much like nature itself goes into dormancy. However, on the solstice, the cycle shifts. The return of the sun heralds new beginnings, hope, and the eventual awakening of the earth. Symbolic acts during Yule, such as lighting candles and burning Yule logs, invoke the sun's light, offering warmth, guidance, and protection against the darkness. The use of evergreen plants like holly, ivy, and mistletoe during Yule rituals embodies the eternal spirit of life, growth, and continuity even in the bleakest of times.

In modern practices, Yule remains a time of introspection, celebrating the renewal of light within and around us. It invites us to shed the old and embrace the new, aligning our energy with the earth's natural rhythm. It is not merely a historical festival but a reminder of the inherent cycles that govern our lives and the universe. By understanding Yule's deep roots and its symbolism of rebirth, light in darkness, and nature's power, we can appreciate its significance and incorporate its magic into our spiritual practice.

Purpose of the Spell Book

"Frost & Flame: The Enchanted Yule Grimoire of 1000 Winter Spells" serves as a bridge between ancient Yule traditions and contemporary magical practices. This spell book is designed to help practitioners harness the potent energy of Yule for personal growth, transformation, and the manifestation of desires in various aspects of life. Each spell within these pages taps into the unique magic of winter—whether it's the stillness of the snow, the warmth of the hearth, or the promise of returning sunlight. The power of Yule lies in its ability to help us reflect on the past year, release what no longer serves us, and set intentions for the new year ahead.

The spells and rituals in this book are crafted to work with the season's natural energies, guiding practitioners in creating positive change and reinforcing connections to the cycles of nature. Whether you seek protection during winter's darkness, wish to manifest prosperity, or want to deepen your relationships, this grimoire provides spells to align your intentions with Yule's magical atmosphere. It also offers tools for personal reflection, self-care, and community connection, promoting balance and harmony during a time when the world is often at its most hectic.

By using this spell book, you can learn to work with the elements of winter—cold and warmth, darkness and light—to create a sacred space for magical workings. Each chapter explores a different facet of Yule magic, offering a rich array of spells, rituals, and practices to incorporate into your spiritual journey. This book is not only a collection of spells but a companion to guide you through the Yule season, helping you embrace its mysteries and gifts fully.

Setting Intentions for Yule

Setting intentions during Yule is an essential practice that aligns your magical work with the energy of the season. As the darkness of the longest night gives way to the returning light, it presents an opportunity to reflect on the past, release burdens, and plant the seeds of new beginnings. Before delving into the spell work, take time to meditate on what you wish to let go of and what you want to invite into your life in the coming year.

To set your intentions, find a quiet, peaceful place where you can sit undisturbed. Begin by lighting a candle, representing the sun's return, and close your eyes. Take several deep breaths, inhaling the crisp, fresh energy of the winter season and exhaling all negativity. Allow your mind to drift to the events, emotions, and experiences of the past year. What do you feel ready to release? What dreams and goals do you wish to cultivate moving forward?

Once you have clarity, write down your intentions in a journal or on a piece of parchment. Use affirmative and specific language, focusing on positive outcomes. For example, instead of saying, "I want to stop feeling stressed," frame it as, "I invite calm and peace into my daily life." Setting intentions in this way aligns your energy with your desires and creates a roadmap for the spell work you will undertake.

After setting your intentions, consider holding a simple ritual to reinforce them. You might bury your written intentions in the earth as a symbolic act of planting the seeds for future growth or burn them in a fire-safe bowl, releasing them to the universe. This act of intention-setting is the first step in your Yule magic, serving as the foundation upon which all other spells and rituals in this book are built.

Tools of Yule Magic

To perform the spells and rituals within this grimoire, certain tools are traditionally associated with Yule magic. Each tool carries a unique energy that enhances your practice, allowing you to connect more deeply with the season's spirit. Here is a guide to some of the essential tools used in Yule spellcasting:

- **Candles:** Representing the returning sun and the light within each of us, candles are a central part of Yule rituals. Use candles in colors like red, green, gold, and white to invoke specific energies. Red symbolizes vitality and courage, green for growth and renewal, gold for prosperity, and white for purity and peace.
- **Herbs and Spices:** Incorporate herbs and spices associated with Yule to infuse your spells with seasonal energy. Holly, mistletoe, pine, cinnamon, cloves, and nutmeg are just a few examples. These herbs can be used in sachets, incense, or as offerings during rituals. Each herb carries its own magical properties; for instance, mistletoe symbolizes protection and love, while cinnamon is known for its power to attract prosperity.
- **Crystals:** Crystals are powerful tools that amplify your intentions and help you connect with Yule's energy. Stones such as clear quartz, snowflake obsidian, garnet, and bloodstone resonate with the season's themes of clarity, protection, and renewal. Place them on your altar, carry them with you, or use them during meditation to enhance your spell work.
- **Symbols:** Yule symbols like the Yule log, sun wheels, holly, and evergreen wreaths can be used to decorate your altar or sacred space, invoking the season's spirit. The Yule log, traditionally burned in the hearth, symbolizes the warmth and light of the returning sun. Sun wheels represent the cycle of the seasons and the rebirth of light.

- **Yule Incense and Oils:** The scents of Yule—pine, cedar, frank-incense, myrrh, and orange—bring the season's energy into your space. Use incense and essential oils to purify your surroundings, uplift your spirit, and set the mood for your rituals. Scents have a powerful impact on our energy, aiding in concentration and opening pathways for magical work.

- **Cauldron or Fire-Safe Bowl:** For burning intentions, herbs, or incense, a cauldron or fire-safe bowl is a must-have tool. The act of burning is deeply symbolic during Yule, representing the transformation and release of old energies to make way for new ones.

- **Altar:** Your Yule altar is the focal point of your magical practice. Decorate it with seasonal items—evergreen branches, pinecones, candles, crystals, and Yule symbols. Use your altar as a place to perform spells, meditate, and set intentions throughout the season.

These tools are conduits for the energy of Yule, allowing you to draw on the season's power in your spell work. As you explore the chapters of this grimoire, you'll find instructions for using these tools in various spells and rituals. Remember that the true magic lies within you, and these tools serve to focus and amplify your intentions. With each spell, you weave your energy into the fabric of the universe, participating in the timeless cycle of creation and renewal that Yule represents.

Chapter 1: Protection Spells for Winter

As winter descends and the nights grow longer, the world enters a time of stillness and introspection. This season can bring about a sense of vulnerability due to the encroaching cold, darkness, and the challenges of the harsher climate. In many cultures, winter is also seen as a time when the veil between worlds is thinner, making it crucial to reinforce boundaries and protect ourselves and our surroundings. The 50 protection spells in this chapter are designed to safeguard your home, family, and spirit against the physical and spiritual challenges that winter can bring. These spells use the power of the season, drawing on its unique elements like snow, ice, fire, and evergreens to create barriers against negativity, illness, and misfortune.

1. Snow Ward Protection Spell

Snow, pure and reflective, is an excellent element for absorbing negativity. For this spell, gather fresh snow in a small bowl and sprinkle a pinch of salt over it. Speak your intention: "Snow, pure and bright, guard my home day and night. As you melt, cleanse away all harm." Place the bowl outside your front door. As the snow melts, it creates a protective barrier around your home, neutralizing any negativity that tries to enter.

2. Evergreen Wreath Shield

Evergreen wreaths symbolize eternal life and protection. Create a wreath using pine branches, holly, and ivy. As you weave the branches together, focus on your intention of protection, visualizing a shield forming around your home. Hang the wreath on your front door, saying, "Evergreen and holly bright, shield this home both day and night. With ivy's strength and pine's might, protect us through winter's darkened light."

3. Candle Flame Guarding Spell

This spell uses the light of a candle to repel darkness and negative forces. Choose a white or gold candle and carve symbols of protection (such as a pentacle or sun) into the wax. Anoint the candle with rosemary or frankincense oil, then light it. As it burns, chant, "Flame so bright, guard this night, keep us safe within your light." Allow the candle to burn for at least 30 minutes each evening to maintain its protective energy.

4. Protective Salt Circle

Salt is a powerful purifier and protector. To create a protective barrier around your home, sprinkle a circle of salt around the perimeter of your property. As you do, say, "Circle of salt, pure and strong, protect this space all winter long." Visualize the salt forming an impenetrable shield against harmful energies and spirits. This spell is particularly effective before a storm or when you sense negative energy nearby.

5. Yule Log Protection Ritual

The Yule log is a traditional symbol of warmth and light. Choose a piece of oak or pine for your Yule log. Carve protective symbols into the wood and decorate it with sprigs of holly, pine cones, and ribbons. On the winter solstice, light the log in your hearth or bonfire, saying, "Yule log bright, burn with might, guard this home on this night." As the log burns, its energy fills your home with a protective shield.

6. Wind Chime Spirit Ward

Wind chimes can ward off negative spirits and energies. Choose a chime made of metal or wood, and hang it near your front door or a window. Before hanging it, pass the chime through sage smoke to cleanse it. As you hang it, say, "Chime of wind, sing so clear, guard this home and all held dear. With every ring, peace you bring, no dark spirit shall pass within."

7. Protective Quartz Grid

Clear quartz amplifies protective energy. Place four pieces of clear quartz at the four corners of your home or property. As you set each stone down, say, "Quartz so clear, shield this space, guard it well with your embrace." Visualize a web of protective energy connecting the stones, forming a grid that encases your home in a protective barrier.

8. Protection Incense Blend

Create a protective incense blend using pine needles, rosemary, and frankincense. Burn this incense daily to cleanse and protect your space. As the smoke rises, walk through each room, saying, "Smoke of pine, rosemary, and frankincense, cleanse this place of all malevolence. May only love and peace remain, all darkness banished, none to gain."

9. Hearth Stone Protection

The hearth has always been a symbol of home and warmth. Find a stone from nature that resonates with you and place it near your fireplace or in your kitchen. Each evening, hold the stone in your hands, focusing on your intention to protect your home and family. Whisper into the stone, "Hearth stone warm, hearth stone bright, guard this home with all your might." Keep the stone in place all winter to maintain its protective energy.

10. Ice Mirror Reflection Spell

Ice has the unique property of reflecting light and energy. On a cold winter's day, fill a shallow dish with water and place it outside to freeze. Once it becomes ice, sprinkle a pinch of salt over it. As you do, say, "Ice so clear, reflect all harm, send it back, keep us warm." Place the ice near the entrance of your home, allowing it to act as a mirror, reflecting negative energy away from your space.

11. Herbal Protection Sachets

Create small sachets using protective herbs such as rosemary, sage, and bay leaves. Add a few cloves for extra strength. Tie the sachets with a red ribbon and hang them over doorways or windows, saying, "Herbs of power, herbs of might, guard this home both day and night."

12. Yule Tree Blessing Spell

Your Yule tree can become a beacon of protection. As you decorate your tree, weave a strand of red ribbon or yarn through the branches. While doing so, chant: "Tree so green, evergreen, guard this space unseen. With branches bright and spirit true, protect us all the season through." Place protective symbols, such as pentacles, small bells, or charms, among the tree's decorations. Each time you add an ornament, visualize it radiating protective light throughout your home. The tree serves as a shield, absorbing negativity and replacing it with warmth and light.

13. Winter Solstice Circle of Light

On the Winter Solstice, gather five candles: one white, one red, one gold, one green, and one black. Place them in a circle on your altar, with the black candle at the northernmost point. Light each candle in a clockwise direction, beginning with the black candle. As you light each one, say: "Light of the north (east, south, west), shine forth and keep this home secure." Sit within the circle of candles, focusing on their glow forming a protective dome around you and your space. Allow the candles to burn until they extinguish naturally.

14. Frozen Charm Spell

Create an amulet for protection using a small pouch, some protective herbs (such as rosemary and sage), a pinch of salt, and a small piece of obsidian or black tourmaline. Place all items inside the pouch, and as you do, say: "Elements of earth, air, fire, and water, freeze all harm and block disaster." Close the pouch, tie it with a black ribbon, and place it outside to freeze overnight. The frozen charm becomes a symbol of strength and protection, holding the power of winter's cold to deter negativity.

15. Protection Through Reflection Ritual

On a full moon night, take a small mirror and place it on your altar. Encircle the mirror with white candles, leaving one candle in your hand. Light each candle, saying: "Moon's reflection, guard this place. Mirror bright, protect with grace." Hold the remaining candle and gaze into the mirror, visualizing it capturing any negative energy and sending it away. Keep this mirror in a safe place by your front door to reflect unwanted energies out of your home.

16. Protective Bay Leaf Burn

Bay leaves are known for their protective properties. On a cold winter night, take three bay leaves and inscribe protective symbols or words on them, such as "safety," "peace," or a sigil of your own making. Hold the leaves in your hands, focusing on your intention to guard your home and loved ones. Then, safely burn the leaves in a fireproof dish or cauldron, saying: "Bay leaves burn, guard and shield, keep all harm from this field." Allow the smoke to fill the room, purifying the space.

17. Hearth Guardian Sigil

Create a sigil for protection using a piece of charcoal. On your hearthstone or fireplace (or on a piece of paper if you do not have a fireplace), draw a sigil that symbolizes protection to you. As you draw, chant: "Guardian of hearth, guardian of flame, shield this home in winter's name." Leave the sigil in place throughout the winter months as a barrier against negative energy.

18. Cinnamon Stick Door Protection

Cinnamon is a powerful protector. Take three cinnamon sticks and tie them together with red ribbon. As you wrap the ribbon, say: "Cinnamon bright, cinnamon strong, guard this door all winter long." Hang the bundle above your front door or place it on a windowsill. The cinnamon will act as a protective charm, deterring negative influences from entering your space.

19. Pine Cone Protection Charm

Collect pine cones during a winter walk. Cleanse them with salt water and allow them to dry. Once dried, anoint each pine cone with rosemary or pine essential oil while saying: "Cone of pine, guardian's might, ward this home both day and night." Place the pine cones near doorways, windows, or on your altar. Their natural energy will help to ward off any unwelcome spirits or energies.

20. Winter Evergreen Sweep

Using an evergreen branch (such as pine or fir), sweep the floors of your home starting from the back of the house towards the front door. As you sweep, say: "Evergreen sweep, darkness leave, make this home a place of reprieve." Visualize any negativity being swept away by the branch, leaving behind a peaceful and safe environment. Dispose of the branch outside, away from your home, to ensure the energy it absorbed does not return.

21. Icicle Sigil Spell

On a frosty day, take an icicle and carve a protection sigil into its surface using a twig or small knife. As you carve, say: "Ice of winter, pure and strong, seal this spell, guard from wrong." Place the icicle outside your home's main entrance. As it melts, it releases the protective energy into your surroundings, creating a barrier against harm.

22. Peppermint Protection Bath

Fill your bathtub with warm water and add peppermint leaves, a few drops of peppermint essential oil, and a handful of sea salt. Before stepping into the bath, say: "Mint so pure, salt so strong, guard my spirit, make it long." Soak in the bath, feeling the cleansing and protective properties of the peppermint enveloping you. When you're done, drain the water, visualizing it carrying away any negative energy clinging to you.

23. Ice Crystal Defense

Gather several small pieces of ice and place them in a bowl. Hold your hands over the bowl and visualize the ice absorbing all negative energy around you. Say: "Ice so clear, ice so bright, absorb all harm, reflect the light." Let the ice melt and pour the water outside, releasing the absorbed energy away from your home.

24. Protective Pentacle Charm

Create a pentacle using small twigs or sticks you find outside. Bind them together with red thread to form a star. As you wrap the thread, say: "Pentacle bright, star of light, guard this home both day and night." Hang the pentacle in a window or place it on your altar to maintain a shield of protective energy around your home.

25. Holly and Ivy Guardian

Holly and ivy have long been symbols of protection and endurance during the winter months. Gather a few sprigs of holly and ivy, and tie them together with a white ribbon. As you weave them together, say: "Holly and ivy, guard and guide, keep harm away from every side." Hang this charm above your doorway or windows. The combined energy of holly's protective spikes and ivy's strength will form a magical barrier to safeguard your home.

26. Full Moon Water Protection

On a full moon night, fill a bowl with water and place it outside or on a windowsill to capture the moon's light. Add a pinch of salt to the water, saying: "Moonlight bright, water pure, protect this place, keep it secure." Use this moon-charged water to sprinkle around the perimeter of your home or on doorframes and windowsills. The moon water creates a protective boundary, repelling negative forces.

27. Yule Broom Cleansing Sweep

Create a simple besom (broom) using twigs and dried herbs tied to a stick. On the first day of Yule, use this broom to sweep the floors of your home. As you sweep, chant: "Besom sweep, clear and free, guard this home, so mote it be." Sweep towards the front door to push out any stagnant or negative energy. The broom becomes a guardian, keeping your space protected throughout the winter.

28. Juniper Smoke Ward

Juniper has potent protective properties. Gather a bundle of dried juniper twigs and leaves, and light them to create a smoldering smoke. Walk through your home, allowing the smoke to waft into every corner and say: "Juniper smoke, cleanse and guard, keep this home from spirits barred." The smoke purifies the space and forms a protective veil to deter unwanted energies.

29. Pine Needle Protection Sachet

Fill a small sachet bag with dried pine needles, cloves, and a piece of black tourmaline. Sew the bag closed with a needle and thread while visualizing a strong protective energy enveloping your home. As you stitch, chant: "Pine so green, cloves so bright, protect this home with all your might." Hang this sachet near the main entrance to keep negativity at bay.

30. Silver Bell Door Charm

Silver bells have long been used to ward off evil spirits and negative energy. Take a small silver bell and tie it with a red ribbon. Before hanging it on your doorknob, say: "Bell of silver, ring so clear, keep out darkness, keep out fear." Every time the door opens and the bell rings, it reactivates the protective charm.

31. Warm Hearth Ash Spell

After burning a Yule log or other wood in your fireplace, collect a small amount of the ash in a jar. Sprinkle a pinch of ash at each entrance to your home (doors, windows, etc.) while saying: "Ash of fire, ash of light, guard this home through winter's night." The ashes carry the energy of the fire, which will continue to protect your space.

32. Red Ribbon Protection Knot

Using a length of red ribbon, tie nine knots along its length. With each knot, speak an intention for protection, such as: "Knot of one, protection begun; knot of two, safeguard through." Continue until all nine knots are tied. Hang this ribbon near your front door or on your altar to create a continuous loop of protective energy.

33. Star Anise Protection Pouch

Fill a small pouch with star anise, cloves, and dried rosemary. Hold the pouch in your hands, close your eyes, and visualize a bright, protective light emanating from it. Chant: "Herbs of power, herbs of might, guard this home both day and night." Hang the pouch in a central area of your home or carry it with you for personal protection.

34. Birch Bark Guardian Spell

Birch is associated with new beginnings and protection. Write your name (or the names of your family members) on a small piece of birch bark using charcoal or a black marker. Wrap the bark in a piece of cloth and bury it near your front door, saying: "Birch bark white, pure and true, guard this home, through and through." The birch bark will act as a guardian, watching over your space.

35. Mirror Window Protection

Place a small mirror on a windowsill, with the reflective side facing outward. As you position the mirror, say: "Mirror bright, mirror clear, reflect all harm away from here." This mirror will deflect negative energy away from your home, keeping it safe and filled with positive vibes.

36. Snow Globe Protective Seal

Create a protective snow globe using a glass jar filled with water, glitter, and a few drops of protective essential oils (such as frankincense or rosemary). Seal the jar tightly, and as you shake it, say: "Snow within, swirling bright, guard this space from harm and fright." Place the snow globe on your altar or a central location in your home to act as a magical seal of protection.

37. Cedar Smoke Protection

Cedar is known for its purifying and protective qualities. Light a cedar stick and walk through your home, allowing the smoke to fill each room. As you do this, say: "Cedar smoke, strong and wise, guard this space, keep all lies." Visualize the smoke forming a protective barrier that blocks out negativity and unwelcome spirits.

38. Nutmeg Circle Protection

Take a whole nutmeg and grind it into a fine powder. Sprinkle a circle of nutmeg powder around your bed or a specific area you wish to protect, while saying: "Nutmeg bright, nutmeg strong, keep me safe all winter long." The nutmeg circle serves as a shield, guarding you during sleep or meditation.

39. Candle Wax Seal of Safety

On a piece of parchment, draw a symbol or sigil that represents protection to you. Light a white or red candle and allow some of the melted wax to drip onto the parchment, sealing your symbol. While the wax is still warm, say: "Wax and fire, seal so strong, protect this home where I belong." Place the sealed parchment on your altar or under your doormat for ongoing protection.

40. Garlic Doorway Protection

Garlic is a traditional protective herb. Peel several cloves of garlic and thread them onto a piece of red string. Hang this garland over your front door, saying: "Garlic strong, keep harm away, guard this home by night and day." The garlic acts as a natural ward against negativity and ill intentions.

41. Evergreen Circle Protection Spell

On a winter solstice night, gather a circle of evergreen branches and place them around your altar or a central space in your home. Stand within the circle, holding a white candle, and say: "Circle of green, circle of light, guard this space through winter's night." Visualize the circle glowing with protective energy that radiates outward, covering your entire home.

42. Moonstone Guardian Amulet

Moonstone is known for its protective properties, especially during the winter months. Cleanse a piece of moonstone by placing it in a bowl of salt overnight. The next day, hold the stone in your hands and say: "Moonstone bright, moonstone clear, protect me now, hold me near." Carry this stone with you or place it under your pillow for protection and peace.

43. Rosemary Bath of Purification

Fill a sachet bag with dried rosemary and place it in your bathwater. As you soak, say: "Rosemary herb, pure and clean, protect my spirit, calm and serene." Visualize the water absorbing any negativity and replacing it with a shield of calm, protective energy.

44. Silver Ring Protection Charm

If you have a silver ring, cleanse it with saltwater. Once cleansed, hold the ring in your hands and say: "Silver bright, silver strong, guard me right, guard me long." Wear the ring daily during the winter months to maintain a circle of protection around you.

45. Frosted Window Sigils

On a frosty morning, use your finger to draw protective symbols or sigils on the frosted windows of your home. As you draw each sigil, say: "Symbols of frost, symbols of light, guard this home both day and night." The frost itself will act as a temporary but potent guardian, dissipating negative energy as it melts.

46. Laurel Leaf Fire Protection

Place a few laurel leaves into your fireplace or a fire-safe bowl. As they burn, say: "Laurel bright, burn so pure, guard this space and make it secure." The smoke from the burning leaves creates a veil of protection around your home.

47. Star of Anise Candle

Carve a star into a white candle, then press a star anise into the wax. Light the candle and say: "Star of anise, star of light, guard this space, protect tonight." Allow the candle to burn for at least 30 minutes, focusing on its flame creating a shield around your home.

48. Winter Spice Floor Wash

Create a floor wash using warm water, salt, a few drops of pine essential oil, and a pinch of cinnamon. Mop your floors with this mixture while saying: "Cleanse and guard, strong and true, keep this space from harm undue." The wash will cleanse away negativity and lay a protective layer throughout your home.

49. Winter Solstice Knot Spell

Take a piece of white yarn and tie nine knots along its length. As you tie each knot, say: "Knot of one, protection begun; knot of two, guard me through." Continue until nine knots are tied. Hang this knotted yarn above your bed or near the main entrance to seal in protective energy throughout the winter season.

50. New Year's Banishing Ritual

On New Year's Eve, fill a bowl with water and add a few drops of peppermint or eucalyptus oil. As the clock strikes midnight, dip your fingers in the water and sprinkle it around your home, saying, "New year begun, old year done, banish all harm, may peace be won." Visualize the energy of the past year leaving your space, making room for new, positive energy.

Chapter 2: Hearth and Home Blessings

As winter wraps the world in its frosty embrace, the hearth becomes the heart of the home. It symbolizes warmth, comfort, and a safe retreat from the biting cold outside. The Yule season is the perfect time to bless and strengthen this sanctuary, filling it with positive energy, love, and peace. The following 30 spells are designed to create a protective and comforting environment in your home, turning it into a haven of tranquility during the darkest time of the year. These spells draw upon the elements of Yule—fire, earth, light, and the evergreens—to infuse your living space with warmth and nurturing energy.

1. Yule Hearth Blessing

For this spell, you'll need a piece of wood (preferably oak or pine), some rosemary sprigs, and a red candle. Light the candle and hold the wood in your hands. Visualize your home filled with light, warmth, and comfort. Sprinkle rosemary over the wood and say: "Hearth of Yule, burn so bright, bless this home with warmth and light." Place the wood in the fireplace and light it. As it burns, feel the energy of peace spreading throughout your home.

2. Evergreen Garland Blessing

Craft a garland using evergreen branches (such as pine, cedar, or fir) and decorate it with pine cones, ribbons, and dried oranges. As you weave the garland, speak your intentions: "Evergreen, evergreen, stay in this space, bring warmth, love, and endless grace." Hang the garland over your mantel or door to bless your home with the enduring spirit of the evergreen trees.

3. Cinnamon Comfort Candle

Create a cozy atmosphere by placing a white candle in a bowl of cinnamon sticks. Light the candle and say: "Cinnamon sweet, cinnamon warm, bless this space, keep us from harm." Allow the candle to burn for an hour each evening during the Yule season, filling your home with the scent of comfort and warmth.

4. Window Blessing with Snowflakes

Cut out paper snowflakes and sprinkle them with a few drops of rosemary or lavender essential oil. Hold each snowflake and whisper: "Snowflake bright, snowflake pure, bless this home, make it secure." Stick the snowflakes on windows to bring a touch of winter's magic inside, infusing the space with peaceful energy.

5. Pine Cone Abundance Spell

Collect pine cones and place them in a decorative bowl at the center of your dining table. Sprinkle them with salt and cinnamon, then say: "Pine cone of earth, pine cone of cheer, bring abundance to this space all year." The pine cones serve as a magnet for prosperity and comfort, blessing your home throughout Yule.

6. Warmth of the Fire Blessing

On a cold winter's night, gather your family around the hearth. Hold hands and light a fire, saying: "Fire so bright, fire so warm, bless this home, keep us from harm." Sit together in silence for a few moments, focusing on the warmth radiating from the flames. Visualize that warmth spreading throughout every room, filling it with peace.

7. Doorway Spruce Protection

Place a small sprig of spruce or pine above your doorway. Hold the sprig in your hands and focus on your intention to create a barrier of comfort and peace. Say: "Spruce so green, guard this door, bless this home forevermore." The evergreen serves as a guardian, welcoming positive energy into your home.

8. Orange and Clove Hanging Charm

Create an aromatic charm by sticking cloves into an orange in a spiral pattern. As you insert each clove, say: "Orange of sun, clove of might, bless this home, fill it with light." Hang the charm near a window or on the mantle to draw in warmth and joy.

9. Honey and Milk Hearth Blessing

On Yule morning, pour a small bowl of honey and another of milk. Place them near your hearth and say: "Honey so sweet, milk so pure, bless this hearth, our warmth secure." Leave the offerings until the next morning, then pour them outside as an offering to nature, asking for continued warmth and blessings in your home.

10. Warming Tea Incantation

Prepare a pot of warming tea with cinnamon, ginger, and cloves. As it brews, hold your hands over the steam and say: "Steam so warm, spice so sweet, bless this home with love replete." Pour the tea and share it with family or guests, imagining the warmth infusing everyone and the space around you.

11. Full Moon Water Blessing

On the night of a full moon, fill a bowl with water and place it where it can soak up the moonlight. Add a pinch of sea salt to the water and say: "Moon so full, water bright, bless this home with your gentle light." Use this blessed water to sprinkle around the perimeter of your home, inviting peace and serenity into each room.

12. Rosemary Hearth Sweep

Tie together a bundle of dried rosemary sprigs and use it as a broom to sweep around your hearth. As you sweep, say: "Rosemary cleanse, rosemary bless, fill this hearth with happiness." This simple act purifies the hearth and invites a warm, loving energy into the space.

13. Cinnamon Stick Wreath

Create a small wreath using cinnamon sticks tied together with red and green ribbons. Hang the wreath in your kitchen or living room, saying: "Cinnamon sweet, bind us tight, bring comfort here, both day and night." The wreath will radiate warmth and joy throughout the Yule season.

14. Sugar and Spice Floor Sweep

Mix a handful of sugar, cinnamon, and salt in a small bowl. Sprinkle the mixture across your floors, starting from the back of your home and moving toward the front door. As you sweep, say: "Sugar, spice, salt so fine, bless this home, keep it divine." After sweeping, discard the sweepings outside, visualizing them taking away any lingering negativity.

15. Candle Circle of Peace

Gather five candles—one white, one green, one red, one gold, and one silver. Place them in a circle on your dining table. Light each candle, saying: "White for peace, green for growth, red for love, gold for warmth, silver for truth." Allow the candles to burn for an hour, their combined light filling the room with harmonious energy.

16. Hearthstone Blessing

Find a stone that feels warm and comforting to you. Cleanse it with saltwater, then place it near your hearth or fireplace. Hold your hands over the stone and say: "Stone of hearth, stone of home, keep us warm, where'er we roam." Leave the stone in place to draw in the hearth's warmth, spreading it throughout your home.

17. Fireplace Salt Blessing

Sprinkle a circle of salt around your fireplace, while saying: "Salt so pure, salt so bright, bless this hearth with calming light." The salt absorbs and neutralizes negative energy, turning the hearth into a center of peace.

18. Protective Oven Blessing

Your oven is a modern-day hearth. To bless it, mix a handful of salt and rosemary in a small bowl. Sprinkle a pinch of this mixture into the oven (when it is cool) and say: "Oven warm, oven bright, bless this home with love and light." The blessed oven brings warmth and positive energy into the home with every meal it prepares.

19. Yule Altar Blessing

Create a small altar using Yule-themed items such as pine cones, candles, holly, and a bowl of water. Light a candle on the altar and say: "Altar bright, altar blessed, fill this home with joy and rest." Let the candle burn as you go about your day, knowing the energy of the altar radiates comfort throughout your home.

20. Evergreen Branch Spritz

Make a simple room spray using pine essential oil and water. Add a sprig of fresh pine to the bottle and shake it gently. Walk through your home, spritzing each room while saying: "Pine so green, pine so pure, bless this space, keep it secure." The pine scent will invoke the forest's tranquility and bring a refreshing, calming energy into your living space.

21. Peaceful Hearth Tea Lights

Place a tealight candle inside a small glass container and add a few drops of lavender oil around its edges. Light the candle and say: "Lavender calm, light of peace, bless this home, bring us ease." Place these tealights around the home to create an atmosphere of warmth and serenity.

22. Warm Blanket Enchantment

Hold a soft, warm blanket in your arms and infuse it with your intention. Say: "Blanket warm, blanket soft, bless with comfort, hold us aloft." Lay the blanket over the back of a couch or chair, ready to envelop anyone who wraps themselves in its warmth.

23. Orange Peel Hearth Offering

Dry some orange peels in the oven until they are crispy. Place them in a small bowl on your hearth. Say: "Orange so bright, citrus cheer, bring warmth and joy to those who gather here." The scent of oranges invokes warmth and happiness, blessing your home with cheerful energy.

24. Gingerbread Blessing Spell

Bake gingerbread cookies with your favorite recipe. Before eating them, hold them in your hands and say: "Gingerbread spice, sugar sweet, bless this home, make it complete." Share the cookies with loved ones to spread the warmth and blessings throughout the household.

25. Heart of the Home Blessing

Stand in the center of your home, holding a piece of rose quartz or another soothing stone. Close your eyes and say: "Heart of the home, beat so true, fill this space with love anew." Visualize a warm, pink light emanating from the stone, expanding to fill every corner of your home with peaceful, loving energy.

26. Sun-Warmed Room Blessing

On a sunny winter's day, open the curtains to let the sunlight flood into your room. As the light enters, say: "Sunlight bright, sunlight pure, bless this home with warmth for sure." Allow the sunlight to fill the room with its comforting energy, driving away any shadows of negativity.

27. Bay Leaf Simmering Potpourri

Fill a pot with water, bay leaves, cinnamon sticks, and cloves. Let it simmer on the stove, filling your home with its aroma. As it simmers, say: "Bay and spice, warmth and cheer, bless this space, keep us near." The scent will invite positive energy and blessings into your space.

28. Candlelit Bath Blessing

Prepare a warm bath and surround the tub with candles. Add a few drops of rose or lavender oil to the water. As you soak, say: "Water warm, candle bright, bless this home, grant peace tonight." This ritual purifies your energy, which then radiates throughout the home, bringing a calming presence to every room.

29. Red Ribbon Wish

Take a red ribbon and tie a knot in it for every blessing you wish upon your home (e.g., peace, joy, warmth). As you tie each knot, say: "Ribbon red, hold my plea, bless this home, so mote it be." Hang the ribbon near a window or on your hearth as a constant reminder of the blessings you've bestowed.

30. Comforting Bread Blessing

Bake a loaf of bread and, as you knead the dough, infuse it with your intentions. Say: "Bread of hearth, bread of life, bless this home, free of strife." After baking, place the bread on the dining table, letting its aroma fill the home with warmth. Share it with your family to spread the blessings.

Chapter 3: Spells for Manifesting New Beginnings

Yule is a time of renewal when the longest night gives way to the growing light, symbolizing the return of the sun and the promise of new beginnings. This chapter is dedicated to 40 spells designed to harness this transformative energy, helping you welcome new opportunities, personal growth, and profound changes in the coming year. Each spell draws upon the natural elements of winter, the symbolism of rebirth, and the energy of the season to plant the seeds of change and manifest your desires.

1. Yule Candle of New Intentions

Light a green candle to symbolize growth and new beginnings. Carve symbols or words representing your desires for the coming year into the candle using a toothpick or small knife. Anoint the candle with rosemary or peppermint oil. As you light the candle, say: "Flame of Yule, burn so bright, grant new beginnings with your light." Sit in meditation, focusing on the flame, and visualize your intentions manifesting in the year ahead. Allow the candle to burn completely to release your wishes into the universe.

2. Snow-Covered Seed Spell

Gather a small seed, such as a sunflower or an acorn, and place it in the palm of your hand. Go outside and scoop up some fresh snow. Gently press the seed into the snow while saying: "Seed of hope, buried deep, grow anew from winter's sleep." Bury the snow and seed in the earth, visualizing the seed absorbing the energy of the season. As it melts and roots into the soil, imagine your intentions taking root and growing in the months to come.

3. Cinnamon and Orange Prosperity Bath

Draw a warm bath and add a handful of dried orange peels and a cinnamon stick. As you soak, close your eyes and imagine all the positive changes you want to welcome into your life. Say: "Orange and spice, warmth of Yule, bring new beginnings, blessings full." Feel the warm water enveloping you, washing away the old and making room for new opportunities.

4. Evergreen Wish Sachet

Fill a small cloth sachet with pine needles, rosemary, and a piece of citrine or clear quartz. Hold the sachet close to your heart and say: "Green of pine, crystal bright, bring new beginnings into sight." Keep the sachet under your pillow or carry it with you to draw fresh energy and new opportunities.

5. Full Moon Renewal Ritual

On the night of a full moon during Yule, fill a bowl with water and place it where it can soak up the moonlight. Add a pinch of salt and a few drops of peppermint oil. Hold your hands over the bowl and say: "Moon so full, moon so bright, cleanse my soul, set things right." Wash your hands and face with the water, visualizing the moon's energy purifying you and making way for new growth.

6. Birch Bark Blessing

Write your intention for the new year on a piece of birch bark. Hold the bark in your hands and say: "Birch of white, pure and new, bring forth change and dreams come true." Place the bark on your altar or keep it in a safe place as a reminder of your intention.

7. Firelight Manifestation

On a quiet evening, light a fire in your fireplace or an outdoor fire pit. Write down what you wish to manifest in the new year on a piece of paper. Hold the paper close to your heart and say: "Fire so warm, fire so bright, bring my wishes into sight." Carefully place the paper into the flames, visualizing your desires being carried into the universe with the smoke.

8. Yule Log Wish

Carve symbols of growth and renewal into a small piece of wood. Anoint the wood with rosemary or cedar oil, then place it in the hearth or burn it in a bonfire. As the wood burns, say: "Wood of Yule, burn so free, bring new beginnings straight to me." Let the fire consume the wood, releasing your intentions into the ether.

9. Frozen Pathway Spell

On a frosty morning, draw a pathway in the frost with your finger. As you trace the path, say: "Path of ice, path of new, clear the way for what is true." Visualize this path leading you to new opportunities and personal growth as the frost melts and evaporates into the air.

10. Evergreen Circle of Growth

Gather pine branches and form them into a circle on your altar. In the center, place a small green candle. Light the candle and say: "Circle of green, circle of might, bring new beginnings into sight." Sit in silence and visualize the evergreen energy surrounding you, nurturing your growth.

11. Seed of Potential Spell

Hold a seed, such as a sunflower or pumpkin seed, in your hand and focus on your intentions. Say: "Seed of life, seed of change, grow in strength, grow in range." Plant the seed in a small pot and nurture it throughout the year as a symbol of your growing potential.

12. Morning Dew Invocation

On a clear winter morning, collect dew from plants outside. Place a drop on your forehead while saying: "Dew of morn, fresh and clear, bring new beginnings throughout the year." Feel the cool dew seeping into your skin, filling you with renewed energy.

13. Candle Drip Manifestation

Take a white candle and light it. Hold a piece of parchment under the candle and let the wax drip onto it. As you watch the wax fall, say: "Wax of white, drip of flame, bring new beginnings in my name." Allow the wax to cool, then place the parchment on your altar as a focus for your intentions.

14. Cinnamon and Honey Offering

Mix a spoonful of honey with a pinch of cinnamon in a bowl. Place the mixture on your altar as an offering to the universe. Say: "Sweet as honey, warm as spice, bring new beginnings, blessings twice." Leave the offering overnight, then discard it outside the next morning, releasing your intentions.

15. Crystal Grid for Change

Create a crystal grid on your altar using clear quartz, citrine, and amethyst. Arrange them in a circle, with a piece of green aventurine in the center. As you place each crystal, say: "Crystals bright, form this ring, bring new growth, to me bring." Keep the grid on your altar throughout the Yule season to attract new opportunities.

16. Pine Cone Transformation Charm

Find a small pine cone and hold it in your hands, focusing on the changes you wish to see. Say: "Pine cone small, pine cone bright, bring transformation with your might." Place the pine cone on your windowsill to draw transformative energy into your home.

17. Cleansing Salt Bowl

Fill a bowl with sea salt and place it on your altar. Add a piece of rose quartz and a sprig of rosemary to the salt. As you mix the items, say: "Salt and stone, herb of grace, cleanse and clear, make new space." Leave the bowl on your altar for seven days to absorb old energy, then scatter the salt outside to release it.

18. New Year's Dawn Ritual

Wake up before dawn on New Year's Day. Light a candle and place it by a window. As the first light of the day appears, say: "Dawn of new, dawn of bright, bring me change with all your might." Focus on the sunrise, welcoming its energy to fill your life with new beginnings.

19. Snow Globe Wish

Create a simple snow globe using a small jar filled with water, glitter, and a tiny pine branch. Close the jar and shake it, saying: "Snow and light, swirl and spin, bring new beginnings to let in." Place the globe on your altar as a visual reminder of your intention.

20. Orange Peel Renewal

Dry orange peels in the oven, then crush them into small pieces. Sprinkle the pieces in a circle on your altar, saying: "Orange peel, bright and new, bring fresh change, through and through." Leave the circle for three days, then gather the peels and bury them in the earth to release their energy.

21. Ribbon of Change Spell

Take a piece of green ribbon and hold it in your hands. Tie a knot at each end, saying: "Ribbon green, tied so tight, bring me change, day and night." Keep the ribbon in your pocket or purse as a talisman for transformation.

22. Full Moon Tea Blessing

Brew a cup of herbal tea with chamomile and peppermint. Hold the cup under the light of the full moon, saying: "Moonlight pure, tea so warm, bring new beginnings, transform." Drink the tea slowly, letting the moon's energy fill you with renewal.

23. Star Anise Prosperity Spell

Place a star anise and a pinch of cinnamon in a small pouch. Hold the pouch in your hands and focus on the energy of new growth and prosperity. Say: "Star of spice, fortune's friend, bring new beginnings without end." Carry the pouch with you to attract fresh opportunities and good fortune.

24. Waxing Moon Manifestation Jar

During the waxing moon phase, fill a small glass jar with items symbolizing growth and newness, such as a sprig of rosemary, a coin, and a small crystal. As you add each item, say: "Waxing moon, growing bright, manifest my dreams in the light." Seal the jar with a lid and place it on your windowsill until the full moon, allowing the moon's energy to amplify your intentions.

25. Evergreen Broom Sweep

Craft a small broom using evergreen branches and tie them together with green ribbon. Sweep the floors of your home, moving from the back to the front, saying: "Sweep away the old, bring in the new, blessings fill this home, pure and true." The broom carries the energy of the evergreens, sweeping out the past to make space for new growth.

26. Pine and Peppermint Simmer Pot

Fill a pot with water, pine needles, and a few drops of peppermint oil. Allow the mixture to simmer on the stove, filling your home with its refreshing scent. As it simmers, say: "Pine and mint, fresh and bright, bring new beginnings, day and night." The steam spreads your intention throughout the house, clearing out stagnant energy.

27. Candle of Self-Transformation

Choose a candle in a color that represents the change you seek (green for growth, blue for wisdom, red for courage). Carve a symbol of your intention into the candle. Light it and say: "Flame of change, burn so free, transform my spirit, set it free." Let the candle burn completely, focusing on the flame's power to bring about transformation within you.

28. Frosted Window Manifestation

On a frosty morning, use your finger to draw symbols or words representing your intentions on a frosted window. As you draw, say: "Frost so clear, frost so bright, bring new beginnings with your light." Watch as the frost melts, visualizing your intentions flowing into reality.

29. Rose Quartz New Love Spell

Hold a piece of rose quartz in your hands, focusing on the type of new relationships you wish to welcome into your life. Say: "Quartz of rose, soft and pure, open my heart, make love secure." Keep the rose quartz near your bed or in your purse to attract new, loving energy into your life.

30. Plant a Wish Spell

Take a small pot of soil and a seed of your choice (sunflower, basil, etc.). Hold the seed in your hands and speak your wish for the new year. Say: "Seed of earth, seed of might, grow my dreams into the light." Plant the seed in the soil and water it regularly. As the seed grows, so too will your intentions manifest.

31. Crystal Wand of Beginnings

Create a simple wand using a stick and a crystal (clear quartz or amethyst). Bind the crystal to the end of the stick using silver thread. Hold the wand over your heart and say: "Wand of crystal, wand of light, guide my path, make it bright." Keep the wand on your altar as a symbol of the changes you are inviting.

32. Evergreen Protection Sachet

Fill a small sachet with pine needles, rosemary, and bay leaves. Tie it with a green ribbon while saying: "Green of pine, bay of might, guard my path, day and night." Keep the sachet in your pocket or hang it by your door to attract opportunities while keeping negativity at bay.

33. Cinnamon Wish Paper

Write your wish for the coming year on a small piece of paper. Roll a cinnamon stick in the paper and tie it with red thread. Hold the cinnamon bundle over a flame (a candle or fireplace) and say: "Cinnamon bright, cinnamon sweet, bring my wish, make it complete." Let the bundle smolder slightly, then bury it in the earth to manifest your desires.

34. Winter Star Manifestation

Cut out a star shape from a piece of paper. Write your intention in the center of the star, then place it on your altar. Surround it with pine cones, cinnamon sticks, and crystals. Say: "Star of light, guide my way, bring new beginnings every day." Leave the star on your altar until the spring equinox as a constant focus for your intentions.

35. Bay Leaf New Year Spell

Write your intention on a bay leaf using a marker. Hold the leaf over a candle flame and say: "Bay leaf bright, burn away, bring my dreams to light today." Allow the leaf to burn completely, visualizing the smoke carrying your intentions into the universe.

36. Rosemary Renewal Bath

Prepare a warm bath and add a handful of dried rosemary and sea salt. Light a white candle and place it near the bath. As you soak, say: "Rosemary pure, rosemary bright, cleanse my spirit, grant new sight." Visualize the water washing away old energy and filling you with the light of new beginnings.

37. Winter Wind Whisper

On a windy winter day, go outside and face the wind. Speak your intention aloud, letting the wind carry your words. Say: "Wind of winter, cold and clear, bring me change, bring it near." As the wind rushes past, feel it taking your intentions into the world to manifest.

38. Pine Needle Circle

Gather pine needles and arrange them in a circle on your altar. In the center, place a small candle. Light the candle and say: "Circle of pine, circle of light, welcome change into my sight." Allow the candle to burn down, envisioning your new beginnings growing with the strength of the pine.

39. Candlelight Blessing

Light a white candle and hold a piece of clear quartz in your hands. Close your eyes and focus on the flame. Say: "Candle bright, flame so true, bring new beginnings, fresh and new." Visualize the candle's light filling you and your surroundings with energy for personal growth and transformation.

40. Pine Cone Burying Spell

Hold a small pine cone in your hands and focus on what you wish to leave behind and what you wish to invite into your life. Say: "Pine cone small, pine cone bright, bury the old, welcome the light." Bury the pine cone outside, imagining it sealing away the past and nourishing the seeds of new opportunities to come.

Chapter 4: Abundance and Prosperity Rituals

Yule marks a time of giving and sharing, a season filled with generosity and the promise of renewal. As the earth rests in the quiet of winter, it also prepares for the growth and abundance that spring will bring. The energy of Yule is ripe for setting intentions to draw prosperity, wealth, and success into our lives. This chapter provides 45 spells and rituals that utilize the season's symbols and elements—evergreens, warmth, light, and the spices of Yule—to attract abundance in its many forms. Through these rituals, you can align your energy with the spirit of giving and the flow of prosperity.

1. Pine Cone Prosperity Spell

Gather a pine cone and place it in a small bowl. Sprinkle cinnamon and nutmeg over it, saying: "Pine cone bright, pine cone strong, draw abundance all year long." Place the bowl near your front door or on your altar to invite prosperity into your home.

2. Cinnamon Stick Wealth Charm

Tie three cinnamon sticks together with a green ribbon. Hold the bundle in your hands and say: "Cinnamon spice, warm and bright, bring me wealth, both day and night." Place this charm in your kitchen or near your cash drawer to attract wealth.

3. Yule Log of Abundance

Choose a small piece of wood and carve symbols of abundance, such as a dollar sign or rune for wealth (Fehu). Anoint the log with cinnamon or frankincense oil. Light it in your fireplace, saying: "Yule log burn, bright and free, bring prosperity unto me." Allow the log to burn completely, releasing your intention into the universe.

4. Golden Orange Blessing

Cut an orange into slices and lay them out on a baking sheet to dry. Once dried, sprinkle them with gold glitter and say: "Golden orange, fruit of light, bring abundance, day and night." Place these slices in a bowl on your altar to draw prosperity.

5. Candle Money Draw

Light a green candle and place a coin at its base. As the candle burns, say: "Green of flame, wealth so bright, fill my life with riches' light." Visualize the flame attracting abundance as it flickers. Allow the candle to burn completely, then keep the coin in your wallet or cash register as a charm.

6. Snowflake Wealth Manifestation

On a snowy day, gather fresh snow in a small dish. Using your finger, draw a dollar sign or other wealth symbols in the snow while saying: "Snow so pure, snow so bright, bring me wealth, day and night." Place the snow outside to melt naturally, visualizing it dissolving financial blocks and opening pathways to abundance.

7. Nutmeg and Rosemary Abundance Bag

Fill a small sachet with nutmeg, rosemary, and a small coin. Hold the bag in your hands, focusing on your intention for financial growth. Say: "Nutmeg and herb, coin of gold, bring abundance, as foretold." Keep this bag in your pocket or near your bed to attract wealth and prosperity.

8. Peppermint Windfall

Prepare a cup of peppermint tea. Hold the cup in your hands and say: "Peppermint bright, mint of wealth, bring abundance, joy, and health." Drink the tea, imagining its warmth filling you with prosperous energy.

9. Full Moon Wealth Jar

On a full moon night, fill a small jar with coins, bay leaves, and a pinch of cinnamon. Seal the jar and place it under the moonlight, saying: "Moon of silver, moon so bright, fill this jar with riches' light." Keep the jar on your altar or in a safe place to draw wealth.

10. Prosperity Hearth Spell

Before lighting a fire in your hearth, sprinkle a mixture of cinnamon, nutmeg, and sugar onto the logs. Light the fire and say: "Hearth of flame, hearth of might, bring abundance through this night." Allow the fire to burn, visualizing its energy radiating prosperity into your home.

11. Bay Leaf Success Ritual

Write your financial goals on a bay leaf using a pen or marker. Hold the leaf in your hand and say: "Bay of wealth, bay of gain, bring success and ease my strain." Burn the leaf in a fire-safe dish, releasing your intentions into the universe.

12. Evergreen Wealth Charm

Tie together small sprigs of pine, cedar, and holly using a gold ribbon. Hang this charm above your doorway while saying: "Evergreen and holly bright, bring me fortune day and night." The charm invites prosperity and growth into your home.

13. Bread of Plenty Spell

Bake a loaf of bread, incorporating seeds like sunflower or poppy for abundance. As you knead the dough, say: "Bread of life, bread of plenty, bring me wealth, both good and steady." Share the bread with loved ones, spreading the energy of abundance.

14. Cinnamon Salt Prosperity Circle

Mix sea salt with ground cinnamon in a small bowl. Sprinkle a circle of this mixture around a green candle. Light the candle and say: "Salt and spice, wealth entice, fill my life with riches nice." Let the candle burn down completely, allowing the circle to draw in prosperity.

15. Yule Coin Planting

Take a coin and bury it in the soil of a potted plant in your home. As you plant the coin, say: "Coin of silver, coin of gold, bring me riches manifold." Water the plant and care for it, watching your intentions for wealth grow.

16. Holly and Pine Abundance Bundle

Tie a bundle of holly and pine branches together with a green ribbon. Hold the bundle over a green candle flame, saying: "Holly and pine, green and free, bring abundance unto me." Hang the bundle near your front door to attract prosperity.

17. Sunlight Wealth Ritual

On a sunny winter day, place a gold or silver coin on your windowsill where it can catch the sunlight. As the sun shines on the coin, say: "Sun of gold, sun of light, bring me wealth, day and night." Leave the coin in the sun for an hour, then keep it in your wallet as a wealth talisman.

18. Gold Glitter Money Spell

Sprinkle a pinch of gold glitter onto a piece of green cloth. Fold the cloth and tie it with a gold ribbon, saying: "Glitter of gold, bright and clear, bring me fortune far and near." Carry this charm in your pocket or keep it on your altar to attract wealth.

19. Prosperity Oil Anointment

Create a prosperity oil by mixing olive oil with a few drops of cinnamon, peppermint, and orange essential oils. Anoint your wallet, front door, and candles with this oil while saying: "Oil of wealth, oil of grace, bring abundance to this place."

20. Wishing Stone Spell

Find a small, smooth stone and hold it in your hands, focusing on your financial desires. Say: "Stone of earth, stone of might, bring me fortune, day and night." Place the stone on your altar or carry it with you to attract abundance.

21. Sugar and Spice Money Draw

Mix sugar, nutmeg, and cloves in a small bowl. Sprinkle a pinch of this mixture near your home's entrance while saying: "Sugar and spice, wealth entice, bring me fortune, neat and nice." The sweetness invites abundance into your home.

22. Wealth Candle Grid

Create a simple grid on your altar using four green candles arranged in a square. Place a small bowl of coins in the center. Light the candles and say: "Candle bright, candle green, bring me riches, pure and clean." Visualize the candles forming a protective circle that draws wealth into the bowl.

23. Pine Needle Abundance Bath

Fill a muslin bag with pine needles and a cinnamon stick. Add it to your bathwater, then soak while saying: "Pine and spice, bath so warm, bring me riches in all forms." Feel the water washing away blocks to prosperity and opening you to abundance.

24. Gold String Wish

Take a piece of gold string or thread and hold it in your hands. Close your eyes and focus on your wish for wealth. Tie three knots in the string, saying: "String of gold, wealth unfold, bring me fortune, both rich and bold." Keep the string in your purse or wallet to attract money.

25. Bay Leaf Money Drawing

Write a dollar sign on a bay leaf and place it in your wallet, saying: "Bay of wealth, bay of might, draw me money day and night." The bay leaf serves as a magnet for financial prosperity.

26. Rosemary and Coin Purse Charm

Place a sprig of dried rosemary and a small coin in your purse or wallet. As you do, say: "Rosemary green, coin of gold, bring me riches as foretold." The rosemary's protective properties, combined with the coin, will attract and safeguard your financial abundance.

27. Yule Bell Wealth Ringing

Hold a small bell and visualize your financial goals. Ring the bell three times, saying: "Bell so clear, bell so bright, bring me fortune with your light." Repeat this ritual each morning throughout the Yule season to keep the flow of prosperity active.

28. Clover and Nutmeg Abundance Jar

Fill a small jar with dried clover leaves, nutmeg, and a pinch of sugar. Close the jar and hold it in your hands, focusing on your intention. Say: "Clover green, nutmeg spice, bring abundance, make it nice." Keep the jar in your home to attract wealth and success.

29. Prosperity Tea Ritual

Brew a cup of peppermint tea and add a spoonful of honey for sweetness. Stir the tea clockwise with a cinnamon stick while saying: "Tea of mint, honey sweet, bring me wealth, make it complete." Sip the tea slowly, imagining each sip filling you with the energy of prosperity.

30. Gold Ribbon Door Blessing

Tie a gold ribbon around the doorknob of your front door. As you tie it, say: "Ribbon gold, wealth and might, bring abundance, both day and night." The ribbon acts as a welcoming beacon for wealth and prosperity to enter your home.

31. Evergreen and Clover Wealth Spell

Place a few sprigs of pine and a four-leaf clover in a small pouch. Add a small coin to the pouch and tie it closed with green thread. Hold the pouch in your hands and say: "Pine of green, clover true, bring abundance, both fresh and new." Keep this charm in a place where you handle money, such as a wallet, cash register, or desk.

32. Cinnamon Pinecone Abundance Charm

Coat a pinecone with honey and sprinkle it with ground cinnamon. Hold the pinecone in your hands and say: "Pinecone sweet, cinnamon bright, bring me fortune, wealth, and light." Place the pinecone on your altar or windowsill to attract prosperity into your home.

33. Sunflower Seed Money Spell

Hold a handful of sunflower seeds in your hands and focus on your financial goals. Say: "Seeds of gold, seeds of light, bring me fortune, day and night." Plant the seeds in a pot of soil and tend to them regularly. As the seeds grow, visualize your wealth expanding.

34. Apple and Cinnamon Money Bowl

Place a whole apple in a bowl and surround it with cinnamon sticks and coins. Hold your hands over the bowl and say: "Apple bright, cinnamon pure, bring abundance, steady and sure." Keep the bowl on your kitchen counter or dining table to draw prosperity into your home.

35. Yule Candle Anointment

Anoint a green candle with a few drops of cinnamon and orange essential oils. Light the candle and say: "Candle bright, green of hue, bring abundance, fresh and true." Allow the candle to burn completely, visualizing the flame attracting wealth and success to you.

36. Silver Coin Night Spell

On a clear winter night, place a silver coin outside where it can catch the moonlight. Say: "Moon so bright, coin of light, draw me fortune through this night." The next morning, place the coin in your wallet or purse to carry the moon's energy of abundance with you.

37. Cinnamon Incense Prosperity Ritual

Light a stick of cinnamon incense and hold it in your hands while focusing on your intention to draw wealth. Say: "Smoke of spice, scent so sweet, bring me riches, make it neat." Waft the incense around your home, letting the scent fill every corner with prosperous energy.

38. Golden Thread Knot Spell

Cut a piece of golden thread and tie three knots along its length. With each knot, speak your intention: "Knot of one, wealth begun; knot of two, fortune true; knot of three, prosperity." Carry the knotted thread with you or place it on your altar as a charm for abundance.

39. Nutmeg and Clove Prosperity Pouch

Fill a small pouch with whole nutmeg and cloves. Hold the pouch in your hands and say: "Nutmeg bright, clove so strong, bring me fortune all year long." Keep the pouch near your workspace to draw financial success into your endeavors.

40. Peppermint Wealth Bath

Prepare a warm bath and add a handful of fresh or dried peppermint leaves. Light a green candle beside the bath and say: "Mint of green, fresh and bright, bring me wealth, day and night." Soak in the bath, feeling its refreshing energy washing away financial blocks and opening you to abundance.

41. Sunwheel Abundance Spell

Create a sunwheel using evergreen branches and gold ribbon. Hang the sunwheel in a prominent place in your home, such as above your hearth or near a window. Say: "Wheel of sun, turn so free, bring abundance unto me." The sunwheel symbolizes the cycle of abundance and prosperity returning to your life.

42. Candle Flame Money Magnet

Light a gold or green candle and hold a coin in your hand. Gaze at the candle flame and say: "Flame so bright, flame so clear, bring me riches far and near." Place the coin in a small dish near the candle as it burns, visualizing it attracting wealth.

43. Cinnamon and Pine Sugar Jar

Fill a small jar with sugar, a cinnamon stick, and a few pine needles. Seal the jar and hold it in your hands, focusing on the sweetness of life and financial abundance. Say: "Sugar sweet, cinnamon strong, bring me wealth all season long." Keep the jar in your kitchen to attract prosperity.

44. Holly and Ivy Wealth Blessing

Gather a sprig of holly and a length of ivy. Wrap the ivy around the holly while saying: "Holly bright, ivy free, bring abundance unto me." Place this charm on your altar or mantle as a magnet for financial blessings throughout the season.

45. Cinnamon Apple Abundance Circle

Slice an apple horizontally to reveal its star-shaped core. Place the slices in a circle on your altar. Sprinkle cinnamon on each slice while saying: "Apple of earth, cinnamon bright, bring me abundance, day and night." Leave the apple slices for three days, then bury them outside to release the energy into the universe.

These spells use the elements of Yule—evergreens, spices, warmth, and light—to draw wealth, success, and prosperity into your life. Through focusing your intentions and working with the energies of the season, you open pathways for abundance to flow to you naturally.

Chapter 5: Love and Friendship Spells

Yule is a time of warmth, togetherness, and renewal, making it a powerful season for fostering love, friendship, and harmony in relationships. The following 30 spells harness the elements of the season—evergreens, spices, light, and warmth—to attract new love, deepen existing connections, and heal rifts. These spells are designed to infuse your life with the gentle, nurturing energy of winter, creating an environment where love and friendship can thrive.

1. Yule Candle of Love

Choose a pink or red candle to symbolize love and affection. Carve a symbol of your choice (such as a heart or your initials) into the candle. Anoint it with rose or cinnamon oil. Light the candle and say: "Flame of love, burn so bright, bring harmony, both day and night." Sit quietly, focusing on the candle's warmth radiating love into your life. Allow the candle to burn out completely to release the energy.

2. Holly and Rose Petal Friendship Charm

Fill a small cloth sachet with dried holly leaves and rose petals. Hold the sachet close to your heart, envisioning the bonds of friendship being strengthened. Say: "Holly strong, rose so sweet, bring friends closer, make love replete." Keep the charm in a drawer or carry it with you to reinforce harmony in friendships.

3. Winter Rose Tea Ritual

Brew a pot of tea using rose petals and honey. Hold the cup in your hands and say: "Rose of love, honey sweet, bring harmony to those I meet." Share the tea with a loved one or friend, drinking it slowly and focusing on the warmth and love filling your relationship.

4. Cinnamon Stick Bonding Spell

Tie two cinnamon sticks together with red ribbon, symbolizing the bond between you and a loved one. As you tie the knot, say: "Cinnamon strong, cinnamon true, bind our hearts, me to you." Place the charm on your mantle or bedside table to strengthen the bond.

5. Yule Tree Blessing for Relationships

As you decorate your Yule tree, choose an ornament that symbolizes love or friendship. Hold it in your hands and say: "Tree of Yule, evergreen and bright, bless this bond with warmth and light." Place the ornament on the tree, visualizing it radiating harmony and love throughout the season.

6. Rose Quartz Love Bath

Prepare a warm bath and add a handful of rose petals and a few drops of rose oil. Place a rose quartz stone in the water, focusing on the energy of love surrounding you. Say: "Rose of love, stone of grace, bring me warmth in every space." Soak in the bath, allowing its soothing energy to fill you with love and open your heart to others.

7. Snowflake Friendship Spell

Cut out a paper snowflake and write the names of friends you wish to strengthen bonds with on each arm of the snowflake. Hold it in your hands and say: "Snowflake bright, bonds of light, keep our friendship ever tight." Hang the snowflake in a window to reflect your intentions into the world.

8. Evergreen Love Knot

Using a small sprig of pine, tie a knot with a piece of red yarn around it. Hold the sprig in your hands and say: "Pine of green, love so true, keep us close, me and you." Place this charm near a photograph of you and your loved one to maintain a bond of love and harmony.

9. Apple and Honey Friendship Ritual

Cut an apple in half horizontally, revealing its star-shaped core. Drizzle honey over each half and say: "Apple sweet, honey pure, bring our friendship warmth and sure." Share the apple with a friend, taking turns feeding each other a slice to symbolize shared love and harmony.

10. Holly and Ivy Love Blessing

Wrap a sprig of holly and ivy together with a pink ribbon. Hold the bundle in your hands, focusing on the love you wish to cultivate. Say: "Holly strong, ivy free, bind our hearts in harmony." Place the charm on your mantle or altar as a symbol of enduring love.

11. Pink Candle Healing Spell

Light a pink candle to symbolize love and healing. Sit quietly and focus on the flame, letting its warmth fill your heart. Say: "Candle pink, flame so true, heal our bond, renew love's hue." Allow the candle to burn completely, releasing its energy into your relationship.

12. Winter Solstice Connection Ritual

On the Winter Solstice, sit with your loved one around a fire or a circle of candles. Hold hands and take turns sharing what you appreciate about each other. Say: "Solstice night, longest of all, deepen our bond, answer love's call." This ritual strengthens your connection by sharing warmth and gratitude.

13. Sugar and Spice Love Jar

Fill a small jar with sugar, cinnamon, and dried rose petals. Seal the jar with a pink ribbon and hold it in your hands, saying: "Sugar and spice, love entice, bring us joy, warmth, and light." Keep this jar in your kitchen to bring harmony into your home.

14. Peppermint Peace Spell

Brew a cup of peppermint tea and stir it clockwise with a cinnamon stick. Hold the cup in your hands, saying: "Mint of calm, spice of peace, bring our love sweet release." Drink the tea with your partner to soothe tension and invite a peaceful energy into your relationship.

15. Friendship Knot Ritual

Take a piece of green thread and tie nine knots along its length. As you tie each knot, say: "Knot of one, friendship begun; knot of two, bond so true." Continue until all nine knots are tied. Place the thread under your pillow to strengthen friendships and maintain harmony.

16. Orange and Clove Attraction Spell

Take an orange and insert cloves into its skin in a spiral pattern. As you insert each clove, say: "Orange of sun, clove of might, bring me love, pure and bright." Place the orange on your altar to attract new love or enhance an existing relationship.

17. Crystal Grid for Harmony

Create a simple crystal grid on your altar using rose quartz, amethyst, and clear quartz arranged in a circle. Place a photograph of you and your loved one in the center. As you lay each crystal, say: "Crystals bright, love so clear, bring us harmony year to year." Keep the grid in place throughout the Yule season.

18. Cinnamon and Sugar Love Sachet

Fill a small cloth sachet with cinnamon sticks and a pinch of sugar. Hold the sachet in your hands and say: "Cinnamon sweet, sugar pure, bring me love that will endure." Place the sachet in your dresser or under your pillow to draw love into your life.

19. Rose Petal New Love Ritual

On a new moon, scatter dried rose petals in a circle on your altar. Place a pink candle in the center and light it, saying: "Rose of love, moon so new, bring me love, warm and true." Allow the candle to burn completely, then bury the rose petals outside to release your intention.

20. Heart of Evergreen Spell

Form a small heart shape using evergreen branches and secure them with red thread. Hold the heart in your hands and say: "Evergreen, heart so true, bring us love, me and you." Hang this heart on your Yule tree or in your room to attract or strengthen love.

21. Love's Reflection Mirror Spell

Take a small hand mirror and write "Love" on the glass with a washable marker. Hold the mirror in your hands and say: "Mirror bright, reflect love's light, bring harmony both day and night." Place the mirror face-up on your altar to reflect loving energy into your life.

22. Winter Love Candle Circle

Place five candles (white, pink, red, green, and gold) in a circle on your altar. Light each candle, saying: "Candle bright, flame so true, bring me love, pure and new." Sit in the circle of light, visualizing love entering your life or strengthening an existing relationship.

23. Cinnamon Heart Love Charm

Bake heart-shaped cookies with cinnamon and sugar. Hold each cookie in your hands, saying: "Cinnamon heart, sugar sweet, bring us love, joy complete." Share the cookies with your loved one to share the warmth and love.

24. Yule Wreath Blessing

Create a Yule wreath using evergreen branches and decorate it with red and pink ribbons. Hold the wreath and say: "Wreath of Yule, wreath of might, bring us love through winter's night." Hang the wreath on your front door to invite love and harmony into your home.

25. Moonlit Love Letter

Write a letter to your partner or a potential love, expressing your desires and intentions for the relationship. Place the letter under the moonlight on a clear winter night. Say: "Moon so bright, hear my plea, bring love's joy to me." Keep the letter in a special place as a reminder of your intentions.

26. Honey and Rose Petal Elixir

Create an elixir by placing dried rose petals in a jar of honey. Seal the jar and hold it in your hands, saying: "Honey sweet, rose so fair, bring me love beyond compare." Add a spoonful of this elixir to tea or use it in baking to sweeten your relationships.

27. Holly Ring of Love

Make a small ring using holly leaves and secure it with red thread. Place a pink candle in the center of the ring and light it, saying: "Holly ring, love's embrace, fill our hearts with gentle grace." Let the candle burn down to infuse the ring with love.

28. Rose Quartz Gift Exchange

Gift a rose quartz crystal to a friend or partner as a token of love. Before giving it, hold the crystal in your hands and say: "Quartz of rose, stone of light, bring us love, pure and bright." This shared crystal strengthens the bond between you.

29. Red Ribbon Affection Spell

Tie a red ribbon around your wrist or ankle, saying: "Ribbon red, warm and bright, bring me love, hold me tight." Wear the ribbon throughout the Yule season to attract love and deepen bonds.

30. Evergreen and Lavender Peace Pouch

Fill a small sachet with evergreen sprigs and dried lavender. Hold the sachet close to your heart, saying: "Evergreen, lavender bright, bring us peace, day and night." Keep the sachet in your bedroom to foster a loving and harmonious atmosphere.

These spells use the symbols and energies of Yule—evergreens, warmth, light, and spices—to enhance love and friendship in your life. Whether you are seeking new love, strengthening a current relationship, or fostering harmony with friends, these rituals will help you open your heart and invite deeper, more fulfilling connections.

Chapter 6: Inner Peace and Reflection Spells

Winter is a season of stillness, introspection, and rest. The quiet of Yule provides the perfect opportunity to retreat inward, reflecting on the past year, releasing emotional burdens, and seeking inner peace. This chapter contains 30 spells designed to guide you through a journey of self-discovery, emotional balance, and mental tranquility. Drawing on the serene energy of winter, these spells employ elements such as candles, herbs, snow, and evergreens to create a sacred space for introspection and inner calm.

1. Yule Candle Meditation

Select a blue or white candle, colors associated with peace and clarity. Light the candle and sit comfortably. Close your eyes and focus on the warmth of the flame, feeling its glow permeate your body. Say: "Flame of winter, burn so bright, grant me peace, both day and night." Allow the candle to burn as you breathe deeply, letting its light clear away mental fog and anxiety.

2. Snow Silence Ritual

On a quiet, snowy day, stand outside and let the stillness of the falling snow surround you. Close your eyes and listen to the silence, breathing in the crisp air. Say: "Snow so pure, snow so still, grant me peace, bend to my will." Let the snow's calm energy fill you, bringing a sense of tranquility and inner balance.

3. Evergreen Tea Reflection

Brew a cup of evergreen tea using pine needles (make sure they are safe to consume) and honey. Hold the cup in your hands and breathe in the earthy scent. As you sip the tea, say: "Evergreen, so strong and free, bring me peace, let me be." Drink slowly, allowing the warmth to center you and open your mind to reflection.

4. Winter Moon Bath

Prepare a warm bath infused with a handful of dried lavender and a few drops of peppermint oil. Light a white candle and place it beside the tub. As you soak, say: "Moon of winter, calm and clear, grant me peace, draw me near." Visualize the water washing away your worries, leaving behind a deep sense of calm and mental clarity.

5. Lavender and Rosemary Peace Pouch

Fill a small cloth sachet with dried lavender and rosemary. Hold the sachet close to your heart, feeling its soothing scent surround you. Say: "Lavender calm, rosemary clear, bring me peace, draw me near." Keep this pouch under your pillow or in your pocket to carry tranquility with you.

6. Birch Bark Reflection Spell

Write your worries or emotional burdens on a piece of birch bark using a pencil. Hold the bark in your hands, focusing on your intention to release these burdens. Say: "Birch of white, pure and clear, grant me peace, dispel my fear." Burn the bark safely in a fire-safe dish or fireplace, visualizing your worries turning to ash and leaving you with a sense of inner peace.

7. Snowflake Meditation

Cut out a paper snowflake and hold it in your hands. As you gaze at its intricate pattern, focus on the uniqueness of each snowflake and how it mirrors your own complexities. Say: "Snowflake bright, snowflake clear, help me see what lies near." Use this time to reflect on the beauty within you and the peace that comes from self-acceptance.

8. Yule Log of Release

Choose a small log and carve symbols of peace, such as runes or simple shapes, into the wood. Place the log in the fireplace, sprinkle it with rosemary, and light it, saying: "Yule log burn, warm and free, grant me peace, let me be." As it burns, visualize it absorbing your inner turmoil and transforming it into calm energy.

9. Morning Dew Reflection

On a frosty morning, collect a small amount of dew or frost in a glass dish. Place it on your altar and sit quietly, focusing on the stillness of the morning. Say: "Morning dew, calm and clear, bring me peace, help me hear." Allow the dew's energy to quiet your mind and aid in introspection.

10. Candlelit Snow Mirror

Fill a small bowl with snow and place a white candle behind it. Light the candle, letting its reflection shine on the snow. Say: "Snow so pure, light so bright, grant me peace on this night." Gaze into the reflection, allowing it to guide your thoughts inward and bring a sense of serenity.

11. Rosemary Cleansing Breath

Hold a sprig of dried rosemary in your hands and close your eyes. Inhale deeply, drawing in the scent of rosemary. Say: "Rosemary strong, scent so clear, bring me peace, draw me near." Take several deep breaths, focusing on the energy of the herb clearing your mind and restoring balance.

12. Crystal Grid for Calm

Create a crystal grid using amethyst, clear quartz, and blue lace agate arranged in a circle. Place a small piece of selenite in the center. As you lay each crystal, say: "Crystals bright, calm and clear, bring me peace, draw me near." Sit quietly beside the grid, allowing its energy to wash over you.

13. Winter Wind Whisper

On a windy day, go outside and face the wind. Close your eyes and allow the wind to carry away your anxieties. Say: "Wind of winter, strong and free, take my worries far from me." Feel the gusts lifting your emotional burdens, leaving you with a sense of lightness.

14. Candle Flame Tranquility

Light a blue candle and sit in a quiet, dimly lit room. Gaze at the candle's flame and say: "Flame of blue, calm and bright, grant me peace this Yule night." Breathe deeply, synchronizing your breath with the flickering of the flame, allowing it to bring a sense of inner stillness.

15. Pine Needle Reflection Bath

Fill a muslin bag with pine needles and place it in your bathwater. As you soak, say: "Pine so green, scent so pure, grant me peace, let me endure." Visualize the pine's energy cleansing your spirit and grounding you in the present moment.

16. Peppermint Tea Calm

Brew a cup of peppermint tea and hold it in your hands. Close your eyes and breathe in the steam. Say: "Mint of calm, breath of peace, soothe my mind, bring release." Drink the tea slowly, feeling its warmth dissolve any mental tension.

17. Birch and Snow Meditation

Gather a small piece of birch bark and a handful of snow. Place the snow in a bowl and set the birch on top. Sit quietly, focusing on the stillness of winter. Say: "Birch of white, snow so clear, grant me peace, quiet my fear." Meditate on the simplicity of the scene, allowing it to center your thoughts.

18. Bay Leaf Release

Write your worries or stresses on a bay leaf. Hold the leaf between your palms and say: "Bay of green, take my plight, grant me peace, day and night." Burn the leaf in a fire-safe dish, visualizing the smoke carrying your troubles away.

19. Lavender and Cedar Room Spray

Create a room spray by mixing water, a few drops of lavender essential oil, and cedar oil in a spray bottle. Walk through your space, misting the air while saying: "Lavender calm, cedar strong, grant me peace, all day long." This spray fills your environment with a calming energy.

20. Evergreen Circle of Peace

Form a small circle using pine branches and place it on your altar. Light a white candle in the center of the circle. Sit quietly and say: "Circle of green, light so pure, bring me peace, let me endure." Allow the candle to burn down, filling the room with tranquility.

21. Morning Journal Spell

On a quiet winter morning, take a notebook and write down your thoughts, worries, and reflections. When finished, hold the notebook close to your heart and say: "Words of mine, thoughts so near, bring me peace, make things clear." Use this practice to gain insight into your inner world.

22. Holly and Pine Meditation

Hold a sprig of holly in one hand and a pine needle in the other. Close your eyes and breathe deeply. Say: "Holly strong, pine so free, grant me peace, let me be." Focus on the contrasting energies of the two plants, finding balance within their union.

23. Snow-Covered Path Reflection

On a snowy day, find a quiet path and walk slowly, observing the silence around you. With each step, say: "Snow so soft, path so clear, bring me peace, quiet my fear." Allow the walk to center your thoughts and ground you in the present moment.

24. Candle and Quartz Balance

Place a piece of clear quartz beside a lit candle. As the light refracts through the quartz, say: "Quartz of clarity, flame of light, bring me balance, day and night." Sit with this setup for a few minutes, letting its energy restore your inner equilibrium.

25. Frosted Window Reflection

Draw a symbol of peace on a frosted window with your finger. As you draw, say: "Frost of night, calm and clear, bring me peace, keep me near." Watch as the frost slowly melts, taking with it your tension and stress.

26. Lavender Pillow Peace

Fill a small pouch with dried lavender and place it under your pillow. As you lay down to sleep, say: "Lavender pure, lavender bright, grant me peace through the night." Let the scent of lavender soothe your mind and guide you into a restful sleep.

27. Candlelit Bath Ritual

Run a warm bath and light several candles around the bathroom. Add a few drops of chamomile oil to the water. As you soak, say: "Water warm, light so bright, bring me peace, calm my sight." Allow the bath to cleanse your spirit and relax your body.

28. Amethyst Tranquility Spell

Hold a piece of amethyst in your hands and close your eyes. Focus on its energy bringing calmness to your mind. Say: "Amethyst bright, stone of peace, calm my spirit, grant release." Carry the stone with you or place it under your pillow for continued serenity.

29. Nutmeg and Orange Oil Anointment

Mix a drop of nutmeg essential oil with a drop of orange oil. Anoint your wrists with this blend while saying: "Nutmeg warm, orange bright, bring me peace, day and night." The scent will help uplift your mood and soothe emotional turbulence.

30. Winter Sunlight Meditation

On a sunny winter day, stand in a patch of sunlight. Close your eyes and let the warmth of the sun wash over you. Say: "Sun of winter, cold yet bright, fill me with peace, grant me light." Allow the sunlight to melt away your worries, leaving behind a sense of inner harmony.

Chapter 7: Releasing the Old

As the year draws to a close, the Yule season offers a powerful opportunity to let go of what no longer serves us. Releasing negativity, bad habits, and lingering issues from the past year is essential for making room for new growth and positive change. This chapter contains 35 spells designed to help you clear emotional clutter, break free from old patterns, and cleanse your spirit. These rituals harness the energies of winter, such as the purifying power of snow, the cleansing properties of evergreens, and the transformative force of fire.

1. Snow Melting Release

On a snowy day, gather a small bowl of snow and place it on your altar. Write down your worries or bad habits on a piece of paper. Tear the paper into small pieces and sprinkle it over the snow, saying: "Snow so pure, melt and flow, take my burdens as you go." Place the bowl outside and let the snow melt naturally, visualizing it absorbing and dissolving your troubles as it seeps into the earth.

2. Evergreen Cleansing Smoke

Burn a bundle of dried pine or cedar in a fireproof dish. As the smoke rises, waft it around yourself or your space, saying: "Smoke of pine, cleanse so clear, release the old, draw it near." As the smoke fills the room, imagine it carrying away lingering negativity.

3. Candle Flame Release Ritual

Light a black candle and sit quietly before it. Write down on a piece of paper the bad habits, negativity, or lingering issues you wish to release. Hold the paper over the candle flame, saying: "Flame of night, burn so bright, release the old, grant me light." Allow the paper to catch fire and burn completely. As it turns to ash, envision the old energy leaving you.

4. Salt and Rosemary Bath

Fill your bathtub with warm water and add a handful of sea salt and a few sprigs of fresh or dried rosemary. As you soak, say: "Salt of earth, rosemary pure, cleanse me now, make me sure." Visualize the water drawing out negative energy, leaving you refreshed and renewed.

5. Winter Wind Release

On a windy winter day, go outside and stand in an open space. Close your eyes and focus on the issues you wish to release. Say: "Wind of winter, strong and free, take my troubles, set them free." As the wind blows past you, imagine it sweeping away your worries and old habits.

6. Pine Cone Burial

Hold a small pine cone in your hands and focus on what you wish to release. Whisper your intentions to the pine cone, saying: "Pine cone small, pine cone bright, take my burdens, clear my sight." Bury the pine cone in the earth, leaving your troubles behind and allowing nature to absorb and transform them.

7. Snow-Covered Stone Spell

Find a small stone and hold it in your hands, focusing on the negativity or habit you wish to let go of. Say: "Stone of earth, cold and clear, take my troubles, draw them near." Cover the stone with snow and place it outside. As the snow melts, imagine the negativity dissolving and being absorbed into the ground.

8. Burning Bay Leaf Release

Write down a word or phrase representing what you wish to release on a bay leaf. Hold the leaf in your hand and say: "Bay of green, cleanse my way, take this burden, clear the day." Burn the bay leaf in a fireproof dish, watching as the smoke carries away your intention.

9. Evergreen Wreath Purging

Create a small wreath using pine branches, holly, and rosemary. As you weave the branches together, focus on the energy of release. Hang the wreath on your door, saying: "Wreath of green, hold my plea, take the old, set me free." Keep the wreath up for three days, then remove it and bury it outside, letting the earth transform the energy.

10. Snow Writing Ritual

Find a patch of undisturbed snow. Use a stick to write in the snow the word or symbol representing what you want to let go of. Say: "Snow so pure, snow so bright, take my troubles out of sight." Walk away, leaving the snow to melt and dissolve your worries.

11. Yule Log Release

Choose a small log and carve symbols or words representing the negative energy you wish to release. Place it in your fireplace and sprinkle it with salt. Light the log, saying: "Yule log burn, warm and free, take this burden far from me." As the log burns, visualize the energy transforming into light.

12. Salt and Sage Doorway Sweep

Sprinkle salt mixed with dried, crushed sage along your doorway. Sweep the mixture out of your house, saying: "Salt and sage, cleanse this space, release the old, leave no trace." This creates a barrier that blocks negativity from re-entering.

13. Candle Circle Cleansing

Arrange four candles (black, white, blue, and green) in a circle on your altar. Sit in the center, focusing on what you need to release. Light each candle, saying: "Circle of light, circle of flame, cleanse my spirit, free my name." Allow the candles to burn down completely, visualizing them absorbing and clearing away the old energy.

14. Holly and Pine Needle Release Pouch

Fill a small pouch with holly leaves and pine needles. Hold the pouch in your hands, focusing on your intention. Say: "Holly strong, pine so green, take my burdens, keep me clean." Leave the pouch in a dark drawer for seven days, then bury it outside to release the energy.

15. Lavender and Chamomile Tea Purge

Brew a cup of lavender and chamomile tea. Hold the cup in your hands, breathing in its calming scent. Say: "Herbs of peace, herbs so free, take my troubles, set me at ease." Drink the tea slowly, imagining it washing away negativity and emotional clutter.

16. Ice Block Release

Fill a small bowl with water and add a pinch of salt. Hold the bowl in your hands and say: "Water freeze, cold and clear, hold my burdens, disappear." Place the bowl in the freezer and let it freeze solid. Once frozen, take the ice outside and shatter it on the ground, imagining the ice breaking apart your troubles.

17. Candle Wax Drip

Light a black candle and let it drip onto a piece of parchment. As the wax pools, say: "Wax of night, drip and flow, take my worries as you go." Allow the wax to harden, then bury the parchment outside, releasing the old energy into the earth.

18. Morning Frost Spell

On a frosty morning, find a quiet spot outdoors. Close your eyes and take a deep breath, focusing on what you want to release. Say: "Frost of morning, cold and bright, take my burdens, make things right." Allow the frost's energy to cleanse you as it evaporates with the rising sun.

19. Rosemary Sprig Release

Hold a fresh sprig of rosemary in your hands. Close your eyes and concentrate on the negative energy you want to let go of. Say: "Rosemary bright, herb of clear, take my troubles, draw them near." Hang the rosemary above your doorway to absorb the energy, then bury it after seven days.

20. Peppermint Wind Spell

On a blustery day, take a peppermint leaf in your hand and hold it up to the wind. Say: "Wind so strong, blow it free, take my troubles far from me." Let the wind take the leaf from your hand, carrying away your negativity.

21. Snowball Release

Pack a small snowball in your hands. Focus on your intention to release the old energy. Say: "Snowball small, snowball bright, take my burdens out of sight." Throw the snowball far, watching as it breaks apart and scatters, releasing your troubles into the air.

22. Selenite Wand Clearing

Hold a selenite wand in your hands, focusing on its cleansing energy. Wave it around your body, saying: "Selenite pure, selenite bright, cleanse my aura, bring me light." This spell clears your energetic field, allowing old, stagnant energy to be released.

23. Pine Needle Door Sweep

Sprinkle a handful of pine needles in front of your door. Sweep them out with a broom, saying: "Needles green, clear the way, take the old, bring the day." The pine needles absorb negative energy as they are swept away.

24. Salt Bowl Release

Fill a small bowl with sea salt. Hold your hands over the bowl, focusing on what you want to release. Say: "Salt so pure, salt so bright, take my burdens, clear my sight." Leave the bowl out overnight, then scatter the salt outside to release the energy.

25. Candle Wax Casting

Light a white candle and let it drip into a bowl of cold water. As the wax hits the water, say: "Wax of white, water clear, take my worries, disappear." Once the wax has cooled, take the hardened pieces and bury them outside.

26. Yule Candle Reflection Spell

Choose a black candle to represent the release of negative energy. Light the candle and sit in a quiet space. Write on a small piece of paper the negative emotions, bad habits, or burdens you wish to let go of. Hold the paper near the candle's flame and say: "Flame of night, burn away, clear my path, show me the way." Let the flame ignite the paper, then drop it into a fireproof bowl to burn completely. As the paper turns to ash, visualize the negativity dissolving into nothingness.

27. Pine and Salt Release Ritual

Gather a small bowl of sea salt and a few fresh pine needles. Place the pine needles in the bowl of salt, focusing on the energy you want to release. Hold the bowl in your hands and say: "Pine and salt, cleanse so pure, take my burdens, make me sure." Leave the bowl out overnight to absorb negativity. The next morning, scatter the salt and pine needles outside, allowing nature to transform the energy.

28. Snowbound Thought Release

On a snowy day, go outside and find a patch of untouched snow. Use a stick or your finger to write the thoughts, patterns, or habits you wish to release into the snow. As you write, say: "Snow so pure, snow so white, take these burdens, out of sight." Walk away, leaving the snow to melt naturally. As it melts, imagine the written words dissolving, releasing their hold on you.

29. Holly Leaf Banishing Spell

Take a fresh holly leaf and focus on what you wish to release—whether it's a bad habit, an old grudge, or lingering negativity. Hold the leaf in your hands and say: "Holly strong, banish and clear, take my burdens far from here." Bury the leaf in the ground, asking the earth to absorb and neutralize the negative energy.

30. Full Moon Snow Cleansing

On the night of a full moon, gather a bowl of fresh snow. Place it on your altar or windowsill to catch the moon's light. Write down on a piece of paper what you wish to release. Fold the paper and place it under the bowl of snow, saying: "Moon so bright, snow so clear, cleanse my spirit, calm my fear." Allow the snow to melt overnight, then pour the water outside, symbolizing the release of your burdens.

31. Eucalyptus and Lavender Smoke Cleansing

Burn a bundle of eucalyptus and lavender in a fireproof dish. As the smoke rises, move it around your body or space, saying: "Smoke so sweet, cleanse this place, take the old, leave no trace." Visualize the smoke absorbing the negative energy, carrying it away and leaving you feeling lighter and more centered.

32. Birch Bark Release Writing

Write down your burdens, bad habits, or negative thoughts on a piece of birch bark using a pencil. Hold the bark in your hands, focusing on your intention to let go. Say: "Birch of white, clear and free, take my burdens, set me free." Tear the bark into small pieces and bury them in the ground, leaving behind the energy you wish to release.

33. Rosemary Bath Release

Prepare a warm bath and add a handful of dried rosemary and a few drops of lavender essential oil. Light a white candle and place it near the bath. As you soak, say: "Rosemary pure, water bright, wash away the old tonight." Close your eyes and visualize the water pulling negativity and stress out of your body, leaving you refreshed and renewed. After the bath, drain the water, imagining it taking away the old energy.

34. Selenite Wand Energy Clearing

Hold a selenite wand in your hands and close your eyes. Take a deep breath and visualize the selenite glowing with a pure, white light. Move the wand around your body, especially over your head, heart, and solar plexus, saying: "Selenite pure, selenite bright, cleanse my aura, bring me light." As you do this, imagine the wand drawing out negativity, stagnant energy, and bad habits from your aura, replacing them with calm and clarity.

35. Burning List of Release

Write a list of everything you wish to release from the past year on a piece of parchment. Light a black candle and use its flame to ignite the paper. As it burns, say: "Flame of night, burn away, take my troubles, clear the way." Let the paper burn completely, and then scatter the ashes outside, envisioning them dissolving into the earth.

Chapter 8: Snow Magic and Winter Elements

Winter holds a unique magic that is deeply connected to the earth's cycles of rest, renewal, and quiet power. Snow, ice, frost, and other elements of the season bring an energy of purification, transformation, and deep reflection. This chapter explores the powerful properties of snow and winter elements, providing 50 spells that tap into their potential for a wide range of magical purposes—protection, manifestation, love, healing, and spiritual growth. Each spell uses the essence of winter to weave magic in its purest and most potent form.

1. Snow Purification Spell

Gather fresh snow in a small bowl and hold it in your hands. Focus on any negative energy or emotional clutter you wish to clear away. Say: "Snow so pure, snow so bright, cleanse my spirit with your light." As the snow melts, imagine it absorbing negativity and washing it away. Pour the water outside, visualizing it carrying away all that you've released.

2. Frost Drawing Manifestation

On a frosty morning, use your finger to draw a symbol or write a word on a frosted window representing what you wish to manifest (e.g., love, peace, strength). As you draw, say: "Frost so clear, cold and bright, bring my wishes into light." Let the frost melt naturally, allowing your intention to flow into the universe.

3. Snowflake Blessing Charm

Catch a snowflake on a piece of black fabric to see its unique pattern. Gaze at it for a moment, focusing on what you wish to bless (a person, object, or situation). Say: "Snowflake bright, crystal clear, bless with magic far and near." Once the snowflake melts, place a drop of the water on the object or your hands to impart the blessing.

4. Ice Crystal Protection Spell

Fill a small bowl with water and place a clear quartz crystal in it. Place the bowl outside to freeze overnight, saying: "Water freeze, crystal bright, guard this space with winter's might." Once frozen, place the bowl near your home's entrance to act as a protective shield. Allow it to melt gradually, imagining it absorbing and neutralizing negativity.

5. Snowball Wish

Form a snowball with fresh, clean snow. Hold it in your hands and focus on a wish you want to make. Whisper your wish into the snowball, saying: "Snowball bright, snowball pure, grant my wish, make it sure." Toss the snowball into the air or into a natural space, letting it dissolve and release your wish into the world.

6. Ice Candle Meditation

Place a small candle inside a bowl of ice. Light the candle and say: "Candle warm, ice so bright, bring me clarity through this night." As the candle burns and the ice melts, meditate on the idea of warmth and light emerging from the cold, bringing insight and inner calm.

7. Snowbound Dream Spell

On a snowy night, gather snow in a small jar and place it beside your bed. Before sleeping, say: "Snow of night, cold and clear, bring me dreams, make them near." The snow's energy will help promote vivid dreams, providing insights into your subconscious. In the morning, pour the melted snow outside, symbolizing the release of dream energies into the world.

8. Snowflake Essence Healing

Catch fresh snowflakes in a clean bowl, letting them melt. Pour the melted water into a small vial. Hold the vial in your hands, focusing on its healing properties. Say: "Snow so pure, water clear, bring me healing, draw me near." Use a drop of this snow essence in a bath, anoint your forehead, or add it to a spell bottle to enhance healing energy.

9. Winter Wind Cleansing

On a windy day, stand outside with your arms outstretched. Close your eyes and say: "Wind of winter, strong and free, cleanse my spirit, set me free." Allow the wind to pass through you, imagining it sweeping away any lingering negativity or stagnant energy.

10. Icicle Binding Spell

Choose a long icicle and hold it in your hands, focusing on something you wish to bind (e.g., a bad habit, a negative influence). Whisper your intention into the icicle, saying: "Icicle sharp, ice so strong, bind this trouble, keep it long." Place the icicle outside in a secure spot. As it melts, visualize the binding energy dissolving and neutralizing the unwanted influence.

11. Snow Circle Protection

On a snowy day, go outside and walk in a circle around yourself or your home, packing the snow with your footsteps. As you complete the circle, say: "Circle of snow, cold and bright, guard this space with winter's might." This snow circle forms a temporary but potent barrier against negative energies.

12. Ice Reflection Scrying

Freeze a bowl of water until a thin layer of ice forms on its surface. Gaze into the ice, focusing on your question or seeking guidance. Say: "Ice so clear, ice so bright, show me truths hidden from sight." Watch as shapes and symbols form in the ice, providing insights into your query.

13. Snow-Covered Herb Spell

Sprinkle a handful of dried rosemary or sage onto fresh snow. Gather the snow and herbs in a cloth pouch, saying: "Snow so pure, herbs so bright, bring protection through the night." Hang the pouch near your doorway to create a protective charm that wards off negativity.

14. Frosted Window Love Spell

On a frosty window, use your finger to draw a heart or other love symbols. Focus on the love you wish to attract or strengthen. Say: "Frost of love, cold and clear, draw love's warmth, bring it near." Let the frost melt naturally, releasing the energy of love into your space.

15. Snowball Banishing

Form a snowball and hold it in your hands, visualizing what you wish to banish (e.g., negativity, bad habits). Say: "Snowball bright, take my plight, banish troubles, out of sight." Throw the snowball away from you, imagining it carrying away the energy you wish to release.

16. Ice and Candle Clarity Spell

Place a small candle inside a bowl surrounded by ice cubes. Light the candle and say: "Ice of night, candle bright, clear my mind, give me sight." As the candle burns and the ice melts, focus on gaining mental clarity and insight.

17. Snow-Covered Pinecone Healing

Place a pinecone in a bowl and cover it with fresh snow. As you do, say: "Pine of earth, snow of white, bring me healing, set things right." Allow the snow to melt over the pinecone. Keep the pinecone on your altar as a symbol of ongoing healing.

18. Icicle Charging

Choose a long, clear icicle and hold it up to the sky. Focus on the energy you wish to draw into it (e.g., protection, love, wisdom). Say: "Icicle sharp, ice so clear, charge with magic, bring it near." Place the icicle outside near your home to absorb and radiate the desired energy.

19. Snow-Dipped Candle Blessing

Dip the base of a white candle in fresh snow, allowing it to freeze slightly. As you light the candle, say: "Candle bright, dipped in snow, bless this space, let it glow." The combination of fire and ice brings balance and calm to your surroundings.

20. Frozen Petal Love Spell

Collect rose petals and place them in a bowl of water. Put the bowl outside to freeze overnight, saying: "Ice of love, hold so tight, bring me love, pure and bright." Once frozen, remove the ice and place it in a safe spot to melt naturally, allowing the loving energy to flow.

21. Icicle Spell of Stillness

Find an icicle and hold it gently in your hands. Focus on the calm, still energy it represents. Say: "Icicle of silence, icicle so still, bring me peace, bend to my will." Place the icicle outside to melt naturally. As it melts, imagine the stillness and peace spreading through your life, quieting chaos and anxiety.

22. Snow Lantern Light Spell

Create a snow lantern by packing snow around a small candleholder or jar. Place a candle inside and light it, saying: "Snow so pure, lantern bright, fill my path with guiding light." Place the lantern outside or on a windowsill to symbolize the light of hope during dark times. Let it burn down completely, filling your space with clarity and purpose.

23. Winter Leaf Transformation

Find a leaf partially covered in snow. Hold the leaf in your hands and focus on a personal trait or habit you wish to change. Say: "Leaf of change, snow of white, transform my spirit, grant me might." Bury the leaf in the snow, allowing the earth to absorb the energy of transformation.

24. Frosted Glass Vision

On a frosty morning, take a glass or mirror and let it frost naturally. Place it on your altar and gaze into its surface, focusing on a question or situation. Say: "Frost of glass, show me true, bring me sight, old and new." As the frost melts, watch for shapes or symbols that provide guidance.

25. Ice Candle Manifestation

Fill a bowl with water and place a small candle in the center. Put the bowl outside to freeze. When the water turns to ice, light the candle and say: "Ice so strong, flame so bright, manifest my dreams this night." Allow the candle to burn down, melting the ice and releasing your intentions into the universe.

26. Snow-Drawn Pentacle Protection

In a snowy area, use a stick to draw a large pentacle on the ground. Stand in the center of the pentacle and say: "Snow so pure, drawn with care, guard my spirit, hold me there." Visualize the pentacle forming a shield of light around you, providing protection and strength.

27. Icicle Focus Spell

Hold a long icicle in your hand and concentrate on an intention or goal you want to focus on. Say: "Icicle sharp, clear and bright, bring my focus to its height." Place the icicle on your windowsill to melt naturally. As it melts, imagine it clearing distractions and honing your mental clarity.

28. Snow-Infused Candle for Peace

Collect a handful of snow and place it in a bowl. Light a white candle and let a few drops of wax fall onto the snow, saying: "Snow of peace, candle bright, calm my spirit, bring me light." Allow the snow to melt, then use the water to anoint your forehead, bringing tranquility to your mind and spirit.

29. Evergreen Snow Blessing

Gather a small branch of pine or fir and dip it in fresh snow. Gently shake the branch over your head, allowing the snow to fall around you. Say: "Evergreen of winter, snow of white, bless me now, fill me with light." Visualize the snow washing away negativity and blessing you with the earth's strength.

30. Snow Mirror Clearing

Find a quiet spot with a snowy surface. Use a small mirror to reflect the snow's light onto yourself, saying: "Snow so clear, mirror bright, cleanse my aura, make it light." Hold the mirror until you feel a sense of purification and clarity.

31. Frozen Herb Purification

Place a few sprigs of rosemary in a bowl of water. Set the bowl outside to freeze overnight. In the morning, hold the frozen bowl in your hands and say: "Herbs of earth, frozen bright, cleanse this space, set things right." Allow the ice to melt in your home, releasing the cleansing energy of the herbs.

32. Snowstorm Visualization

During a snowstorm, sit quietly by a window and watch the snow fall. Close your eyes and imagine the storm swirling around your worries and fears. Say: "Snowstorm wild, fierce and free, take my troubles far from me." Visualize the storm carrying away the negativity and leaving behind calm and peace.

33. Ice Heart Spell for Emotional Healing

Fill a heart-shaped mold with water and place a rose petal in it. Freeze it, then hold the ice heart in your hands, focusing on emotional wounds you wish to heal. Say: "Heart of ice, rose so true, heal my pain, bring peace anew." Allow the heart to melt naturally, releasing the energy of healing and love.

34. Snow-Dipped Branch Protection

Find a small branch and dip it into fresh snow. Place it on your altar and say: "Branch of earth, snow of light, guard this space, protect with might." Keep the branch on your altar throughout winter to ward off negativity and invite protection.

35. Frost on Glass Release

Breathe onto a cold glass surface to create frost. Use your finger to write a word representing something you wish to release (e.g., fear, anger). Say: "Frost so cold, hold this plight, take it from me, fade from sight." Watch as the frost dissipates, carrying away the energy you've released.

36. Icicle Water Elixir

Melt an icicle in a small bowl, then add a pinch of sea salt. Hold the bowl in your hands and say: "Water of ice, salt of earth, grant me strength, show my worth." Drink a small sip of the water to absorb the energy of resilience and fortitude.

37. Snow-Drawn Sigil Spell

Find a patch of undisturbed snow and draw a sigil representing your intention (e.g., protection, love, success) using a stick. As you draw, say: "Snow so white, sigil bright, bring my will into the light." Leave the sigil to melt naturally, releasing its energy into the universe.

38. Ice-Encased Candle Binding

Place a small candle in a bowl of water and let it freeze. Write down what you wish to bind (e.g., a bad habit) on a piece of paper. Place the paper under the frozen bowl and light the candle, saying: "Ice and flame, bind and hold, keep this trouble in your fold." As the ice melts and the candle burns, visualize the energy of binding taking effect.

39. Snowflake Visualization

Catch a snowflake on your glove or hand. Study its pattern and focus on a problem or situation in your life. Say: "Snowflake bright, pattern true, show me insight, guide me through." Watch the snowflake melt, allowing it to reveal clarity and guidance regarding your situation.

40. Frozen Fruit Prosperity

Place a small piece of fruit (such as a berry) in a bowl of water and set it outside to freeze. Hold the frozen bowl and say: "Fruit of earth, frozen pure, bring me wealth, make it sure." Place the bowl on your altar and let it melt, releasing prosperity energy into your home.

41. Icicle Energy Charging

Hold an icicle in your hand and focus on the energy you wish to charge it with (e.g., love, courage, peace). Say: "Icicle strong, ice so clear, charge with power, draw it near." Place the icicle outside near your home to release the charged energy as it melts.

42. Snow-Swept Pathway

Walk along a snowy path, focusing on a goal or intention. With each step, say: "Snow beneath, path so bright, lead me forward, show me right." Visualize the snow guiding you toward your desired outcome, clearing obstacles from your path.

43. Ice and Candle Purification

Fill a small glass with water and freeze it. Place a candle on top of the ice and light it. As the candle burns, say: "Ice so cold, flame so bright, cleanse this space with your light." Allow the ice to melt and the candle to burn down, purifying the area and filling it with light.

44. Snowball of Strength

Form a snowball and hold it in your hands. Visualize it absorbing the strength and fortitude of winter. Say: "Snowball strong, cold and bright, fill me with strength, grant me might." Throw the snowball into the air or against a tree, releasing the energy of strength into yourself.

45. Snow-Encased Herb Spell

Place a sprig of rosemary in a small bowl of water and freeze it. Hold the frozen bowl in your hands and say: "Herb of earth, ice so clear, cleanse my spirit, calm my fear." Place the bowl on your altar to melt, releasing the cleansing and calming energy of the herb.

46. Frosted Crystal Charging

Leave a piece of clear quartz outside on a frosty night. In the morning, hold the crystal in your hands and say: "Crystal clear, frost so bright, charge with power, fill with light." Use the crystal in future spells to enhance their potency with the energy of winter.

47. Snowstorm Empowerment

During a snowstorm, stand outside and let the snow swirl around you. Close your eyes and say: "Storm of snow, fierce and free, fill me with power, let me be." Imagine the storm energizing you, filling you with the strength to face challenges.

48. Ice Scrying for Insight

Fill a bowl with water and freeze it. Hold the bowl up to the light and gaze into the ice, looking for patterns or symbols that appear. Say: "Ice of sight, ice so clear, show me truth, bring it near." Use this scrying method to gain insight into questions or situations in your life.

49. Snow-Covered Stone Wish

Find a small stone and cover it with fresh snow. Hold the stone in your hands and focus on a wish you want to make. Say: "Snow of earth, stone so bright, grant my wish, take its flight." Let the snow melt naturally, then carry the stone with you as a charm for your wish to manifest.

50. Snow Globe Meditation Spell

Create a simple snow globe using a glass jar filled with water, glitter, and a small evergreen branch. Seal the jar tightly and hold it in your hands, shaking it gently. Say: "Snow so bright, swirl and flow, bring me calm, let peace grow." Place the snow globe on your altar or in a quiet space. Use it as a focus during meditation, watching the glitter settle to calm your mind and spirit.

Chapter 9: Sun Spells and Returning Light

Yule marks the return of the sun, the turning point where the longest night gives way to increasing light. This rebirth of the sun symbolizes hope, renewal, and the promise of brighter days ahead. As the days slowly lengthen, we celebrate the light's return and invite its warmth into our lives. This chapter contains 40 spells to honor the sun's return and encourage growth, positivity, and light in every aspect of life. Each spell harnesses the energy of the sun and the growing light to bring warmth, inspiration, healing, and transformation.

1. Sun Candle Blessing

Choose a gold or yellow candle to represent the sun. Carve a symbol of the sun or rays into the candle's surface. Anoint it with a few drops of rosemary or orange oil. Light the candle and say: "Candle bright, flame of gold, bring me light, let warmth unfold." Place the candle on your altar and let it burn for at least an hour, focusing on the growing light filling your life.

2. Sun Rise Intention Setting

On a sunny morning, stand outside and face the rising sun. Hold a piece of citrine or clear quartz in your hands and close your eyes. As you feel the sun's warmth, say: "Sunrise bright, dawn so new, fill my soul, renew and true." Focus on setting your intentions for the day, visualizing the sun's energy fueling your goals and dreams.

3. Sun Wheel Ritual

Create a sun wheel using evergreen branches woven into a circle. Decorate it with gold and yellow ribbons. Hang the wheel in a prominent place in your home, saying: "Wheel of light, wheel of sun, turn the darkness, joy begun." This sun wheel serves as a beacon, inviting the sun's growing light into your space.

4. Gold Thread Sun Talisman

Cut a piece of gold thread or ribbon and hold it in your hands. Focus on the light and warmth you wish to draw into your life. As you tie a knot at each end, say: "Thread of gold, light so bright, bring me joy, day and night." Carry the thread with you as a talisman to keep the sun's energy close to you.

5. Sun-Infused Water

Fill a clear glass jar with fresh water and place it in direct sunlight for several hours. Hold the jar in your hands and say: "Water of light, water so clear, fill me with warmth, bring me cheer." Drink a few sips of this sun-infused water whenever you need a boost of energy or positivity.

6. Solar Candle Circle

Arrange five candles (yellow, orange, gold, red, and white) in a circle on your altar. Light each candle, saying: "Circle of flame, circle of light, bring me strength through day and night." Sit within this circle and meditate on the light filling your heart and mind.

7. Orange and Cinnamon Sun Offering

Slice an orange and place the slices on a plate. Sprinkle them with cinnamon, then hold the plate up to the sunlight. Say: "Fruit of sun, spice so sweet, bring me warmth, joy replete." Place the offering on your altar or outside to honor the sun and invite its blessings into your life.

8. Golden Mirror Reflection

Take a small mirror and hold it up to the sunlight, allowing the light to reflect into your home. As you do, say: "Mirror bright, reflect the sun, bring me joy, darkness shun." Use the mirror to fill your space with sunlight, dispelling shadows and inviting clarity.

9. Sun Blessing for Prosperity

At noon, when the sun is at its peak, hold a gold coin in your hands and stand in direct sunlight. Say: "Sun so high, sun so bright, bring me fortune, bring me light." Keep the coin in your wallet or cash drawer as a charm to attract prosperity and abundance.

10. Golden Citrine Meditation

Hold a piece of citrine in your hands and sit in the sunlight. Close your eyes and focus on the warmth of the sun entering the stone. Say: "Citrine bright, stone of light, fill me with joy, set things right." Carry the citrine with you to maintain the sun's energy throughout the day.

11. Sunflower Seed Manifestation

Hold a handful of sunflower seeds in your hands, focusing on your desires and dreams. Say: "Seeds of sun, seeds of light, grow my wishes, bring them bright." Plant the seeds in a pot and nurture them, watching your intentions grow as the seedlings reach for the light.

12. Orange Peel Blessing

Dry orange peels in the sunlight, then place them in a small bowl. Hold the bowl up to the sun and say: "Peel of gold, sun's delight, bring me warmth, guide my sight." Keep the bowl on your altar to draw the sun's energy into your space.

13. Sunstone Energizing Spell

Hold a piece of sunstone in your hand while standing in the sunlight. Close your eyes and say: "Stone of sun, bright and clear, fill me with energy, draw it near." Use this charged stone whenever you need a burst of motivation or energy.

14. Solar Candle Reflection

Light a yellow candle and place it in front of a mirror. As the candle's flame reflects, say: "Flame of light, mirror's glow, bring me clarity, let it show." Sit quietly and meditate on the reflected light, allowing it to bring insights and illumination.

15. Sunlight Cleansing Ritual

Choose a personal item (such as a piece of jewelry or a small stone) and place it in direct sunlight for several hours. Say: "Sun so bright, clear and pure, cleanse this item, make it sure." Allow the sunlight to purify and energize the object.

16. Dawn of Hope Spell

Wake up at dawn and face the rising sun. Hold a piece of clear quartz and say: "Dawn of hope, light so new, fill my heart, make it true." Keep the quartz in a special place as a reminder of the hope and light that the sun brings each day.

17. Sun Herb Tea Ritual

Brew a tea using herbs associated with the sun, such as chamomile, rosemary, or mint. Hold the cup up to the sunlight, saying: "Herbs of sun, warmth so bright, fill my soul, bring me light." Drink the tea slowly, absorbing the sun's energy through the herbs.

18. Solar-Powered Dream Charm

Place a small pouch filled with dried marigold petals in the sunlight for a day. Before bed, hold the pouch in your hands and say: "Sun of day, moon of night, bring me dreams of hope and light." Place the pouch under your pillow to invite positive, illuminating dreams.

19. Sun Crystal Charging

Leave a clear quartz crystal outside in direct sunlight for several hours. Hold the crystal in your hands and say: "Crystal clear, sun so bright, charge with power, fill with light." Use this charged crystal in future spells to enhance their energy with the sun's power.

20. Sunflower Petal Protection

Collect sunflower petals and place them in a small bowl. Hold the bowl up to the sunlight and say: "Petals bright, gold and strong, guard me well, all day long." Sprinkle the petals around your home to create a protective barrier filled with the sun's energy.

21. Sun-Melted Candle Cleansing

Melt a small candle in the sunlight. As the wax softens, say: "Candle of sun, melt and flow, cleanse my spirit, let light show." Allow the wax to cool, then use the candle in a future spell for purification and renewal.

22. Morning Sun Affirmation

Each morning, face the sun and say: "Sunrise bright, fill my day, bring me light, guide my way." Repeat this affirmation to set a positive tone for the day and to invite the sun's energy into your life.

23. Solar-Water Cleansing

Fill a bowl with water and place it in the sunlight for several hours. Use this solar-charged water to wash your hands or face, saying: "Water of light, cleanse my soul, fill me with warmth, make me whole." This ritual clears away negativity and fills you with solar energy.

24. Sun-Thread Knotting Spell

Cut a piece of yellow thread and hold it in the sunlight. Tie three knots in the thread, saying: "Knot of one, light begun; knot of two, bring me through; knot of three, joy to me." Carry the knotted thread as a charm for happiness and positivity.

25. Golden Candle Meditation

Select a golden or yellow candle to symbolize the sun's energy. Light the candle and place it on your altar. Sit comfortably and gaze into the flame, focusing on its warmth and glow. Say: "Candle of gold, flame so bright, fill my spirit with pure light." Close your eyes and meditate on the light expanding within you, illuminating your inner world and dispelling shadows.

26. Orange Sun Charm

Peel an orange, keeping the peel in one continuous spiral if possible. As you peel, say: "Orange bright, sun's delight, bring me joy, guide my sight." Hang the peel near a sunny window to invite the energy of the sun into your home, promoting happiness and clarity.

27. Sunlit Room Blessing

On a sunny day, open the curtains or blinds of your home to let sunlight flood in. Stand in the center of the room and say: "Sunbeam bright, fill this space, bring warmth, joy, love, and grace." Visualize the sunlight spreading warmth and positive energy to every corner of the room, clearing out darkness and negativity.

28. Sunstone Pendant Empowerment

Hold a piece of sunstone or a sunstone pendant in your hands. Stand in direct sunlight and say: "Stone of sun, warm and clear, fill me with light, draw it near." Wear the sunstone as a pendant to carry the sun's energy with you throughout the day, enhancing your confidence and vitality.

29. Golden Ribbon Affirmation

Cut a length of golden ribbon and hold it in your hands. Each morning, take the ribbon and recite an affirmation of light and positivity. For example: "Golden light, warm and true, fill my heart, guide me through." Keep the ribbon in your pocket or tie it around your wrist as a reminder of your daily affirmation.

30. Sunlight Infusion for Herbs

Place a jar filled with dried herbs (such as rosemary, chamomile, or mint) in a sunny spot for a day. As the herbs soak in the sunlight, say: "Herbs of light, herbs so bright, fill me with warmth, grant me might." Use these sun-infused herbs in teas or spells to enhance their potency with solar energy.

31. Solar Plexus Charging Ritual

Sit outside in the sunlight, close your eyes, and place your hands over your solar plexus (the area just above your stomach). Say: "Sun so bright, fill my core, bring me strength, forevermore." Visualize the sun's energy entering your body, filling your solar plexus with warmth and power, boosting your confidence and willpower.

32. Sun Mirror Spell for Inner Light

Take a small hand mirror and hold it up to the sunlight, reflecting the light onto yourself. As the light touches you, say: "Mirror bright, sunbeam clear, shine within, bring light here." Close your eyes and visualize the sunlight filling you with radiant energy, illuminating your inner world with positivity.

33. Lemon Sun Cleansing

Slice a lemon into thin rounds and place them in a clear bowl. Pour a bit of sea salt over the slices, then place the bowl in direct sunlight. Say: "Lemon bright, salt so clear, cleanse my spirit, draw light near." Leave the bowl in the sun for an hour to cleanse negative energy. Afterward, dispose of the lemon slices by burying them outside to complete the cleansing process.

34. Sunflower Seed Ritual for Growth

Hold a handful of sunflower seeds in your hands while standing in the sunlight. Close your eyes and say: "Seeds of gold, seeds of light, bring me growth, day and night." Plant the seeds in a pot or garden and nurture them as they grow. As the sunflower reaches for the light, visualize your intentions growing and manifesting alongside it.

35. Dawn Gratitude Spell

Wake up early and face the rising sun. Take a moment to express gratitude for the new day and the light returning to your life. Say: "Sunrise new, dawn of day, bring me joy, light my way." Breathe deeply and let the sun's energy fill you with a sense of peace and purpose, setting a positive tone for the rest of the day.

36. Marigold Sun Jar

Fill a small jar with dried marigold petals and hold it up to the sunlight, saying: "Marigold bright, sun's delight, bring me warmth, fill me with light." Seal the jar and place it on your altar or carry it with you as a charm to invoke the sun's energy whenever you need an uplifting boost.

37. Sunbeam Wish

Find a sunny spot outside and close your eyes. Hold your hands out, palms facing the sky, and focus on a wish you want to bring into your life. Visualize the sunbeams filling your hands with light and warmth. Say: "Sunbeam bright, carry my plea, bring my wish to reality." Stand there until you feel the wish has been charged with the sun's power, then release it into the universe.

38. Solar Waxing Moon Spell

Perform this spell during the waxing moon phase to align with the sun's growing light. Light a yellow candle and place it in a sunny spot. As the candle burns, say: "Moon of growth, sun so bright, bring me strength, guide my light." Allow the candle to burn for at least an hour to enhance the energy of growth and new beginnings in your life.

39. Sunbeam Crystal Bath

On a sunny day, gather clear quartz, citrine, or sunstone crystals and place them in a bowl of water. Set the bowl in direct sunlight for several hours to charge the water and crystals. Say: "Sunbeam bright, crystal clear, charge this water, fill with cheer." Use this sun-charged water in a bath or sprinkle it around your home to infuse the space with warmth and positive energy.

40. Sunbeam Reflection Ritual

Sit in a room where sunlight streams through a window. Hold a piece of selenite in the beam of light, allowing the sun's rays to pass through it. Say: "Beam of sun, pure and bright, fill my soul, guide my sight." Meditate on the light filling you with clarity, hope, and a renewed sense of purpose.

Chapter 10: Yule Feast and Kitchen Magic

The Yule season is a time of gathering, feasting, and sharing warmth with family and friends. Food prepared during this period can be imbued with magical intent, transforming simple dishes and drinks into powerful, enchanting concoctions. In this chapter, we explore the magic of the kitchen, offering 30 spells that involve cooking, baking, and brewing to bring prosperity, protection, love, healing, and joy into your life. Each recipe uses traditional Yule ingredients like spices, fruits, herbs, and festive spirits to connect with the energies of the season.

1. Yule Wassail of Abundance

Prepare a pot of wassail using apple cider, orange slices, cloves, cinnamon sticks, nutmeg, and a splash of cranberry juice. As it simmers, stir clockwise and say: "Spices warm, fruit so sweet, bring abundance, joy replete." Pour the wassail into mugs and share it with loved ones, visualizing each sip filling them with warmth, prosperity, and good fortune for the coming year.

2. Rosemary Bread of Protection

Bake a loaf of bread and add fresh rosemary to the dough. As you knead, focus on your intention for protection and say: "Herb of strength, bread of might, guard this home, day and night." As the bread bakes, imagine the aroma filling your home with a protective barrier. Serve the bread at your Yule feast, letting each slice reinforce the protective energy.

3. Apple and Cinnamon Blessing Pie

Prepare an apple pie, adding cinnamon, nutmeg, and cloves to the filling. As you arrange the apple slices in the crust, say: "Apple of earth, spice of light, bring us blessings, pure and bright." Bake the pie and serve it as the centerpiece of your Yule meal, inviting blessings and positive energy into your home.

4. Candied Orange Peel Prosperity Snack

Slice oranges and remove the peel, cutting it into strips. Simmer the strips in sugar water until they become candied. As they cook, say: "Orange peel, sweet and bright, bring prosperity, day and night." Once the peels have cooled and dried, share them with friends and family, spreading the energy of abundance.

5. Sun-Infused Honey for Love

Fill a jar with honey and add a few dried rose petals and a sprig of rosemary. Place the jar in direct sunlight for a few hours, allowing it to absorb the sun's warmth. As it sits, say: "Honey sweet, sunbeam bright, fill this jar with love and light." Use the honey in teas, on toast, or in desserts to infuse your meals with the energy of love.

6. Cinnamon-Spiced Hot Chocolate Comfort

Prepare hot chocolate and add a pinch of cinnamon, a splash of vanilla extract, and a sprinkle of nutmeg. Stir clockwise, saying: "Chocolate rich, spice so warm, bring comfort, joy in every form." Share this drink with loved ones to create a warm, comforting atmosphere filled with love and connection.

7. Yule Log Cake of Renewal

Bake a Yule log cake (Bûche de Noël) and decorate it with sugared cranberries, rosemary sprigs, and powdered sugar for snow. As you roll the cake, say: "Log of sweet, log of might, bring renewal on this night." Serve it during your Yule feast, allowing each bite to symbolize the return of light and renewal in the coming year.

8. Spiced Cider Healing Brew

Simmer apple cider with cinnamon sticks, cloves, ginger, and honey. As it simmers, say: "Spices warm, cider clear, bring me health, draw it near." Drink this healing brew when feeling under the weather to boost your spirits and promote physical well-being.

9. Sun-Seeded Bread for Growth

Add sunflower seeds to a bread dough, kneading the seeds into the mixture. As you do, focus on your intentions for growth and say: "Seeds of sun, seeds of light, grow my dreams, bring them bright." Serve the bread at your Yule meal, envisioning each bite nourishing your personal growth in the coming year.

10. Cranberry Sauce of Love

Prepare a cranberry sauce with fresh cranberries, sugar, orange zest, and a splash of orange juice. As you stir, say: "Cranberries bright, sugar so sweet, bring love's warmth, joy complete." Serve this sauce during your feast to enhance love and harmony among those present.

11. Herb Butter for Harmony

Mix softened butter with finely chopped herbs such as rosemary, thyme, and parsley. As you blend the herbs into the butter, say: "Herbs of green, butter so fine, bring us peace, harmony divine." Serve the herb butter with bread or vegetables to promote harmony in your household.

12. Yule Spice Cookies for Joy

Bake cookies using spices like cinnamon, nutmeg, ginger, and cloves. While mixing the ingredients, say: "Spices warm, sugar sweet, bring me joy, make it complete." Decorate the cookies with symbols of the sun, stars, or Yule trees. Share them with family and friends, spreading joy with every bite.

13. Mulled Wine for Relaxation

In a pot, combine red wine, cloves, cinnamon sticks, orange slices, and honey. As the wine simmers, stir clockwise and say: "Wine of red, spices so true, bring me peace, renew and soothe." Serve this mulled wine during quiet evenings to promote relaxation and reflection.

14. Honey-Glazed Carrots for Sweetness

Glaze carrots with honey and sprinkle with a pinch of cinnamon before roasting. As you prepare the dish, say: "Carrots bright, honey sweet, bring me joy, make life replete." Serve them as part of your Yule meal to attract sweetness and positivity into your life.

15. Spiced Nut Snack for Protection

Toast a mixture of nuts with a drizzle of olive oil, honey, and a blend of spices like cinnamon, cayenne pepper, and salt. As they toast, say: "Nuts of earth, spices warm, bring me strength, protect from harm." Share these nuts during gatherings to create a shield of protection around those present.

16. Gingerbread Luck

Bake gingerbread cookies and use cookie cutters to create festive shapes. Before baking, hold the tray and say: "Ginger and spice, warmth and cheer, bring me luck throughout the year." Share these cookies with family and friends to spread good fortune.

17. Orange and Clove Pomander Spell

Create an orange pomander by sticking whole cloves into the peel. As you work, say: "Orange and clove, bright and clear, bring me warmth, joy, and cheer." Place the pomander on your dining table to fill the room with warmth and positive energy during your Yule feast.

18. Rosemary and Lemon Tea for Clarity

Steep fresh rosemary and lemon slices in hot water to create a cleansing tea. As it steeps, say: "Rosemary bright, lemon so clear, grant me clarity, draw it near." Drink this tea in the morning to start your day with a clear mind and a refreshed spirit.

19. Oat and Honey Prosperity Cakes

Mix oats, honey, and dried fruits to make small, energy-boosting cakes. As you form each cake, say: "Oats of gold, honey bright, bring prosperity, day and night." Bake and serve these cakes during Yule to attract wealth and abundance into your home.

20. Spiced Apple Rings for Harmony

Slice apples into rings and sprinkle with cinnamon, nutmeg, and sugar. Bake them until they become soft and fragrant. As they bake, say: "Apple rings, warm and sweet, bring us harmony, make us complete." Serve these rings to create a loving, harmonious atmosphere during family gatherings.

21. Golden Yule Porridge for Energy

Cook porridge using oats, milk, and honey. Stir in a pinch of turmeric for a golden hue. As you stir, say: "Porridge warm, golden bright, bring me strength, fill me with light." Enjoy this meal in the morning to energize and empower yourself for the day.

22. Chocolate-Dipped Strawberries for Love

Melt chocolate and dip fresh strawberries into it. As you work, say: "Chocolate rich, fruit of red, bring me love, warmth widespread." Share these sweet treats with your partner to deepen affection and enhance the energy of love.

23. Cinnamon Honey Butter for Wealth

Combine honey with softened butter and a pinch of cinnamon. As you blend them together, say: "Honey bright, cinnamon spice, bring me wealth, fortune's device." Use this butter on bread or pastries to attract prosperity into your life.

24. Herb-Crusted Roasted Vegetables for Grounding

Coat a selection of root vegetables with olive oil, rosemary, thyme, and garlic before roasting. As you prepare them, say: "Roots of earth, herbs of green, keep me grounded, strong, and keen." Serve these vegetables to promote grounding and connection to the earth's energies.

25. Clove-Studded Ham for Abundance

Stud a ham with whole cloves before roasting, adding a glaze made of honey, mustard, and a splash of orange juice. As the ham cooks, say: "Ham so sweet, cloves so strong, bring me abundance all year long." Serve this dish as the main course of your Yule feast to invite wealth and prosperity into your home.

26. Peppermint Hot Cocoa for Comfort

Prepare hot cocoa and stir in a drop of peppermint extract. As you stir, say: "Cocoa rich, mint so cool, bring me comfort, make me full." Share this drink with loved ones to create a cozy and comforting environment during cold winter nights.

27. Almond Joy Cakes for Happiness

Bake small almond cakes, adding a touch of vanilla extract and honey. As you mix the batter, say: "Almonds bright, honey sweet, bring me joy, make life complete." Share these cakes during your feast to promote happiness and joy.

28. Spiced Pumpkin Soup for Protection

Cook pumpkin soup with garlic, cinnamon, nutmeg, and a dash of chili powder. As you stir, say: "Pumpkin bold, spices warm, guard this home, protect from harm." Serve this soup to create a warm, protective energy that fills your space.

29. Yule Feast Herb Wine

Infuse a bottle of red wine with rosemary, thyme, and orange peel. Let it steep overnight and, as you pour the wine the next day, say: "Herbs of earth, wine of red, bring me peace, joy widespread." Share this wine during your Yule feast to strengthen bonds and invite harmony.

30. Yule Herb Oil for Cooking Magic

Prepare an herb-infused oil using olive oil, rosemary, thyme, garlic, and a pinch of salt. As you mix the herbs into the oil, say: "Oil of light, herbs of might, bless this meal, fill with light." Use this oil in your cooking to infuse each dish with protective and nurturing energy.

Chapter 11: Gift-Bearing Rituals

The Yule season is a time of giving and receiving, a celebration of abundance, generosity, and the joy of sharing with others. In the spirit of the season, gifts can become magical conduits, carrying intentions of love, prosperity, protection, and goodwill. This chapter explores 25 gift-bearing rituals, where the act of giving is transformed into a powerful spell to enhance positive energy exchange. Whether you're crafting a handmade item or gifting something purchased, each spell in this chapter guides you in imbuing your gifts with magic and intention.

1. Rosemary-Infused Oil Gift for Protection

Prepare a small bottle of olive oil infused with rosemary sprigs. As you pour the oil into the bottle, say: "Oil of warmth, herb of might, protect this heart, day and night." Seal the bottle and tie a red ribbon around the top. Gift this oil to friends or family to bless them with protection and good health.

2. Cinnamon Wish Jar

Fill a small jar with cinnamon sticks, bay leaves, and a piece of citrine. As you add each item, say: "Cinnamon warm, bay of might, bring good fortune day and night." Gift this jar to someone with a note explaining that they should shake it whenever they wish to attract luck and positive energy.

3. Sunlight-Infused Candle for Happiness

Craft a candle using yellow or orange wax, representing sunlight. Before pouring the wax into the mold, hold the mixture up to the sunlight and say: "Candle bright, sunlight pure, bring joy and warmth evermore." Gift this candle with instructions to light it whenever the recipient needs an infusion of joy and happiness in their life.

4. Healing Herb Sachet

Create a small sachet filled with dried lavender, rosemary, and mint. As you fill the sachet, say: "Herbs of healing, herbs of light, bring peace and health, day and night." Sew the sachet closed with a green thread, and gift it to someone who could use a boost of health and tranquility.

5. Pine Cone Abundance Ornament

Decorate a pine cone with golden paint, glitter, and small charms. Hold the pine cone in your hands and say: "Pine so strong, golden light, bring abundance, day and night." Add a ribbon loop so it can be hung as a Yule ornament. Gift it to invite prosperity and abundance into the recipient's home.

6. Love-Infused Tea Blend

Mix dried rose petals, chamomile, and a pinch of cinnamon in a jar to create a love-infused tea blend. As you mix the herbs, say: "Tea of love, tea of grace, bring warmth and joy to this place." Attach a small note to the jar, explaining that the tea should be sipped whenever the recipient needs to feel surrounded by love and comfort.

7. Crystal-Embedded Bath Bombs

Make bath bombs using ingredients like baking soda, citric acid, and essential oils. Embed a small crystal (such as rose quartz or amethyst) into each bomb, saying: "Crystal clear, calm and bright, bring peace and love with each light." Gift these bath bombs as a way for the recipient to enjoy a soothing and magical bath ritual.

8. Cinnamon Stick Prosperity Wand

Tie together three cinnamon sticks with a gold ribbon to form a small wand. As you tie the ribbon, say: "Cinnamon warm, wand so bright, bring prosperity in day and night." Gift this wand with a note explaining that it can be used to stir drinks or wave over their wallet to attract financial success.

9. Hand-Poured Love Candles

Create candles using pink or red wax and rose or vanilla essential oils. As you pour the wax into the molds, say: "Candle of love, flame so pure, bring warmth and joy, evermore." Wrap the candle in tissue paper and gift it to a loved one, with the intention of strengthening the bonds of love between you.

10. Snow Globe of Peace

Create a simple snow globe using a jar, water, glitter, and a small evergreen sprig. Seal the jar tightly and hold it in your hands, saying: "Snow so calm, water clear, bring peace and joy throughout the year." Gift the snow globe with a note encouraging the recipient to shake it whenever they need a moment of calm and reflection.

11. Sunstone Bracelet for Positivity

Thread sunstone beads onto a bracelet and hold it in the sunlight. Say: "Sunstone bright, filled with cheer, bring positivity, draw it near." Gift the bracelet to someone who could use more warmth and positivity in their life, explaining that the bracelet is charged with the sun's energy.

12. Herbal Protection Wreath

Create a small wreath using sprigs of rosemary, bay leaves, and pine branches. As you weave the herbs together, say: "Wreath of green, herbs so strong, bring protection all year long." Gift this wreath as a talisman of protection to hang on a door or in a room for year-round safety.

13. Lavender Sleep Sachet

Fill a small sachet with dried lavender flowers and add a few drops of lavender essential oil. Hold the sachet in your hands and say: "Lavender calm, scent so bright, bring restful sleep, peaceful night." Gift this sachet with instructions to place it under their pillow to promote restful sleep.

14. Abundance Salt Jar

Layer sea salt, dried orange peel, and bay leaves in a small jar. As you layer, say: "Salt of earth, orange bright, bring abundance, day and night." Gift this jar with a note instructing the recipient to sprinkle a pinch of the salt in their wallet or around their home to invite prosperity.

15. Golden Sun Charm

Mold a piece of clay into a small sun shape and paint it gold. Hold the charm in your hands and say: "Golden sun, warmth so true, bring joy and light in all I do." Gift this charm as a symbol of light and positivity, explaining that it can be carried or placed on an altar to invoke the sun's energy.

16. Rosemary-Infused Soap for Cleansing

Make handmade soap infused with rosemary and lavender essential oils. As you mix the ingredients, say: "Herbs of earth, cleanse so pure, bring peace and calm, evermore." Gift the soap to someone who could use a little extra self-care and relaxation in their life.

17. Cinnamon Garland for Joy

String dried orange slices, cinnamon sticks, and star anise onto a garland. As you work, say: "Cinnamon bright, fruit so sweet, bring joy and warmth, make life complete." Gift this garland to be hung over doorways or windows, filling the home with warmth and positive energy.

18. Winter Spice Sachet

Fill a small sachet with cloves, cinnamon sticks, and dried apple slices. As you close the sachet, say: "Spices warm, scent so bright, bring happiness, love, and light." Gift this sachet to be placed in a drawer or hung in a closet to fill their space with the energy of the season.

19. Solar-Powered Crystal Gift

Place a clear quartz crystal in a small bag and leave it in the sunlight for several hours. Hold the bag and say: "Crystal bright, sun's embrace, bring warmth and light to this place." Gift this crystal to someone in need of clarity and positive energy, explaining that it has been charged with the sun's light.

20. Herbal Tea Blessing

Mix a blend of dried mint, chamomile, and rose petals. As you blend the tea, say: "Herbs of peace, herbs of light, bring calm and joy day and night." Place the blend in a small jar or pouch and gift it with instructions to brew the tea whenever they need to feel a sense of calm and comfort.

21. Bay Leaf Money Jar

Write words like "prosperity," "wealth," and "abundance" on bay leaves using a marker. Place the bay leaves in a jar and say: "Bay of green, bring me gold, wealth and riches, manifold." Gift the jar to someone with a note explaining that they can shake it whenever they want to attract financial abundance.

22. Cedar Bundle Cleansing Gift

Tie together small sprigs of cedar with a green ribbon. Hold the bundle in your hands and say: "Cedar green, scent so clear, cleanse this space, draw peace near." Gift the bundle with instructions for using it to cleanse their home by waving it through the air.

23. Sunflower Seeds of Growth

Fill a small pouch with sunflower seeds. Hold the pouch in the sunlight and say: "Seeds of sun, seeds of might, bring growth and strength, day and night." Gift this pouch with a note explaining that they can plant the seeds to symbolize growth in their life.

24. Yule Bath Salts for Rejuvenation

Mix sea salt with dried rosemary, lavender, and a few drops of peppermint oil. As you mix, say: "Salt of earth, herbs so bright, bring renewal, grant me light." Place the bath salts in a jar and gift them to someone, encouraging them to use the salts for a relaxing and rejuvenating bath.

25. Candle of Hope

Create a candle using white wax and a few drops of lemon or orange essential oil. As you pour the wax into the mold, say: "Candle of hope, flame so bright, bring me strength, guide my light." Gift this candle with a note instructing the recipient to light it whenever they need hope and guidance.

Chapter 12: Nature and Animal Spells

Winter transforms the natural world, covering the earth in a blanket of snow and creating a stillness that allows for deeper connections with nature and its spirits. During Yule, nature and animals take on a special significance as they embody the cycle of rest, renewal, and the promise of spring's return. This chapter contains 35 spells that honor the winter season by connecting with plants, animals, and nature spirits. These rituals involve the energies of evergreens, forest creatures, winter birds, and snow-covered landscapes, creating a bridge between the practitioner and the natural world.

1. Evergreen Protection Circle

Gather pine, spruce, or fir branches and form a circle on the ground. Stand in the center of the circle and say: "Evergreen strong, evergreen bright, guard my spirit, day and night." Visualize the evergreen circle creating a protective barrier around you. Leave the circle outside to honor the forest spirits and invite their guardianship.

2. Animal Offering for Winter Blessings

Prepare a small offering of seeds, nuts, or dried fruit and place it in a bowl outside for the woodland creatures. As you place the bowl, say: "To the animals of winter, I give this gift, bring me blessings, the seasons shift." Leave the offering as a token of respect for the animals' resilience during the cold months, asking them to watch over you.

3. Pine Cone Wish Spell

Find a pine cone and hold it in your hands, focusing on a wish you wish to manifest. Say: "Pine cone strong, seeds so bright, grant my wish, bring it light." Bury the pine cone under the snow or in the earth, trusting the nature spirits to nurture your wish until it comes to fruition.

4. Birch Tree Communication

Approach a birch tree and place your hands on its trunk. Close your eyes and take a deep breath, feeling the tree's energy. Whisper your worries or wishes to the tree, saying: "Birch of white, hear my plea, share your wisdom, guide me free." Listen for any subtle messages or feelings from the tree spirits as a response.

5. Snow Footprint Spell

In a quiet, snowy area, walk barefoot or in soft shoes, leaving footprints behind you. As you walk, say: "Snow so pure, earth below, guide my steps, show me the flow." Imagine the snow absorbing your energy, clearing your path, and inviting guidance from the nature spirits.

6. Winter Bird Feeding Ritual

Fill a bird feeder with seeds and hang it near your home. As you fill the feeder, say: "Birds of winter, friends in flight, bring me joy, bless my sight." Watch the birds come and go, seeing them as messengers of the natural world. Offer gratitude for their presence, inviting peace and harmony into your life.

7. Snow-Covered Crystal Charging

Place a crystal (such as clear quartz or moonstone) outside in the snow overnight. In the morning, retrieve the crystal and say: "Snow so pure, crystal bright, charge with magic, fill with light." Carry the crystal with you to maintain a connection with the cleansing energy of winter.

8. Pine Needle Renewal Bath

Collect a handful of pine needles and add them to your bathwater. As you soak, say: "Pine so green, scent so clear, renew my spirit, draw me near." Visualize the energy of the evergreen renewing and cleansing you, releasing the old and welcoming new growth.

9. Winter Animal Spirit Invocation

Sit quietly outdoors or by a window overlooking a natural landscape. Close your eyes and visualize the animals of winter (such as deer, foxes, and owls) gathering around you. Say: "Spirits of winter, creatures of grace, guide my path, light my space." Meditate on their wisdom and messages, allowing their energy to infuse you with strength and clarity.

10. Snowfall Peace Invocation

Stand outside during a gentle snowfall and close your eyes. Let the snowflakes fall on your skin, feeling their cool touch. Say: "Snow so soft, falling light, bring me peace, through the night." Imagine the snow absorbing your worries and transforming them into peace.

11. Nature Spirit Guardian Ritual

Choose a quiet spot in a forest or park. Build a small stone circle and place an evergreen sprig in the center. As you do, say: "Spirits of nature, spirits of green, guard this place, keep it serene." Leave an offering of seeds or nuts within the circle as a gift to the nature spirits, asking for their protection and guidance.

12. Animal Companion Blessing

For those with pets, sit quietly with your animal companion. Gently place your hand on their head and say: "Friend so dear, heart so true, bless our bond, old and new." Visualize a golden light surrounding both of you, strengthening your bond and inviting harmony and love.

13. Snow-Dusted Tree Connection

Select a tree covered in snow and place your hand on its bark. Close your eyes and focus on the tree's energy, feeling its strength and endurance. Say: "Tree of winter, tree so wise, share your strength, help me rise." Absorb the tree's grounding energy, letting it fill you with stability.

14. Holly Berry Protection Charm

Gather a few sprigs of holly with bright red berries. Hold them in your hands and say: "Holly bright, berries red, guard my home, keep it fed." Hang the holly above your door to ward off negativity and invite nature's protection.

15. Snow-Covered Grounding

Find a patch of snow-covered ground and kneel, placing your hands on the earth. Close your eyes and take deep breaths, saying: "Earth so cold, snow so white, ground me now, set things right." Visualize your energy sinking into the earth, connecting with the deep roots of winter.

16. Winter Deer Connection

If you see deer tracks in the snow, kneel beside them and place your hand gently on the track. Say: "Deer so swift, gentle and bright, guide my steps, day and night." Visualize the deer's grace and alertness becoming a part of you, enhancing your intuition.

17. Moonlit Owl Calling

Stand outside on a moonlit night and listen for the call of an owl. Close your eyes and say: "Owl of night, wisdom's flight, share your sight, guide me right." Allow the owl's energy to enhance your inner wisdom and clarity.

18. Pine Cone Cleansing Spell

Collect a pine cone and place it in a bowl of snow. As the snow melts, say: "Pine cone clear, snow so pure, cleanse this space, make it sure." Keep the pine cone on your altar or in your home as a cleansing charm throughout the winter season.

19. Animal Track Spell

Follow animal tracks in the snow until they disappear. Stand at the end of the trail and say: "Tracks so faint, spirit so free, guide my steps, let me see." Visualize the animal's path merging with your own, providing guidance for your personal journey.

20. Forest Offering of Gratitude

Take an offering of seeds, nuts, or dried fruit to a forested area. Place it on the ground beneath a tree, saying: "Forest deep, spirits old, accept this gift, stories untold." Leave the offering as a sign of respect and gratitude for the nature spirits and animals.

21. Evergreen Wreath Invocation

Create an evergreen wreath using pine, holly, and mistletoe. Hold the wreath in your hands and say: "Green of earth, life so bright, bring me strength, day and night." Hang the wreath on your door to invoke the spirit of nature and its protection.

22. Snowflake Reflection Meditation

Catch a snowflake on your glove or a piece of fabric. Gaze at its intricate design and say: "Snowflake bright, pattern true, bring me insight, guide me through." Meditate on the snowflake's unique pattern, allowing its delicate beauty to inspire reflections on your own path.

23. Mistletoe Love Blessing

Hold a sprig of mistletoe and say: "Mistletoe bright, sacred and pure, bless this love, make it sure." Hang the mistletoe in your home to encourage love and harmony among those who dwell within.

24. Animal Spirit Guidance Charm

Choose a small object (such as a stone or a piece of wood) and sit outside in nature. Close your eyes and invite an animal spirit to connect with the object. Say: "Animal spirit, friend so wise, guide my path, open my eyes." Keep the charm with you to maintain a link with the animal spirit's guidance.

25. Pine Needle Cleansing Broom

Gather a bundle of pine needles and tie them together to create a small broom. Use it to sweep your home, saying: "Pine so green, cleanse this space, bring protection, grant me grace." Visualize the broom clearing away negative energy and replacing it with nature's purity.

26. Winter Bird Feather Spell

If you find a feather on the ground, hold it up to the sky and say: "Bird of flight, spirit so free, bring me peace, let it be." Carry the feather with you as a token of the bird's energy, reminding you to stay lighthearted and free-spirited.

27. Ice Crystal Connection

Pick up an icicle and hold it in your hand. Close your eyes and say: "Crystal clear, ice so bright, connect my soul, give me sight." Let the icicle's energy connect you with the deep wisdom of winter's stillness.

28. Nature Spirit Stone Circle

Create a small stone circle outside as an offering to nature spirits. Place a sprig of pine in the center and say: "Spirits of nature, guardians old, accept this gift, tales untold." This circle acts as a space for nature spirits to gather and bless the land around you.

29. Pine Cone Animal Shelter Spell

Fill a pine cone with peanut butter and birdseed, then hang it outside. As you hang it, say: "Cone of seeds, gift of earth, feed the creatures, warmth and worth." This act of kindness creates a bond between you and the local wildlife, inviting their blessings.

30. Snowfall Shield of Calm

Stand outside during a gentle snowfall and close your eyes. Say: "Snow so light, shield so clear, guard my heart, bring me near." Visualize the falling snow forming a protective shield around you, creating a bubble of peace and serenity.

31. Holly Protection Pouch

Place holly leaves, pine needles, and a small crystal into a pouch. Hold the pouch and say: "Holly bright, pine so clear, guard this space, keep it near." Keep the pouch in your home for protection against negative energies.

32. Animal Track Offering

Follow an animal track and place a small offering of seeds or nuts along the path. Say: "Tracks of earth, guide so true, take this gift, blessings through." Leave the offering as a sign of gratitude for the guidance and presence of nature spirits.

33. Frost-Covered Leaf Spell

Find a frost-covered leaf and hold it gently in your hands. Close your eyes and say: "Leaf of frost, beauty bright, bring me insight, day and night." Meditate on the leaf's delicate structure, allowing it to reveal hidden truths.

34. Tree Root Connection

Sit at the base of a large tree and place your hands on its roots. Close your eyes and say: "Roots so deep, strength so old, connect my spirit, keep me bold." Feel the tree's energy rising through the roots, grounding and empowering you.

35. Animal Spirit Candle Ritual

Light a white candle and place it on your altar. Surround it with symbols of animals (such as feathers, stones, or small figurines). Say: "Spirits of animals, guides so near, share your wisdom, banish fear." Meditate on the candle's flame, inviting the animal spirits to connect with you and offer their guidance.

Chapter 13: Crystal Magic for Yule

The winter season, with its cool, serene energy, is the perfect time to work with crystals to enhance your magic. During Yule, crystals like snowflake obsidian, garnet, and clear quartz resonate deeply with the themes of rest, renewal, protection, and light. Snowflake obsidian, with its dark beauty speckled by light spots, mirrors the balance of darkness and hope. Garnet, with its deep red hue, symbolizes warmth, strength, and grounding during the cold months, while clear quartz amplifies intention and reflects the purity of snow. This chapter explores 30 spells that use these and other crystals to harness the powerful energy of Yule for protection, love, healing, and transformation.

1. Snowflake Obsidian Protection Pouch

Place a piece of snowflake obsidian, a sprig of pine, and a pinch of salt into a small pouch. Hold the pouch in your hands and say: "Obsidian dark, speckled light, guard my spirit, day and night." Carry this pouch with you to ward off negativity and protect your energy during the winter months.

2. Garnet Hearth Blessing

Hold a garnet stone in your hands and sit quietly by your hearth or a candle flame. Say: "Garnet bright, flame of red, bless this home, keep us fed." Place the garnet on your mantle or in the kitchen to invite warmth, abundance, and familial harmony.

3. Clear Quartz Renewal Bath

Place a clear quartz crystal in a bowl of water and set it under the moonlight overnight. The next day, add the quartz-infused water to your bath along with a handful of sea salt. As you soak, say: "Quartz of light, water so clear, cleanse my spirit, draw me near." Visualize the water renewing your energy, washing away negativity, and filling you with light.

4. Snowflake Obsidian Grounding Ritual

Hold a piece of snowflake obsidian in your hands and sit on the ground, preferably outside or near a window. Close your eyes and take deep breaths. Say: "Stone of night, speckled bright, ground my spirit, hold me tight." Imagine roots growing from the stone, connecting you deeply to the earth, providing balance and stability.

5. Garnet Love Spell

Place a garnet stone on a piece of red cloth and sprinkle dried rose petals around it. Hold your hands over the stone and say: "Garnet red, warm and true, bring love's fire, old and new." Wrap the stone in the cloth and carry it with you to attract love and enhance passion in your relationships.

6. Clear Quartz Manifestation Grid

Create a simple crystal grid using clear quartz points arranged in a circle on your altar. Place a small candle in the center. Light the candle and say: "Quartz of light, amplify, bring my wishes to the sky." Focus on your intention as the candle burns, visualizing the energy of the quartz enhancing and projecting your desires into the universe.

7. Snowflake Obsidian Nightly Protection

Place a piece of snowflake obsidian under your pillow before bed. As you do, say: "Obsidian of night, calm and clear, protect my dreams, keep me near." Sleep with the stone to ward off nightmares and promote restful, protected sleep during the long winter nights.

8. Garnet Prosperity Candle Spell

Carve symbols of abundance (such as a dollar sign, a pentacle, or a sun) into a green candle. Place a garnet stone at the base of the candle and light it, saying: "Garnet bright, flame so green, bring prosperity, wealth unseen." Let the candle burn for at least an hour, allowing the garnet's energy to attract abundance and wealth.

9. Clear Quartz Snowfall Meditation

Sit quietly by a window and hold a piece of clear quartz in your hand as you watch the snow fall. Say: "Quartz of clear, snow so bright, bring me peace, guide my sight." Focus on the snowflakes and the quartz, letting their energy quiet your mind and bring clarity to your thoughts.

10. Snowflake Obsidian Mirror Scrying

Place a snowflake obsidian stone beside a small mirror. Light a candle and let its light reflect off the obsidian onto the mirror. Say: "Obsidian dark, mirror bright, show me truth within the night." Gaze into the mirror, using it as a portal to scry for insights and guidance from the shadowy depths of winter.

11. Garnet Heart Healing Spell

Hold a garnet stone against your heart chakra and close your eyes. Breathe deeply and say: "Garnet red, warm and true, heal my heart, make it new." Visualize the stone's energy radiating warmth into your heart, healing emotional wounds and filling you with love and compassion.

12. Clear Quartz Light Invocation

Stand outside during the day and hold a clear quartz crystal up to the sunlight. Say: "Quartz so clear, sun so bright, fill me with warmth, bring me light." Let the sunlight pass through the quartz and into you, filling you with positive energy and dispelling the winter blues.

13. Snowflake Obsidian Shadow Work

Hold a piece of snowflake obsidian in your hand and sit in a dimly lit room. Reflect on the aspects of your shadow self that you wish to understand or transform. Say: "Obsidian dark, speckled with light, reveal my shadows, guide me right." Allow the stone to help you explore and integrate your shadow, bringing balance to your inner world.

14. Garnet Confidence Boost

Before an important event or meeting, hold a garnet in your dominant hand and say: "Garnet strong, filled with might, boost my spirit, shine so bright." Carry the stone with you to enhance your confidence, courage, and personal power.

15. Clear Quartz Crystal Water for Cleansing

Place a clear quartz crystal in a glass of water and let it sit for an hour. Use the charged water to wash your hands or sprinkle around your space, saying: "Quartz of light, water so clear, cleanse my spirit, banish fear." This ritual purifies both your energy and your environment.

16. Snowflake Obsidian Peace Grid

Create a circle using snowflake obsidian stones around a white candle. Light the candle and sit within the circle, saying: "Stones of night, speckled calm, bring me peace, like a soothing balm." Meditate within this circle to cultivate a sense of inner peace and quiet reflection.

17. Garnet and Rose Love Sachet

Place a garnet stone, rose petals, and a few drops of rose oil in a small sachet. Hold the sachet in your hands and say: "Garnet bright, rose so fair, bring me love, warmth to share." Place the sachet under your pillow or give it to a loved one to strengthen bonds of love and passion.

18. Clear Quartz Full Moon Ritual

Place a clear quartz crystal outside under the full moonlight overnight to charge. The next day, hold the crystal in your hands and say: "Moon of light, quartz so clear, bring me power, year to year." Use the crystal in future spells to amplify your intentions with the moon's energy.

19. Snowflake Obsidian Transformation

Hold a piece of snowflake obsidian in your hands and focus on a habit or trait you wish to transform. Say: "Obsidian dark, spots of white, aid my change, guide me right." Keep the stone with you to remind you of your commitment to personal transformation.

20. Garnet Hearth Renewal

Place a garnet stone near your fireplace or a lit candle in the living room. Say: "Garnet red, warmth so bright, renew this home, bring me light." Allow the stone to absorb and radiate warmth and positivity, renewing the energy of your living space.

21. Clear Quartz Solar Energy Spell

Hold a clear quartz crystal up to the midday sun and say: "Quartz of clear, sun of might, fill me with energy, pure and bright." Carry the crystal with you to harness the sun's energy, boosting your vitality and mental clarity throughout the day.

22. Snowflake Obsidian Dream Shield

Place a snowflake obsidian stone under your bed or near your headboard. Before sleeping, say: "Obsidian dark, calm and clear, shield my dreams, keep them near." This creates a protective shield around your dream state, guarding against negative energies.

23. Garnet Fire Ritual

Light a small fire in your fireplace or outdoor fire pit. Hold a garnet stone in your hands and say: "Garnet warm, flame so bright, bring me courage, strength, and might." Gaze into the flames, allowing their energy to empower and strengthen your spirit.

24. Clear Quartz Snow Cleansing

On a snowy day, bury a clear quartz crystal in the snow for a few hours. Retrieve it and say: "Snow so pure, quartz so clear, cleanse this stone, draw it near." Use this crystal in future rituals, now purified and charged with the cleansing energy of snow.

25. Snowflake Obsidian Shadow Release

Hold a snowflake obsidian stone in your hands and focus on a shadow aspect of yourself you wish to release. Say: "Obsidian dark, speckled light, release this shadow into the night." Visualize the stone absorbing this aspect, helping you release it and find balance.

26. Garnet Strength Bath

Place a garnet stone in a bowl of warm water. Let it sit for an hour, then pour the water into your bath. As you soak, say: "Garnet red, warmth and might, fill me with strength, day and night." Imagine the garnet's energy infusing you with strength and resilience.

27. Clear Quartz Clarity Pouch

Place a clear quartz crystal, a sprig of rosemary, and a pinch of sea salt in a small pouch. Hold the pouch and say: "Quartz of clear, herb of sight, bring me clarity, guide me right." Carry this pouch with you to enhance mental clarity and focus.

28. Snowflake Obsidian Scrying Bowl

Place a snowflake obsidian stone in a shallow bowl of water. Gaze into the water, focusing on the stone's reflection. Say: "Obsidian dark, water deep, show me truths that I seek." Use this as a scrying tool to reveal hidden insights and guidance.

29. Garnet and Cinnamon Love Charm

Wrap a garnet stone in a piece of red cloth sprinkled with cinnamon. Hold it in your hands and say: "Garnet bright, spice of fire, bring me love, heart's desire." Place the charm under your pillow to attract love and passion into your life.

30. Clear Quartz Winter Meditation

Hold a clear quartz crystal and sit in a quiet space. Close your eyes and say: "Quartz so pure, calm and bright, bring me peace, inner light." Meditate with the quartz, using its energy to find inner peace and connect with the stillness of winter.

Chapter 14: Candle Magic and Light Rituals

Candle magic is a central practice during Yule, a time of year when the longest night gives way to the growing light of the sun. The soft glow of candlelight symbolizes hope, warmth, and the return of the sun's power, guiding us through winter's darkness. Candles can serve as potent tools for focus, intention-setting, and spiritual illumination, helping to manifest desires, cleanse energy, and bring peace and joy into our lives. This chapter offers 45 detailed candle spells that harness the transformative energy of light, each designed to inspire hope, welcome warmth, and illuminate your spirit during the winter season.

1. Yule Night Illumination

On the night of Yule, light a white candle and place it on your windowsill to symbolize the return of the sun. As you light the candle, say: "Candle bright, light of Yule, guide us through the dark and cool." Let the candle burn down completely to welcome light and warmth into your home.

2. Candle of Protection

Carve symbols of protection (such as a pentacle, an eye, or a rune) into a black candle. Anoint the candle with rosemary or sage oil, saying: "Candle of night, shield of light, protect this space, guard it tight." Light the candle at dusk to ward off negativity and protect your home.

3. Solar Renewal Candle Spell

Use a yellow or gold candle to represent the sun's energy. Carve the symbol of the sun into the candle's surface. Hold the candle in your hands and say: "Golden light, sun's embrace, bring renewal to this place." Light the candle at dawn on Yule morning to welcome the sun's return and inspire personal renewal.

4. Candle for Self-Love

Choose a pink candle and carve a heart symbol on its surface. Anoint it with rose oil, saying: "Candle of love, pink and true, fill my heart, make it new." Light the candle and focus on the flame, allowing its warmth to fill you with self-love and compassion.

5. Flame of Clarity

Carve the symbol of an eye or a spiral into a blue candle. Anoint the candle with lavender oil, saying: "Candle of blue, calm and clear, bring me sight, draw me near." Light the candle when seeking insight or clarity, letting the flame illuminate your mind and spirit.

6. Hearth Blessing Candle

Select a red candle to represent warmth and home. Carve the symbols of a hearth or flame into the wax. Hold the candle in your hands and say: "Candle of red, hearth so bright, bless this home, bring warmth and light." Light this candle in your kitchen or living room to invite harmony and comfort.

7. Candle of Gratitude

Choose a yellow candle and inscribe words of gratitude on its surface (such as "thanks," "blessings," "gratitude"). Light the candle and say: "Candle bright, flame so true, I give my thanks, old and new." Sit quietly and reflect on the blessings in your life as the candle burns.

8. Candle Magic for New Beginnings

Carve the word "beginning" or a symbol of rebirth (such as a sprout or sunrise) into a green candle. Anoint the candle with peppermint oil, saying: "Candle of green, life renew, open paths, clear my view." Light this candle to mark a new start, whether it's a project, a relationship, or a personal journey.

9. Peaceful Sleep Candle Ritual

Carve moon symbols and stars into a lavender or light blue candle. Anoint it with chamomile oil, saying: "Candle of calm, light so true, bring me peace, sleep anew." Light this candle before bedtime to invite restful and peaceful sleep.

10. Candle of Abundance

Choose a green candle and carve the symbols of prosperity (such as a dollar sign, coins, or leaves) into its surface. Anoint the candle with cinnamon or patchouli oil, saying: "Candle of green, wealth of earth, bring abundance, joy, and mirth." Light this candle on your altar to attract prosperity and financial success.

11. Candlelight Meditation

Select a white candle and place it in a quiet space. Light the candle, saying: "Candle white, purest flame, still my mind, call my name." Sit in silence, focusing on the candle's flame. Allow your mind to clear and your spirit to find peace as you meditate.

12. Joyful Heart Candle

Carve a smile or heart symbol into a pink or orange candle. Anoint it with citrus oil (such as orange or lemon), saying: "Candle bright, flame of cheer, fill my heart, bring joy near." Light this candle whenever you feel down or need to lift your spirits.

13. Candle of Cleansing

Choose a black candle for clearing negativity. Anoint the candle with sage or rosemary oil, saying: "Candle of night, burn so clear, cleanse this space, draw out fear." Light the candle while visualizing it absorbing and burning away all negativity in your home or mind.

14. Candle Wish Spell

Write your wish on a piece of paper and place it under a small white candle. Light the candle and say: "Flame of light, candle bright, hear my wish, bring it to flight." Allow the candle to burn down completely, envisioning your wish being carried into the universe.

15. Snow-Covered Candle Protection

Roll a white candle in salt, then carve protective symbols into its surface. Say: "Candle bright, snow's pure might, guard this space, day and night." Light this candle during times of uncertainty to invoke protection and strength.

16. Solar Power Candle

Select a yellow or gold candle and carve the symbol of the sun into it. Hold it up to the sunlight for a few minutes, saying: "Sun of day, candle bright, fill this flame with purest light." Light the candle indoors to bring solar energy into your space, especially on cloudy winter days.

17. Love-Attracting Candle

Carve the symbols of Venus or a heart into a pink or red candle. Anoint it with rose or jasmine oil, saying: "Candle of love, flame so bright, attract my love, day and night." Light this candle while focusing on the kind of love you wish to invite into your life.

18. Candlelight Circle of Friends

Arrange a circle of small candles (one for each friend you wish to bless) on your altar. Light each candle and say: "Candle's flame, friendship's light, bring them joy, day and night." Allow the candles to burn for at least an hour, sending warmth and blessings to your friends.

19. Candle for Inner Strength

Carve symbols of strength (such as a mountain, oak tree, or rune) into a purple or red candle. Anoint the candle with cedar or frankincense oil, saying: "Candle of might, burn so strong, give me courage, right all wrong." Light the candle when you need an extra boost of inner strength.

20. Candle of Forgiveness

Choose a light blue candle and inscribe a water symbol (such as waves) on its surface. Anoint it with lavender oil, saying: "Candle of calm, water so clear, bring me peace, draw me near." Light this candle to release anger and embrace forgiveness, allowing its flame to wash away resentment.

21. Spirit Guide Candle

Carve the symbols of a star or moon into a white or silver candle. Anoint it with sandalwood oil, saying: "Candle of light, spirit so clear, guide my path, draw me near." Light this candle when seeking guidance from your spirit guides or ancestors.

22. Prosperity Candle Grid

Create a simple grid of green candles in a square shape. Place a small coin or piece of pyrite in the center. Light each candle, saying: "Candles of green, wealth of earth, bring abundance, joy, and mirth." Meditate on the growing light, imagining it drawing prosperity into your life.

23. Yule Tree Candle Blessing

Place a small candle at the base of your Yule tree. Light the candle and say: "Candle bright, tree so green, bless this space, make it serene." Let the candle burn for a few minutes to fill your home with the tree's blessing and warmth.

24. Morning Candle for Energy

Light an orange candle upon waking, saying: "Candle of dawn, flame of day, fill me with strength, guide my way." Allow the candle to burn while you prepare for your day, infusing you with energy and motivation.

25. Candle of Serenity

Carve waves or the word "peace" into a light blue candle. Anoint it with lavender or chamomile oil, saying: "Candle of blue, calm and clear, bring me peace, draw it near." Light this candle when you need to soothe stress and anxiety, allowing its flame to fill your space with tranquility.

26. Candle of Hope

Select a white candle and carve the word "Hope" or a symbol of hope (such as a star or sunrise) into its surface. Anoint the candle with jasmine or bergamot oil, saying: "Candle of white, flame so bright, fill me with hope, day and night." Light this candle whenever you feel uncertain or need encouragement, letting its glow fill you with optimism and strength.

27. Harmony Candle Ritual

Choose a light blue or green candle and carve the word "Harmony" into its surface. Anoint it with eucalyptus or chamomile oil, saying: "Candle of peace, flame so calm, bring harmony, like a soothing balm." Light the candle during family gatherings or when you need to create a peaceful atmosphere in your home.

28. Banishing Candle Spell

Use a black candle to banish negativity from your life. Carve a symbol representing what you want to banish (e.g., a broken chain, a crossed-out word) into the candle's surface. Anoint it with clove oil, saying: "Candle of night, burn away, clear my path, light my way." Light the candle and focus on the flame absorbing and banishing the unwanted energy from your space.

29. Gratitude Circle Candle

Create a circle of small tea light candles on your altar. In the center, place a note listing things you are grateful for. Light each candle, saying: "Flames so bright, warm and clear, I give my thanks, bring them near." Allow the candles to burn down, radiating gratitude and drawing more blessings into your life.

30. Candle of Creativity

Choose a yellow or orange candle and carve symbols of creativity (such as a spiral, sun, or feather) into its surface. Anoint it with rosemary or citrus oil, saying: "Candle of gold, flame so bright, inspire my mind, fill me with light." Light this candle before starting any creative work to enhance your inspiration and focus.

31. Healing Light Candle

Select a green or white candle to represent healing. Carve a healing symbol (such as a caduceus or a heart) into the wax. Anoint the candle with eucalyptus or tea tree oil, saying: "Candle of green, flame of light, heal my body, make it right." Light this candle while focusing on the flame, visualizing it filling you or your loved one with healing energy.

32. Candle of Joy

Carve a smiley face or a sun symbol into a yellow candle. Anoint it with orange or lemon oil, saying: "Candle of joy, flame so bright, fill my heart with pure delight." Light this candle when you need a mood boost, letting its warmth and light uplift your spirit.

33. Protection Candle for Loved Ones

Carve the names or initials of loved ones you wish to protect into a white or purple candle. Anoint it with lavender or rosemary oil, saying: "Candle of light, shield so clear, protect my loved ones, far and near." Light this candle while visualizing a protective bubble of light surrounding each person you wish to guard.

34. Candle for Letting Go

Choose a black or dark blue candle to symbolize release. Carve a symbol representing what you need to let go of (such as a chain or knot) into its surface. Anoint the candle with sage or cedar oil, saying: "Candle of night, burn so true, release my past, make me new." Light the candle and watch it burn, imagining the flame dissolving your attachments and freeing you from burdens.

35. Spiritual Awakening Candle

Select a purple candle to represent spiritual growth and awakening. Carve symbols of spiritual power (such as a spiral, eye, or moon) into its surface. Anoint the candle with frankincense or myrrh oil, saying: "Candle of purple, flame of sight, open my mind, bring me light." Light this candle during meditation or ritual work to deepen your spiritual awareness and intuition.

36. Candle of New Opportunities

Choose a green or gold candle and carve a door or key symbol into its surface to represent new opportunities. Anoint the candle with mint or basil oil, saying: "Candle of green, door so wide, bring new chances, open wide." Light this candle whenever you seek to attract new possibilities into your life, focusing on the flame as it draws these opportunities to you.

37. Sunlight Candle Spell

Place a yellow candle on a sunny windowsill during the day to absorb the sun's energy. At dusk, light the candle and say: "Candle of sun, bright and true, bring me warmth, the whole night through." Use this spell on cloudy days or long winter nights to invite the sun's warmth and energy into your space.

38. Wishing Candle for the New Year

Write your wishes for the coming year on a piece of parchment. Place the parchment under a white candle and light it, saying: "Candle of hope, flame of new, bring my wishes, make them true." Let the candle burn for at least an hour, visualizing your wishes taking form as the new year approaches.

39. Grounding Candle Ritual

Select a brown or green candle to represent grounding energy. Carve a tree or root symbol into the candle. Anoint it with cedar or patchouli oil, saying: "Candle of earth, flame so bright, ground my spirit, keep me right." Light this candle during meditation or grounding exercises, focusing on the flame to connect with the earth's stabilizing energy.

40. Candle of Inner Peace

Choose a light blue candle and carve the symbol of a dove or wave into its surface. Anoint it with lavender or chamomile oil, saying: "Candle of blue, calm and clear, bring me peace, draw me near." Light this candle during stressful times or before sleep to invite tranquility and relaxation into your space.

41. Family Unity Candle

Carve symbols representing family (such as a tree, heart, or initials) into a white or gold candle. Anoint the candle with rosemary or lemon oil, saying: "Candle of light, family so near, bring us unity, love sincere." Light this candle during family gatherings or meals to foster harmony and strengthen familial bonds.

42. Moonlit Candle Reflection

Use a white or silver candle to connect with the moon's energy. Carve moon symbols (such as crescents or stars) into the candle. Anoint it with sandalwood or jasmine oil, saying: "Candle of moon, silver light, guide my spirit, through the night." Light this candle on moonlit nights to reflect on your emotions and gain deeper insights into your inner world.

43. Candle of Courage

Choose a red candle and carve a lion or sword symbol into its surface. Anoint the candle with clove or cinnamon oil, saying: "Candle of red, flame of might, grant me courage, through this fight." Light this candle whenever you need to summon courage, focusing on the flame's strength to empower you.

44. Ancestor Connection Candle

Select a white or grey candle to honor your ancestors. Carve the symbols of a tree, cross, or family crest into the candle's surface. Anoint it with sandalwood or myrrh oil, saying: "Candle of old, flame so wise, connect me now, to ancestors' eyes." Light this candle during rituals to invite the presence and guidance of your ancestors.

45. Yule Circle of Light

Create a circle of 12 candles on your altar, representing the 12 months of the year. Light each candle clockwise, saying: "Circle of light, circle of year, bring us joy, cast out fear." Sit within the circle, reflecting on the past year and setting intentions for the coming year. Allow the candles to burn down to welcome the new cycle of growth and change.

Chapter 15: Dream and Vision Spells

Dreams have long been regarded as gateways to the subconscious, offering profound insights, messages from the divine, and glimpses of possible futures. During the quiet and introspective season of Yule, the power of sleep and dreams becomes a potent tool for spiritual growth, personal discovery, and setting intentions. This chapter delves into 30 detailed spells aimed at enhancing dreams, gaining insights, and harnessing the magical power of sleep to shape your waking reality.

1. Lavender Dream Pillow

Create a small pillow filled with dried lavender, chamomile, and mugwort. Sew the pillow shut, focusing on its intention. As you hold it, say: "Herbs of sleep, scent so bright, bring me dreams, through the night." Place the pillow under your regular pillow to invite restful sleep and vivid dreams.

2. Moonstone Dream Enhancement

Place a moonstone under your pillow before sleep. Close your eyes and hold your intention for deeper, more meaningful dreams. Say: "Moonstone bright, dreams take flight, reveal the truth in silent night." Sleep with the moonstone nightly to enhance dream recall and intuitive insights.

3. Mugwort Tea for Lucid Dreams

Brew a cup of mugwort tea and drink it an hour before bedtime. Hold the cup in your hands and say: "Herb of dreams, visions clear, guide my spirit, bring them near." As you sip, set the intention to become conscious within your dreams. Mugwort enhances the likelihood of lucid dreaming and vivid dream experiences.

4. Full Moon Dream Invocation

On the night of a full moon, stand at your window or outside, holding a white candle. Light the candle and say: "Moon so full, dreams so bright, reveal the truths this sacred night." Place the candle by your bedside and let it burn for an hour as you sleep, inviting the moon's energy to enhance your dreams.

5. Sigil of Sleep

Draw a simple sigil representing restful sleep and clear dreams on a piece of paper. Place the paper under your pillow and say: "Sigil of sleep, calm and true, guide my dreams, show me through." Keep the sigil under your pillow to improve dream quality and aid in dream recall.

6. Quartz Crystal Dream Clarity

Hold a clear quartz crystal in your hand before bed. Close your eyes and say: "Quartz of light, dreams so clear, show me truths, bring them near." Place the crystal under your pillow to enhance the clarity of your dreams and improve your ability to remember them upon waking.

7. Protection Dream Circle

Place a black candle at the head of your bed and light it before sleep. Draw a circle of salt around the candle, saying: "Circle of night, guard my dreams, keep me safe from troubled streams." Allow the candle to burn for a few minutes before extinguishing it. The protective circle will shield your dreams from negative energies.

8. Dream Mirror Vision Spell

Place a small mirror under your pillow before going to sleep. As you lie down, say: "Mirror of dreams, reveal to me, the visions clear, let me see." The mirror acts as a portal, helping you gain insights and glimpses of potential futures in your dreams.

9. Chamomile Dream Tea

Brew a cup of chamomile tea before bed. As you stir the tea, say: "Chamomile calm, dreams so bright, bring me peace, guide my night." Sip the tea slowly, setting the intention for peaceful and insightful dreams. Chamomile promotes relaxation and dream recall.

10. Candle of Intention

Select a light blue or lavender candle and carve symbols of peace and sleep into its surface. Light the candle and say: "Candle of rest, flame so true, guide my dreams, through the night blue." Place the candle by your bedside and let it burn for a short time before extinguishing it. Its energy will aid in setting intentions for your dreams.

11. Amethyst Vision Spell

Hold an amethyst stone in your hands before sleep. Close your eyes and say: "Amethyst clear, dreams reveal, visions bright, truths unseal." Place the amethyst under your pillow to invite prophetic and vivid dreams.

12. Rosemary Dream Cleansing

Before bed, place a sprig of rosemary under your pillow. Say: "Rosemary pure, guard my night, cleanse my dreams, keep them light." The rosemary will cleanse your dreams of negative energies and promote positive visions.

13. Dream Journal Spell

Keep a journal and pen by your bedside. Before sleep, hold the journal and say: "Book of dreams, paper so clear, catch my visions, bring them near." Each morning, write down any dreams you recall. This practice helps improve dream recall and increases awareness of recurring themes or messages.

14. Herbal Sleep Pouch

Fill a small pouch with dried lavender, chamomile, and mugwort. Sew the pouch shut and hold it in your hands. Say: "Herbs of dreams, calm and bright, guide my sleep, show me light." Place the pouch under your pillow or hang it near your bed to promote restful sleep and vivid dreams.

15. Candle of Nightmares

Carve the word "Nightmare" or a banishing symbol into a black candle. Anoint it with clove oil, saying: "Candle of night, flame so bright, banish nightmares, guard my sight." Light the candle before bed for a few minutes, then extinguish it, visualizing it absorbing and dispelling any negative dream energy.

16. Saltwater Dream Protection

Fill a small bowl with water and add a pinch of salt. Place the bowl by your bedside, saying: "Water clear, salt so bright, protect my dreams, through the night." The saltwater acts as a protective barrier, absorbing negative energies that could disturb your sleep.

17. Moonlit Amulet for Dream Recall

Place a piece of moonstone or amethyst outside under the moonlight for an hour. Hold the stone and say: "Moon so bright, stone so clear, bring me dreams, draw them near." Wear the stone as an amulet or place it under your pillow to improve dream recall.

18. Dream Incense

Burn a blend of mugwort, lavender, and sandalwood incense before bed. Waft the smoke around your bedroom, saying: "Incense of dreams, visions clear, guide my sleep, bring truth near." The incense will create a dream-friendly atmosphere, enhancing your ability to receive messages during sleep.

19. Dream Path Candle

Carve a path or spiral symbol into a white candle. Anoint it with jasmine oil, saying: "Candle of light, dreams take flight, show me paths, through the night." Light this candle before bed, visualizing it guiding your spirit on a journey through the dream world.

20. Candle of Prophetic Dreams

Choose a purple candle and carve symbols of the moon, stars, or eyes into its surface. Anoint it with sandalwood or mugwort oil, saying: "Candle of purple, flame of sight, bring me visions, through the night." Light this candle on the night of the full moon to invoke prophetic dreams.

21. Dream Talisman Spell

Choose a small object (such as a stone or piece of jewelry) to act as your dream talisman. Hold it in your hands and say: "Talisman bright, dreams so true, guide my sleep, bring them through." Keep the talisman under your pillow to enhance dream experiences and recall.

22. Lavender and Rose Dream Bath

Prepare a warm bath and add a handful of dried lavender and rose petals. Stir the water clockwise, saying: "Bath of dreams, calm and clear, guide my sleep, bring me near." Soak for at least 15 minutes before bed to relax your body and open your mind to deeper dream states.

23. Candle of Past Life Dreams

Choose a silver or blue candle and carve symbols representing the past (such as an hourglass or spiral) into the wax. Anoint the candle with frankincense oil, saying: "Candle of time, dreams so clear, show me lives, past and near." Light the candle and focus on the flame as you fall asleep, inviting dreams of past lives.

24. Night Vision Elixir

Mix a few drops of peppermint oil into a cup of water. Drink it before bed, saying: "Peppermint bright, dreams take flight, bring me visions, through the night." The elixir promotes mental clarity and the potential for vivid dreams.

25. Dreamer's Knot Spell

Tie a simple knot in a piece of white string or ribbon, focusing on your dream intention. Place the knot under your pillow, saying: "Knot so tight, dreams take flight, show me truths, through the night." The knot holds your intention, guiding your dreams toward the desired insight.

26. Dream Mirror Placement

Place a small mirror facing the window beside your bed to capture moonlight. Say: "Mirror of dreams, moon so bright, reflect my visions, through the night." The mirror channels the moon's energy into your dreams, enhancing their clarity.

27. Candle for Inner Sight

Carve an eye or star symbol into a purple or white candle. Anoint it with jasmine or sandalwood oil, saying: "Candle of sight, dreams so true, open my mind, bring them through." Light this candle before bed to enhance your inner sight and intuitive dream experiences.

28. Rosemary Night Calm

Burn a sprig of dried rosemary in a fireproof dish before bed. Waft the smoke around your room, saying: "Rosemary bright, guard my sleep, bring me calm, dream paths deep." The rosemary's smoke purifies your space and calms your mind for clearer dreams.

29. Moon Oil for Dreams

Create a moon oil by adding a few drops of sandalwood and lavender oils into a carrier oil. Anoint your forehead and temples before bed, saying: "Oil of moon, dreams so bright, open my mind, through the night." The moon oil enhances your connection to the dream world and spiritual visions.

30. Yule Night Dream Candle

On Yule night, light a white candle and place it by your bedside. Carve the symbol of the sun or a spiral into the candle, saying: "Candle of Yule, light so true, guide my dreams, bring them through." Allow the candle to burn for a few minutes before extinguishing it, inviting the energy of Yule into your dream world.

Chapter 16: Ancestor Connection Rituals

The winter season, especially around Yule, is a time when the veil between worlds is thinner, allowing us to connect more deeply with our ancestors. Honoring those who came before us not only pays respect to their legacy but also opens pathways to their wisdom, guidance, and protection. In this chapter, you'll find 40 detailed spells and rituals that help to honor ancestors, seek their counsel, and draw on their strength. These spells involve candles, offerings, personal items, symbols, and natural elements to facilitate a meaningful connection with your ancestral line.

1. Ancestral Candle Invocation

Light a white candle on your altar and place a photograph or symbol of your ancestors beside it. As you light the candle, say: "Ancestors of old, spirits bright, guide me now, with your light." Sit quietly and meditate on the flame, allowing it to serve as a bridge to your ancestors. Ask them for guidance or simply honor their presence.

2. Ancestral Altar Creation

Set up a small altar space dedicated to your ancestors. Place photographs, heirlooms, or items that remind you of them on the altar. Light an incense stick, saying: "Altar of old, memories clear, honor my kin, draw them near." Spend a few moments each day at the altar, speaking to your ancestors and offering gratitude for their influence.

3. Family Tree Meditation

Draw or visualize your family tree, focusing on each branch and leaf. Sit before the image and light a green candle. Say: "Tree of kin, roots so deep, guide me now, as I seek." Meditate on the strength and wisdom passed down through your family line, feeling their support surrounding you.

4. Ancestral Herb Offering

Place dried herbs associated with ancestors (such as rosemary, sage, or mugwort) in a small dish on your altar. Light a white candle and say: "Herbs of earth, scent so clear, honor my kin, bring them near." Offer these herbs as a sign of respect and invite the presence of your ancestors into your space.

5. Ancestor Dream Request

Before going to sleep, write a letter to your ancestors, asking for their guidance in your dreams. Fold the letter and place it under your pillow, saying: "Ancestors wise, spirits true, guide my dreams, see me through." Sleep with the letter for several nights to receive messages in your dreams.

6. Candle of Ancestral Guidance

Carve symbols of your ancestry (such as a family crest, totem animal, or traditional symbols) into a white or grey candle. Anoint the candle with sandalwood oil and say: "Candle of old, light so true, guide me now, show me through." Light this candle during meditation or ritual work to invite ancestral guidance.

7. Ancestral Feast Ritual

Prepare a meal using traditional family recipes. Set an extra plate at the table for your ancestors and serve them portions of the food. As you eat, say: "Food of earth, flavors old, honor my kin, stories told." Share memories and stories of your ancestors, inviting them to join the feast.

8. Ancestral Offering Bowl

Place a small bowl of water, salt, or wine on your altar as an offering. Hold your hands over the bowl and say: "Water of life, salt of earth, honor my kin, respect their worth." Keep the offering on the altar for a week, replacing it as needed to maintain the connection with your ancestors.

9. Ancestral Protection Amulet

Choose an object that belonged to an ancestor (such as jewelry, a key, or a coin). Hold the item in your hands and say: "Amulet of old, guard my way, ancestors bright, protect this day." Carry the item with you as a protective charm, drawing on the strength and protection of your lineage.

10. Candle Prayer for the Departed

Light a candle for each departed ancestor you wish to honor. As you light each one, say: "Candle of light, flame so bright, honor my kin, spirits in flight." Spend time reflecting on the lives and legacies of each ancestor as the candles burn, offering prayers or words of gratitude.

11. Ancestor Connection Stone

Hold a stone (such as obsidian or amethyst) in your hands and close your eyes. Say: "Stone of earth, guide so true, connect me now, to those I knew." Place the stone on your altar or carry it with you to maintain a connection with your ancestors.

12. Ancestral Tea Ritual

Brew a cup of tea using herbs connected to ancestral wisdom, such as rosemary, sage, or mugwort. Stir the tea clockwise and say: "Herbs of earth, steeped in might, bring me wisdom, guide my sight." Drink the tea while meditating on the guidance and support of your ancestors.

13. Ancestral Vision Spell

Place a photograph of an ancestor on your altar, along with a white candle and a clear quartz crystal. Light the candle and say: "Vision bright, ancestors near, show me truths, bring them clear." Close your eyes and hold the crystal, inviting visions or insights from your ancestor.

14. Ancestral Circle of Light

Gather a circle of white candles around a family heirloom or photograph on your altar. Light each candle clockwise, saying: "Circle of light, kin of old, bring me strength, wisdom untold." Sit within the circle and focus on the energy and guidance of your ancestors surrounding you.

15. Ancestor Dream Journal

Keep a special journal dedicated to recording dreams related to your ancestors. Each night, place the journal under your pillow, saying: "Book of dreams, ancestors true, guide my sleep, bring me through." Write down any dreams or insights that come to you upon waking.

16. Ancestor's Herb Sachet

Create a sachet using herbs that resonate with ancestral energy (such as sage, rosemary, and lavender). Hold the sachet in your hands and say: "Herbs of old, scent so clear, guide me now, bring you near." Place the sachet under your pillow to strengthen your connection to your ancestors while you sleep.

17. Candle of Family Strength

Carve a tree or family symbol into a green or white candle. Anoint the candle with cedar oil, saying: "Candle of might, flame so bright, bring me strength, day and night." Light this candle whenever you need to draw on the strength and support of your ancestral line.

18. Ancestor Message Ritual

Write a letter to an ancestor you wish to communicate with. Burn the letter in a fireproof dish, saying: "Words of old, flame so true, send my message, bring me through." Sit quietly and listen for any messages or feelings that come to you after the ritual.

19. Offering of the Ancestors

Leave an offering of food, drink, or flowers on your altar to honor your ancestors. As you place the offering, say: "Gift of earth, food so fair, honor my kin, spirits who care." Replace the offering regularly to maintain a continuous bond with your ancestral line.

20. Candle of Ancestral Protection

Select a black or grey candle and carve symbols of protection into its surface. Anoint it with rosemary oil, saying: "Candle of night, guard my way, ancestors bright, keep harm at bay." Light this candle in times of uncertainty to invoke the protective presence of your ancestors.

21. Ancestral Guidance Crystal Grid

Create a crystal grid using stones such as amethyst, clear quartz, and obsidian. Place a photograph or symbol of your ancestor in the center. As you arrange the stones, say: "Grid of light, stones so clear, guide me now, bring you near." Meditate on the grid to invite ancestral wisdom and guidance.

22. Ancestral Storytelling Candle

Light a white candle on your altar and sit before it. Say: "Candle of light, memories old, share their stories, wisdom untold." Speak aloud the stories of your ancestors, passing down their legacy and drawing strength from their experiences.

23. Moonlit Ancestor Connection

On the night of the full moon, stand outside and light a white candle. Hold a family heirloom or photograph in your hands and say: "Moon so bright, guide so clear, ancestors true, bring you near." Allow the moonlight to bathe the object, filling it with ancestral energy.

24. Ancestral Knot Ritual

Tie a knot in a piece of thread or cord for each ancestor you wish to honor. Hold the cord in your hands and say: "Knots of kin, bond so true, guide my path, see me through." Hang the cord on your altar as a representation of your ancestral line.

25. Ancestral Feast of Remembrance

Prepare a simple meal of foods that were significant to your ancestors. Set an extra place at the table and light a white candle. Say: "Feast of kin, food of old, honor their lives, stories told." Eat the meal in silence or while sharing memories of your ancestors, inviting them to join in the feast.

26. Ancestor Rune Carving

Carve an ancestral rune or symbol into a piece of wood or stone. Hold the carved item in your hands and say: "Rune of old, carved so true, guide my path, bring me through." Place the rune on your altar or carry it with you as a talisman for ancestral guidance.

27. Ancestor's Candle for Insight

Carve the initials or name of an ancestor into a white candle. Anoint it with sandalwood or frankincense oil, saying: "Candle of light, name so clear, guide me now, bring you near." Light this candle during meditation to connect with that ancestor's wisdom.

28. Ancestral Meditation Chant

Sit quietly and light a candle. Close your eyes and chant: "Ancestors of mine, spirits so true, guide my steps, show me through." Repeat the chant until you feel a sense of their presence, then sit quietly to receive any messages.

29. Candle of Ancestral Healing

Carve a healing symbol (such as a heart or cross) into a white or green candle. Anoint it with lavender or rose oil, saying: "Candle of light, healing so near, bring peace and calm, to those held dear." Light this candle to send healing energy to your ancestral line, healing past wounds and bringing peace.

30. Ancestor Offering of Wine

Pour a small glass of wine and place it on your altar. Hold your hands over the glass and say: "Wine of earth, drink so fine, honor my kin, spirits divine." Leave the glass overnight as an offering to your ancestors.

31. Candle of Ancestral Dreams

Carve a dream symbol (such as a star or eye) into a silver or purple candle. Light it before sleep, saying: "Candle of dreams, guide me through, ancestors wise, show me true." Let the candle burn for a short time, inviting ancestral messages into your dreams.

32. Ancestral Story Pouch

Fill a small pouch with herbs like rosemary and sage, and a piece of paper listing the names of your ancestors. Sew the pouch shut and say: "Pouch of stories, kin so true, guide my steps, bring me through." Keep the pouch on your altar or carry it to maintain a connection with their stories.

33. Ancestral Water Ritual

Fill a small bowl with water and place it on your altar. Hold your hands over the water, saying: "Water of life, clear and bright, honor my kin, spirits in flight." Leave the water on the altar for a day as an offering to the ancestors, then pour it outside to complete the ritual.

34. Ancestor Candle for Strength

Carve a mountain or tree symbol into a grey or brown candle. Light it while saying: "Candle of might, flame so high, bring me strength, see me by." Focus on the flame, drawing on the resilience and power of your ancestors.

35. Ancestral Communication Jar

Fill a jar with salt, rosemary, and a piece of paper listing the names of your ancestors. Seal the jar, saying: "Jar of truth, ancestors near, guide my path, bring me clear." Keep this jar on your altar as a means of staying connected to your ancestral line.

36. Candle of Ancestral Wisdom

Choose a purple candle and carve symbols of wisdom (such as an owl or book) into its surface. Anoint it with frankincense oil, saying: "Candle of wisdom, flame so clear, show me truths, ancestors near." Light this candle when seeking guidance on a difficult decision.

37. Ancestral Connection Crystal

Place a piece of obsidian or amethyst on your altar. Hold the stone and say: "Crystal of earth, guide so true, connect me now, to those I knew." Use this stone during meditation to strengthen your bond with your ancestors.

38. Ancestral Blessing Candle

Carve a blessing symbol (such as a cross, heart, or pentacle) into a white or green candle. Light it while saying: "Candle of light, flame so true, bless my kin, both old and new." Focus on sending blessings to your ancestors, both past and future generations.

39. Candle for Ancestral Messages

Carve a spiral or eye symbol into a blue candle. Anoint it with sandalwood oil, saying: "Candle of sight, flame so bright, bring me messages, through the night." Light this candle when you wish to receive messages or signs from your ancestors.

40. Yule Night Ancestral Vigil

On Yule night, place a photograph or heirloom on your altar along with a white candle. Light the candle and say: "Yule of old, kin so near, honor your lives, guide me here." Allow the candle to burn for an hour as you sit in reflection, honoring the ancestors and seeking their wisdom.

Chapter 17: Protection Wards and Talismans

Winter is often associated with darkness, cold, and a heightened sense of vulnerability. As the days grow shorter and the nights longer, we seek warmth, light, and protection for ourselves and our homes. In the spirit of Yule, this chapter focuses on crafting protective wards, amulets, and talismans to shield against the season's darker energies. These 50 detailed spells involve using natural elements, symbols, herbs, crystals, and candles to create items that ward off negativity, provide comfort, and create a safe haven during the winter months.

1. Rosemary Protection Charm

Tie together three sprigs of rosemary with a red ribbon. As you wrap the ribbon around the sprigs, say: "Rosemary bright, herb of might, guard this space, day and night." Hang the charm near the entrance of your home to protect against negative energies.

2. Snowflake Obsidian Amulet

Hold a piece of snowflake obsidian in your hands and focus on your intention for protection. Say: "Obsidian dark, speckled with light, guard me now, day and night." Wear the obsidian as a pendant or carry it in your pocket to shield yourself from negative influences.

3. Pine Cone Warding Spell

Collect a pine cone and hold it in your hands. Visualize it absorbing and reflecting any harmful energies. Say: "Pine cone strong, forest's guard, shield my home, keep watch hard." Place the pine cone near your door to act as a protective guardian for your household.

4. Salt Circle Ward

Pour a circle of salt around your home or room to create a protective barrier. As you pour, say: "Salt of earth, pure and bright, guard this space, protect with might." The salt will absorb negativity and prevent unwanted energies from entering your space.

5. Iron Nail Protection Amulet

Wrap an iron nail in black thread, focusing on your intention for protection. As you wrap, say: "Nail of iron, strong and true, ward off harm, keep me through." Carry the nail in a small pouch to ward off malevolent forces and provide strength.

6. Lavender and Sage Protection Sachet

Fill a small sachet with dried lavender and sage. Hold the sachet in your hands and say: "Herbs of peace, herbs of might, guard this place, protect with light." Hang the sachet near your bed or carry it with you for a shield of calm and protection.

7. Black Candle Banishment

Carve a protection symbol (such as a pentacle or rune) into a black candle. Anoint it with clove or rosemary oil and say: "Candle of night, flame so bright, banish darkness, bring me light." Light the candle to burn away negative energies in your home.

8. Pine Needle Door Wreath

Create a wreath using pine needles and holly branches. As you weave the wreath, say: "Pine so green, holly bright, guard this door, with all its might." Hang the wreath on your front door to invite positive energy and protect your household.

9. Moonstone Night Protection

Place a moonstone under your pillow before bed. Hold it in your hands and say: "Moonstone bright, guard my sleep, shield my dreams, safety keep." The moonstone will provide protective energy while you rest, warding off nightmares and harmful influences.

10. Rosemary Water Purification

Boil a handful of rosemary in a pot of water. Let the steam fill the room, saying: "Steam so pure, rosemary bright, cleanse this space, protect with light." Use the cooled rosemary water to wash your floors, windows, and doorways, creating a protective boundary in your home.

11. Candlelight Shield

Light a white candle and hold your hands around the flame, visualizing a shield of light forming around you. Say: "Flame of white, burning clear, guard my spirit, draw me near." Keep the candle burning for an hour to strengthen your personal shield against negativity.

12. Protective Rune Stone

Carve a rune of protection (such as Algiz) into a small stone. Hold the stone in your hand and say: "Rune of guard, stone of earth, ward off harm, prove your worth." Place the stone on your windowsill or carry it with you as a ward against negative forces.

13. Herbal Protection Jar

Fill a small jar with salt, rosemary, and cloves. Seal the jar and hold it in your hands, saying: "Herbs and salt, strong and clear, guard this space, keep harm near." Place the jar on your windowsill or in a hidden corner to absorb and block negative energies.

14. Cinnamon Stick Ward

Tie three cinnamon sticks together with a red ribbon. As you tie the knot, say: "Cinnamon warm, spice so true, guard my home, see me through." Hang the bundle in your kitchen to invite warmth, prosperity, and protection into your household.

15. Iron Key Amulet

Select an old iron key and hold it in your hand. Focus on its strength and history, saying: "Key of iron, lock of might, guard my path, day and night." Carry the key with you as a talisman to lock out negativity and unwanted influences.

16. Pine Branch Floor Sweep

Gather a pine branch and use it to sweep the floor of your home. As you sweep, say: "Pine of green, sweep away, negativity go, peace will stay." The branch clears away stagnant energy and leaves a protective aura in your space.

17. Star Anise Charm

Place a star anise in a small pouch with a piece of black tourmaline. Hold the pouch in your hands and say: "Star of strength, stone so clear, guard my heart, bring me near." Keep this pouch in your pocket to shield against negative energies.

18. Candle of the Watchful Eye

Carve an eye symbol into a white candle. Light the candle and say: "Candle bright, eye so clear, guard this home, keep harm near." Allow the candle to burn down, invoking its protective watchfulness over your home.

19. Protection Sigil

Draw a simple sigil representing protection on a piece of paper. Fold the paper and place it under a candleholder, saying: "Sigil of guard, hidden sight, protect this space, day and night." Light a candle over the sigil to activate its protective energy.

20. Salted Window Seal

Place a line of salt along your windowsills, saying: "Salt so pure, line so clear, guard this home, keep harm near." The salt forms a protective barrier against unwanted energies attempting to enter your home.

21. Garlic Ward for the Threshold

Hang a clove of garlic near your front door. As you hang it, say: "Garlic bright, scent so clear, ward off harm, keep all dear." The garlic serves as a natural protective charm, guarding your home from negativity.

22. Cedar Branch Protection

Place a small cedar branch above your doorway, saying: "Cedar strong, guardian bright, keep this home, safe in light." The cedar creates a barrier against harmful energies and invites harmony into your home.

23. Snow Water Purification

Collect snow in a bowl and let it melt. Use the water to sprinkle around your home, saying: "Snow so pure, water bright, cleanse this space, bring me light." The snow water purifies and blesses your space with the tranquility of winter.

24. Amethyst Door Ward

Hang an amethyst crystal near your front door. Hold the crystal and say: "Amethyst bright, stone of guard, keep this space, ever barred." The amethyst serves as a spiritual guard, blocking negativity from entering your home.

25. Bay Leaf Protection

Write the word "Protection" on a bay leaf and place it under your doormat, saying: "Bay leaf guard, ever true, protect this home, see us through." The bay leaf acts as a shield, warding off unwanted energies.

26. Mistletoe Home Blessing

Hang a sprig of mistletoe in your home, saying: "Mistletoe bright, guard this space, bring us love, protect this place." The mistletoe blesses your household with love and serves as a protective charm.

27. Stone Circle Ward

Place four stones at the corners of your home, forming a protective boundary. As you place each stone, say: "Stone of guard, circle true, protect this space, old and new." The stones create a shield, preventing negative energies from crossing the threshold.

28. Eggshell Powder

Crush eggshells into a fine powder. Sprinkle it around your home's perimeter, saying: "Eggshell white, guard so clear, protect this space, bring peace near." The powder acts as a natural protective barrier, reflecting negative energies.

29. Iron Nail Door Guard

Place an iron nail above your doorway, saying: "Nail of iron, guard so strong, protect this home, all year long." The iron nail serves as a ward, preventing malevolent spirits from entering your space.

30. Yule Candle Protection

Light a green candle on Yule night, saying: "Candle bright, Yule so near, guard this home, keep harm clear." Let the candle burn for an hour to imbue your space with protective and nurturing energy.

31. Feather Wind Ward

Hang a feather near your window, saying: "Feather light, guardian free, ward off harm, come to me." The feather catches and disperses negative energies, letting in only positive and peaceful ones.

32. Black Tourmaline Shield

Place a piece of black tourmaline at each corner of your room, saying: "Tourmaline dark, shield so bright, guard this space, day and night." The stones absorb negativity and create a protective energy field.

33. Candle Circle Ward

Arrange a circle of white candles around the room. Light each one clockwise, saying: "Circle of light, guard this space, bring protection, leave no trace." Sit within the circle to enhance the protective energy around you.

34. Crossroads Dirt Protection

Collect a small amount of dirt from a crossroads. Place it in a jar and say: "Dirt of path, guard so true, protect this home, see me through." Keep the jar on your altar or near your door to guard against wandering spirits.

35. Mirror Ward Spell

Place a small mirror facing outward near your entrance. Hold the mirror and say: "Mirror bright, reflect all harm, guard this space, keep it warm." The mirror reflects negative energies away from your home.

36. Protective Knot Spell

Tie three knots in a piece of black cord while focusing on protection. As you tie each knot, say: "Knot of guard, knot of light, protect this space, with all its might." Hang the knotted cord near your door as a protective charm.

37. Candle Flame Shield

Hold a white candle in your hands and focus on its flame. Say: "Flame of light, burning strong, guard my spirit, all night long." Visualize the candle's light expanding into a shield around you, offering ongoing protection.

38. Garlic Sachet

Place a few cloves of garlic in a sachet with salt and rosemary. Sew the sachet shut, saying: "Garlic guard, herb so true, keep me safe, all night through." Hang the sachet near your bed for protective energy while you sleep.

39. Protective Ash Circle

Burn a protective herb bundle (such as sage, cedar, or rosemary) and collect the ashes. Sprinkle the ashes around your home's perimeter, saying: "Ashes of guard, circle of might, protect this space, day and night."

40. Oak Leaf Charm

Select an oak leaf and hold it in your hands. Say: "Oak of strength, leaf of guard, protect this home, keep harm barred." Hang the leaf near a window or door to draw on the oak tree's protective energy.

41. Protective Knot Bracelet

Braid a cord using three colors (black, white, and red) while focusing on protection. Knot the ends, saying: "Cord of guard, knot of light, shield my spirit, day and night." Wear the bracelet as a protective talisman.

42. Birch Bark Shield

Collect a piece of birch bark and hold it in your hands. Say: "Birch of guard, tree so bright, protect this home, with all your might." Place the bark near your front door to shield your space from negative energies.

43. Candle Wax Seal

Light a black candle and let the wax drip onto a piece of paper with a protective sigil. Say: "Wax of night, seal so clear, guard this space, bring peace near." Place the wax-sealed sigil under your doormat for protection.

44. Salt and Rosemary Floor Wash

Mix salt and rosemary in a bucket of water. Mop your floors, saying: "Wash of earth, clean and true, guard this home, see me through." The wash purifies and protects your space.

45. Candlelight Reflection Ward

Place a small mirror behind a lit candle. Say: "Flame of light, reflect all harm, guard this space, keep it warm." The mirror amplifies the candle's protective light throughout the room.

46. Anise and Clove Protection Pouch

Fill a pouch with star anise and cloves. Hold it in your hands and say: "Spices of guard, scent so bright, protect this space, day and night." Hang the pouch in your home to repel negativity.

47. Cedar and Pine Garland

String together cedar and pine branches with red thread. As you hang the garland, say: "Garland green, protection bright, guard this home, day and night." Place it above a doorway to invite positive energy and ward off harm.

48. Black Obsidian Doorstep

Place a piece of black obsidian at your doorstep, saying: "Obsidian dark, shield so true, guard this home, see me through." The obsidian absorbs and neutralizes harmful energies before they enter your space.

49. Iron Horseshoe Ward

Hang an iron horseshoe above your front door, saying: "Horseshoe strong, iron guard, protect this home, keep harm barred." The horseshoe serves as a classic protective charm, inviting good fortune and repelling negative spirits.

50. Yule Pine Candle

Carve symbols of protection into a green candle. Anoint it with pine oil, saying: "Candle of Yule, pine so clear, guard this home, keep harm near." Light the candle on Yule night to invoke the protective power of the season.

Chapter 18: Sacred Circle and Altar Spells

Yule is a time for reflection, introspection, and the rekindling of light during the darkest part of the year. Creating a sacred space or altar for Yule magic allows you to harness the season's energy, focusing your intentions, prayers, and spells in a dedicated and purified area. This chapter offers 30 detailed spells for setting up sacred circles and altars specifically for Yule, using natural elements, symbols, candles, and crystals to create spaces that radiate warmth, protection, and spiritual focus.

1. Yule Circle of Light

Create a circle of 12 white candles around your altar space, representing the 12 months of the year. Light each candle clockwise, saying: "Circle of light, warmth of sun, guard this space, till the year is done." Sit within the circle to connect with the protective and renewing energy of the Yule season. This circle will amplify the power of your rituals.

2. Altar of Evergreen Blessing

Gather pine, cedar, and holly branches to adorn your altar. As you place each branch, say: "Evergreens bright, winter's guard, bless this space, keep watch hard." These evergreen elements symbolize life, protection, and the enduring spirit of Yule.

3. Sacred Circle Salt Line

Outline your circle using sea salt to create a boundary of protection. As you pour the salt, say: "Salt of earth, pure and bright, guard this space, seal it tight." The salt line establishes a sacred boundary, shielding your rituals from negative energies.

4. Four-Element Altar Setup

Arrange items representing the four elements on your altar: a candle for fire, a bowl of water, a crystal for earth, and incense for air. As you place each item, say: "Fire, water, earth, and air, guide this circle, keep it fair." This balanced altar setup invites the elements to bless and empower your Yule magic.

5. Pine Cone Altar Centerpiece

Place a large pine cone at the center of your altar to symbolize rebirth and renewal. Hold the pine cone in your hands and say: "Pine cone strong, nature's might, bless this space, fill it with light." The pine cone serves as a focal point for your intentions during Yule rituals.

6. Yule Candle Altar Blessing

Select a red, green, and gold candle for your altar. Light each candle, saying: "Candle of warmth, candle of cheer, bless this altar, bring Yule near." Allow the candles to burn for a while, filling your sacred space with warmth and positive energy.

7. Snow-Infused Circle

Collect fresh snow in a bowl and sprinkle it around the edge of your sacred circle. As you do, say: "Snow so pure, cold and bright, guard this space, hold the light." The snow symbolizes the purity and calm of winter, creating a serene atmosphere for your rituals.

8. Crystal Grid for Yule

Create a crystal grid on your altar using clear quartz, amethyst, and snowflake obsidian. Arrange them in a star or spiral pattern, saying: "Crystals bright, energy flow, bless this altar, let magic grow." This grid amplifies your intentions and connects your altar to the season's energy.

9. Holly and Ivy Protection Circle

Lay holly and ivy branches around the boundary of your circle. As you place each branch, say: "Holly and ivy, guard and hold, protect this circle, strong and bold." These plants invoke the protective and enduring qualities of the winter season.

10. Altar Purification with Rosemary Smoke

Light a bundle of dried rosemary and waft the smoke over your altar, saying: "Rosemary bright, herb of clear, cleanse this space, draw spirits near." The smoke purifies the altar, clearing away negative energies and inviting benevolent spirits to aid in your Yule workings.

11. Candlelit Altar of Wishes

Arrange seven small candles in a circle on your altar, each representing a wish for the new year. Light each candle, saying: "Candle bright, flame of hope, bring forth wishes, help me cope." This altar setup focuses your intentions on manifesting your desires for the coming year.

12. Sacred Circle with Evergreen Boughs

Lay a ring of evergreen boughs (pine, fir, or spruce) around the boundary of your sacred circle. As you arrange the boughs, say: "Boughs of green, guard this space, hold the light, in winter's grace." This circle enhances protection and life-force energy during your rituals.

13. Sun and Moon Altar Candles

Place a golden candle representing the sun and a silver candle representing the moon on your altar. Light both candles and say: "Sun and moon, light and dark, bless this altar, ignite the spark." This altar configuration honors the balance of light and dark during the Yule season.

14. Salt and Herb Altar Circle

Mix salt with dried rosemary, thyme, and lavender. Sprinkle this mixture around the perimeter of your altar, saying: "Salt and herbs, blend so bright, guard this space, through Yule's night." The blend protects your altar and enhances its magical properties.

15. Candle of Yule's Blessing

Select a large green candle to place at the center of your altar. Carve symbols of Yule (such as a pine tree, holly, or sun) into the candle. Light it, saying: "Candle of green, light so clear, bless this space, draw Yule near." The candle serves as a beacon, drawing in Yule's blessings.

16. Altar of Ancestral Honor

Arrange photographs, heirlooms, or symbols of your ancestors on the altar. Light a white candle in their honor, saying: "Spirits of old, guide this night, bless this space, with your light." This altar invites the wisdom and protection of your ancestors during your Yule practices.

17. Snowflake Crystal Circle

Place snowflake obsidian stones in a circle around your altar to form a protective barrier. As you lay each stone, say: "Snowflake stone, cold and bright, guard this space, protect with might." The obsidian absorbs and deflects negative energies.

18. Yule Tree Altar Decor

Decorate a small branch or miniature tree on your altar with pinecones, holly berries, and ribbons. As you decorate, say: "Tree of Yule, adorned with care, bless this altar, magic fair." This setup represents the life and renewal of Yule, bringing nature's blessings indoors.

19. Incense Circle of Purification

Place four incense sticks at the cardinal points (north, south, east, west) around your sacred circle. Light each one, saying: "Incense of earth, wind, fire, and sea, purify this space, so mote it be." Allow the smoke to cleanse and sanctify your circle.

20. Altar of Sunlight

Create an altar dedicated to the return of the sun. Place gold candles, yellow crystals (such as citrine), and symbols of the sun. Light the candles, saying: "Sun's return, light so bright, bless this altar, with warmth and might." This altar radiates the energy of renewal and hope.

21. Stone Boundary Circle

Mark the edges of your circle with small stones. As you lay each stone, say: "Stone of earth, guard this line, protect this space, so pure, divine." The stones ground the energy of your circle, providing a solid foundation for your rituals.

22. Fire and Ice Altar

Place a red candle (fire) and a bowl of ice (water) on your altar. Light the candle, saying: "Fire of warmth, ice so cold, bring balance here, new and old." This altar setup honors the balance of opposites present in winter, creating harmony in your sacred space.

23. Altar Circle of Light and Shadow

Arrange a ring of alternating black and white candles around your altar. Light each candle, saying: "Light and dark, shadow and flame, bless this space, by Yule's name." This circle acknowledges the balance of light and darkness, welcoming their guidance into your magic.

24. Evergreen Pentacle Altar

Create a small pentacle using evergreen branches on your altar. As you lay each branch, say: "Pentacle bright, evergreen clear, guard this space, draw spirits near." This symbol draws in protective energy and the life force of the natural world.

25. Yule Altar with Bells

Hang small bells around the edges of your altar or circle. Ring each bell, saying: "Bells of Yule, sound so clear, ward off harm, bring good cheer." The bells create a vibrational shield, repelling negative energies and inviting joy.

26. Sacred Circle of Crystals

Use crystals such as clear quartz, amethyst, and rose quartz to mark the boundary of your circle. Place them in a circle, saying: "Crystals bright, energy flow, guard this space, let magic grow." These stones amplify the protective and harmonious energy of your circle.

27. Yule Herb Altar

Place bundles of dried Yule herbs (such as holly, mistletoe, and pine) on your altar. As you arrange them, say: "Herbs of Yule, nature's might, bless this altar, with your light." The herbs draw in the protective and nurturing energies of winter.

28. Candle Altar of Guidance

Select a purple candle to represent spiritual guidance. Place it on your altar and light it, saying: "Candle of spirit, flame so bright, guide this altar, with your light." This candle serves as a spiritual beacon, enhancing the intuition and guidance available in your sacred space.

29. Yule Log Altar Centerpiece

Carve symbols of protection and renewal into a small log, then place it at the center of your altar. As you place it, say: "Yule log strong, symbols so clear, guard this space, through the year." The log embodies the rebirth and strength of the Yule season.

30. Circle of Sunflowers

Place dried sunflower petals or small sunflower seeds around the boundary of your circle. As you lay them, say: "Sunflowers bright, seeds of sun, guard this space, till Yule is done." This circle invites the energy of the sun into your rituals, fostering growth and positivity.

Chapter 19: Yule Tree Rituals

The Yule tree stands as a central symbol of hope, renewal, and the promise of brighter days. Its evergreen branches remind us of nature's resilience and the continuity of life, even in the heart of winter. In Yule traditions, the tree is often used as a magical focal point for wishes, protection, and blessings. This chapter provides 25 detailed spells involving the Yule tree, guiding you to transform it into a beacon of positivity, a guardian of your space, and a vessel for your intentions.

1. Yule Tree Wish Ornament

Write your wish for the coming year on a small piece of paper. Roll it into a scroll and tie it with a red or green ribbon. As you do, say: "Wish of hope, tied so bright, hang on this tree, take its flight." Hang the scroll on the Yule tree. Leave it there throughout the season, trusting that your wish will be carried into the universe.

2. Evergreen Blessing

Before setting up your Yule tree, hold a sprig of its branches in your hands. Close your eyes and say: "Evergreen, life's true might, bring your blessings, day and night." Visualize the tree's energy spreading throughout your home as you set it up, bringing peace, joy, and harmony to all within.

3. Pine Cone Protection Charm

Collect a small pine cone and tie it with a red ribbon. Hold it in your hands, focusing on your intention for protection. Say: "Pine cone small, power so great, guard this space, protect my gate." Hang the pine cone on the Yule tree to act as a protective charm for your home during the winter.

4. Yule Tree of Gratitude

Create paper ornaments in the shape of stars, hearts, or snowflakes. On each one, write something you are grateful for. As you hang each ornament on the tree, say: "Gratitude bright, blessing so clear, thank you, spirits, for all I hold dear." This ritual fills the tree with the energy of gratitude, attracting more blessings into your life.

5. Crystal Tree of Light

Select small crystals (such as clear quartz, amethyst, and citrine) and attach them to ribbons. As you tie each crystal onto the tree, say: "Crystal bright, filled with light, bring your magic, through the night." The crystals absorb and radiate positive energy, turning your Yule tree into a beacon of light.

6. Tree of Wishes and Hopes

Cut small paper ornaments in various shapes (stars, moons, suns). Write your wishes and hopes for the new year on each one. As you hang them on the tree, say: "Hopes and dreams, wishes so true, hang on this tree, till they come through." Visualize each wish becoming reality as it rests among the branches.

7. Cinnamon Stick Tree Blessing

Tie cinnamon sticks with red ribbons and hang them on the tree. As you hang each one, say: "Cinnamon warm, spice of cheer, bless this tree, through the year." The cinnamon not only adds a pleasant scent but also draws in positive energy and blessings.

8. Holly and Ivy Protection Garland

Create a garland using holly and ivy and wrap it around the tree. As you drape it, say: "Holly and ivy, protect this tree, keep us safe, so mote it be." This garland serves as a protective shield for your home, using the magical properties of these traditional plants.

9. Candlelit Tree Blessing

On Yule Eve, place small, battery-operated candles on the branches of the tree. Turn them on one by one, saying: "Lights of Yule, flame so bright, bless this tree, through the night." The glow symbolizes the return of the sun and fills the space with warmth and positive energy.

10. Yule Tree Circle of Protection

Gather around your Yule tree with family or friends. Hold hands and form a circle, saying: "Tree of life, tree of light, guard this home, day and night." Visualize a protective shield emanating from the tree, expanding to encompass everyone present.

11. Salt Dough Ornaments for Peace

Make salt dough ornaments in shapes like stars, moons, or hearts. Before baking, press symbols of peace (like the peace sign or a dove) into the dough. As you hang the ornaments on the tree, say: "Ornaments bright, symbols of peace, bring calm and joy, never to cease." The ornaments absorb your intention, promoting peace in your space.

12. Yule Tree Renewal Ritual

After decorating the tree, sit quietly before it. Place your hands on your heart, then extend them toward the tree. Say: "Tree of green, life so bright, bring me renewal, strength and light." Visualize the tree's energy flowing into you, renewing your spirit and filling you with hope.

13. Yule Tree Pine Cone Offering

Place small pine cones at the base of your tree as offerings to nature spirits. Hold each cone in your hands and say: "Pine cone true, nature's gift, bring your blessings, spirits lift." This offering invites nature's guardians to bless and protect your home.

14. Ribbon Tree of Protection

Cut ribbons in red, green, and gold. As you tie each ribbon onto the branches, say: "Ribbon of red, green, and gold, guard this tree, as stories are told." The ribbons serve as a colorful protective charm, binding the energy of warmth, prosperity, and love into the tree.

15. Yule Tree Crystal Grid

Place crystals such as clear quartz, rose quartz, and citrine around the base of your tree, forming a grid. As you place each crystal, say: "Crystals bright, energy flow, protect this tree, let blessings grow." This grid enhances the tree's energy and creates a protective field.

16. Tree of Peace and Harmony

Hang blue and white ornaments on the tree to symbolize peace and harmony. As you place each one, say: "Ornaments of calm, colors so clear, bring peace and joy, year to year." These colors imbue the tree with tranquility, radiating a peaceful atmosphere throughout your space.

17. Candlelit Yule Tree Reflection

Sit before your tree with a candle. Light the candle and gaze at the tree, saying: "Tree of light, tree of green, reflect my dreams, visions unseen." Reflect on your hopes and desires, letting the tree serve as a mirror to your innermost wishes.

18. Sun and Moon Ornaments for Balance

Create ornaments in the shapes of the sun and moon. As you hang them on the tree, say: "Sun and moon, light and dark, bless this tree, ignite the spark." These symbols represent balance and harmony, bringing equilibrium to your space.

19. Tree of Ancestral Honor

Hang small photographs or symbols representing your ancestors on the tree. As you place each one, say: "Ancestors old, spirits near, bless this tree, bring us cheer." This ritual honors your lineage and invites ancestral guidance into your home during the Yule season.

20. Snowflake Ornament Protection

Create or purchase snowflake-shaped ornaments. As you hang each one on the tree, say: "Snowflake bright, pure and clear, guard this home, draw spirits near." The snowflakes represent purity and protection, warding off negativity from your space.

21. Star Toppers for Guidance

Place a star at the top of your tree to symbolize guidance and hope. As you set it in place, say: "Star of light, guide so bright, lead our way, through the night." The star serves as a focal point, guiding your intentions and actions in the year ahead.

22. Cinnamon and Orange Tree Blessing

Tie dried orange slices and cinnamon sticks with red thread, then hang them on the tree. As you do, say: "Citrus and spice, warmth and cheer, bless this tree, through the year." The scent of cinnamon and citrus fills your space with positive energy and warmth.

23. Herb Bundle Tree Protection

Create small bundles of protective herbs (such as rosemary, sage, and bay leaves) tied with twine. Hang them on the tree, saying: "Herbs of guard, scent so true, protect this space, old and new." The herbs purify the energy of your home and strengthen the protective aura of the tree.

24. Yule Tree Candlelight Meditation

Place battery-operated candles throughout the tree. Turn off all other lights and sit before the tree. As you gaze at the candlelit branches, say: "Lights of Yule, warm and bright, fill this space, with peace tonight." Meditate on the warmth and light of the candles, drawing in calmness and inner peace.

25. Yule Tree Blessing Spray

Mix water, a few drops of pine essential oil, and a pinch of sea salt in a spray bottle. Shake well and spray lightly over the tree, saying: "Water and pine, salt so pure, bless this tree, make it sure." This spray cleanses and blesses the tree, enhancing its positive energy.

Chapter 20: Fire and Hearth Rituals

Yule is a celebration of light's return amidst winter's darkness. Fire, in its many forms—whether a crackling fireplace, a blazing bonfire, or the flickering candle flame—represents warmth, protection, renewal, and transformation. Fire magic harnesses this elemental energy to bring hope, release negativity, and manifest intentions. This chapter contains 40 spells centered on fire magic, ranging from hearth rituals to candle blessings, each designed to kindle warmth, illuminate the spirit, and empower your Yule practices.

1. Hearth Blessing for Warmth

Stand before your fireplace with a piece of pine or cedar. Light the kindling in the fireplace and say: "Fire of warmth, hearth so bright, bless this home, day and night." As the fire grows, visualize it spreading warmth and comfort throughout your home. Let the fire burn while you sit and meditate on the protective energy it provides.

2. Yule Bonfire of Renewal

If you have access to an outdoor space, gather friends and family for a Yule bonfire. Before lighting it, say: "Bonfire bright, winter's might, bring renewal, chase the night." Light the fire and invite everyone to write down something they wish to release from the past year. Toss the papers into the flames, allowing the fire to transform and renew your energy.

3. Candle Flame Meditation

Sit in a quiet space with a single white candle. Light the candle and say: "Flame of white, pure and clear, bring me peace, draw me near." Gaze into the flame, allowing its glow to calm your mind and guide you into a meditative state. Visualize the candlelight expanding to fill you with warmth and clarity.

4. Fireplace Gratitude Ritual

Before lighting your fireplace, place a small bowl of herbs (such as rosemary, sage, and lavender) near the hearth. Say: "Herbs of thanks, fire of light, bless this hearth, through the night." Sprinkle a pinch of herbs into the flames as they grow, expressing gratitude for the warmth and protection the hearth provides.

5. Candle of Transformation

Carve symbols of change (such as a spiral or butterfly) into a black candle. Anoint it with frankincense or myrrh oil and say: "Flame of dark, light the way, transform my life, clear the gray." Light the candle and focus on releasing what no longer serves you, letting the flame symbolize transformation and new beginnings.

6. Bonfire of Wishes

During a bonfire, gather small pieces of dried herbs or leaves. Hold them in your hands and whisper your wishes for the coming year into them. Toss them into the fire, saying: "Flames so high, wishes take flight, grant my dreams, day and night." Watch as the flames consume the herbs, carrying your wishes into the universe.

7. Hearth of Protection

Light your fireplace and sit before it with a handful of sea salt. Toss a pinch of salt into the fire, saying: "Flame of warmth, salt so pure, guard this home, make it sure." Visualize the fire creating a protective shield around your home, keeping it safe from harm.

8. Candlelight Reflection

Sit in a dimly lit room with a single candle. Light the candle and say: "Flame so bright, guide my sight, show me truths, in the night." Allow your thoughts to flow as you gaze into the flame, using its light to reflect on the past year and gain insight for the future.

9. Fireplace Renewal Spell

Write down a habit or belief you wish to release on a small piece of paper. Fold the paper and hold it over the fireplace, saying: "Flame of old, fire so true, burn this burden, make me new." Toss the paper into the fire, watching it burn and transform, releasing its hold on you.

10. Yule Log Candle Ritual

If you don't have a fireplace, use a candle to represent the Yule log. Select a large green candle and carve symbols of Yule (such as stars, trees, or sun) into the wax. Light it, saying: "Yule log bright, candle of cheer, bless this space, throughout the year." Let the candle burn while you meditate on the season's warmth and renewal.

11. Hearth Cleansing Smoke

Before lighting your fireplace, sprinkle dried rosemary on the hearth. As you light the fire, say: "Rosemary bright, smoke so clear, cleanse this space, draw spirits near." Let the smoke waft throughout your home, clearing away negativity and inviting peaceful energies.

12. Candle Circle of Protection

Arrange a circle of red and green candles around you. Light each candle clockwise, saying: "Circle of fire, light and might, guard my spirit, through the night." Sit within the circle to feel its warmth and protection, letting the flames shield you from negative influences.

13. Yule Fire of Abundance

Gather pinecones and place them by your fireplace. Before lighting the fire, say: "Pinecones small, nature's gift, bring abundance, fortunes lift." Toss the pinecones into the fire, visualizing the flames bringing prosperity and blessings to your home.

14. Candle of Inner Strength

Carve symbols of strength (such as a mountain or tree) into a purple candle. Anoint it with cedar oil and say: "Flame of strength, burn so bright, give me courage, through the night." Light the candle during times of doubt to connect with your inner strength and resolve.

15. Fireplace of Ancestral Honor

Place photographs or symbols of your ancestors near the hearth. Light the fire, saying: "Fire of old, hearth so bright, honor the spirits, guide this night." Sit before the fire, offering gratitude to your ancestors for their wisdom and protection.

16. Bonfire of Dreams

During a bonfire, write your dreams for the future on small pieces of parchment. Toss each into the flames, saying: "Dreams take flight, in flames so high, carry my hopes, to the sky." As the parchment burns, visualize your dreams being carried out into the universe.

17. Candle Flame for Clarity

Select a blue candle and carve an eye symbol into the wax. Light the candle and say: "Flame of blue, calm and clear, bring me insight, draw me near." Sit quietly, focusing on the flame, allowing it to illuminate the answers you seek.

18. Hearth of Peace

Before lighting your fireplace, sprinkle lavender around the hearth. As the fire grows, say: "Lavender bright, flames so clear, bring me peace, draw me near." The fire and lavender's scent will fill your home with a calming energy, soothing frayed nerves and fostering tranquility.

19. Candle of Self-Love

Carve a heart symbol into a pink candle. Anoint it with rose oil and say: "Flame of love, burn so bright, fill my heart, with gentle light." Light the candle and sit before it, focusing on cultivating love and compassion for yourself.

20. Fireplace Blessing of Health

Write the names of those you wish to bless with good health on small pieces of paper. Light the fireplace and toss the papers into the flames, saying: "Flame of health, burn so clear, bring them strength, throughout the year." Visualize the fire surrounding them with warmth and healing.

21. Candle Flame of Release

Hold a black candle and carve symbols representing what you need to release (such as chains or knots). Light the candle and say: "Flame of dark, burn away, cleanse my spirit, clear the gray." Let the candle burn as you focus on releasing the burdens it represents.

22. Hearth Meditation for Renewal

Light the fireplace and sit quietly before it. Focus on the dancing flames, saying: "Fire of life, flame so bright, renew my spirit, with your light." Use the fire's energy to meditate on letting go of the old and embracing the new.

23. Candle of Hope

Select a yellow candle and carve a sun symbol into its surface. Light it, saying: "Flame of hope, burn so clear, bring me joy, throughout the year." Sit with the candle, allowing its light to fill you with optimism and warmth.

24. Bonfire of Cleansing

Write down feelings or situations that have caused you distress on small pieces of paper. During a bonfire, toss the papers into the flames, saying: "Fire so high, burn away, cleanse my soul, clear the way." Watch as the flames consume the papers, transforming your burdens into ash.

25. Candle of Balance

Place a white candle and a black candle side by side. Light both, saying: "Flame of dark, flame of light, bring me balance, through the night." Gaze at the twin flames, contemplating the harmony between light and shadow within yourself.

26. Hearth Protection Spell

Before lighting your fireplace, place a bowl of salt near the hearth. Say: "Salt of earth, flame of might, guard this home, day and night." Let the fire burn, using the salt as a protective barrier against negative energies.

27. Candle of Prosperity

Carve symbols of abundance (such as coins or wheat) into a green candle. Anoint it with patchouli oil and say: "Flame of green, wealth of earth, bring me fortune, joy and mirth." Light the candle while focusing on attracting prosperity into your life.

28. Bonfire of Joy

Gather around a bonfire with friends and family. Toss dried orange peels into the flames, saying: "Flames of joy, burn so bright, bring us laughter, through the night." Allow the fire to fill the atmosphere with joy and warmth.

29. Candle Flame for Guidance

Carve a spiral into a white candle. Light it and say: "Flame so pure, guide my way, show me answers, clear the gray." Gaze into the flame, seeking guidance on the questions you hold in your heart.

30. Hearth of Abundance

Before lighting your fireplace, place coins around the hearth. As the fire grows, say: "Fire of gold, warmth so near, bring abundance, through the year." Visualize the fire's energy drawing prosperity into your life.

31. Candle Circle of Light

Arrange nine candles in a circle on your altar. Light each candle clockwise, saying: "Circle of flame, light so true, bless this space, renew me too." Sit within the circle to feel its protective and revitalizing energy.

32. Fireplace of Reflection

Light the fireplace and place a mirror near the hearth. Say: "Fire of life, mirror bright, show me truths, in the night." Gaze into the mirror, using the flame's reflection to gain insight into your inner self.

33. Candle of Serenity

Select a light blue candle and carve symbols of water (such as waves) into the wax. Light it, saying: "Flame of blue, calm and clear, bring me peace, draw me near." Allow its soft glow to fill your space with tranquility.

34. Hearth Blessing for Family

Gather family members around the fireplace. Light the fire, saying: "Hearth of warmth, flame so bright, bless this home, with love's light." Sit together, sharing stories and laughter, letting the fire strengthen family bonds.

35. Candle of Cleansing

Carve symbols of water (such as drops or waves) into a white candle. Light it, saying: "Flame so bright, burn so clear, cleanse my spirit, draw me near." Use the candle's flame to cleanse your energy, releasing what no longer serves you.

36. Fireplace of New Beginnings

Before lighting the fireplace, place a sprig of pine at the hearth. Light the fire, saying: "Flame of green, light so true, bring me courage, to start anew." The fire ignites the energy of new beginnings, empowering you to move forward.

37. Candle of Inner Light

Hold a yellow candle and carve symbols of the sun into its surface. Light it, saying: "Flame of gold, burn so bright, fill my spirit, with your light." Focus on the flame, feeling its warmth infuse you with confidence and inner radiance.

38. Bonfire of Unity

During a bonfire, hold hands with those around you. Say: "Flames of life, flames of cheer, bring us close, year to year." The fire strengthens the bonds between you, fostering unity and community.

39. Hearth Fire of Forgiveness

Write down words of forgiveness on a piece of paper. Light the fireplace and toss the paper into the flames, saying: "Fire so warm, burn so clear, cleanse my heart, draw me near." Let the fire consume the paper, symbolizing the release of past hurts.

40. Candle of the Returning Sun

Carve a sun symbol into a golden candle. Light it on Yule morning, saying: "Flame of sun, bright and high, bring me joy, as days go by." This candle welcomes the return of longer days and the promise of new growth in the year to come.

Chapter 21: Healing and Renewal Spells

Yule is a time of deep reflection and renewal, making it the perfect season to focus on healing emotional, physical, and spiritual wounds. Just as the winter solstice marks the return of the sun, we too can harness the energy of winter's quiet and the promise of new beginnings to heal and grow. This chapter provides 35 detailed spells for healing various aspects of our lives. These rituals use elements such as herbs, candles, crystals, and the calming energy of winter to bring forth soothing, restorative power, allowing for a gradual and powerful renewal.

1. Snow Meditation for Clarity

Find a quiet spot outside during a snowfall, or sit near a window where you can watch snowflakes fall. Close your eyes, breathe deeply, and say: "Snow so pure, falling light, cleanse my mind, clear my sight." Allow the gentle sound and energy of the snow to calm your mind, bringing clarity and peace.

2. Yule Bath of Renewal

Draw a warm bath and add a handful of sea salt, dried lavender, and rose petals. As you stir the water, say: "Water so warm, herbs so pure, cleanse my body, let it cure." Soak in the bath, visualizing the water drawing out physical tension and emotional pain, leaving you renewed.

3. Winter Rose Healing Ritual

Hold a dried or fresh white rose in your hands. Close your eyes and focus on your intention for healing. Say: "Rose of white, pure and bright, heal my heart, grant me light." Place the rose on your altar to absorb any remaining negativity, allowing it to fill with soothing, healing energy.

4. Candle of Emotional Release

Carve symbols of water (such as waves or drops) into a blue candle. Light the candle and say: "Flame of blue, calm and clear, wash away pain, draw me near." Focus on the flame, visualizing it gently washing away emotional burdens, leaving a sense of peace in their place.

5. Pine Needle Healing Charm

Collect a small bundle of pine needles and wrap them in a white cloth. Tie it with a silver thread while saying: "Pine so green, healing true, grant me strength, make me new." Keep the charm near your bed to absorb and transform any emotional or spiritual wounds as you sleep.

6. Healing Snowflake Meditation

Close your eyes and visualize a beautiful snowflake glowing in front of you. Say: "Snowflake bright, pure and clear, bring me peace, draw me near." Imagine the snowflake entering your heart, spreading its cooling, healing energy throughout your body.

7. Candle of Forgiveness

Carve a heart symbol into a pink candle. Light it and say: "Flame of love, soft and bright, fill my heart, make it light." Sit quietly and focus on forgiving yourself and others, allowing the flame to melt away bitterness and anger.

8. Winter Crystal Healing Grid

Create a crystal grid using amethyst, clear quartz, and snowflake obsidian. Place the crystals in a star pattern on your altar and say: "Crystals bright, energy flow, bring me healing, let it grow." Sit with the grid, feeling its energy flow into your body, cleansing and renewing you.

9. Tea of Serenity

Brew a cup of chamomile and lavender tea. Hold the cup in your hands and say: "Herbs of calm, warmth so clear, bring me peace, draw me near." Sip the tea slowly, letting its soothing warmth fill you with serenity and wash away stress.

10. Candlelight Healing Meditation

Sit in a quiet space with a white candle. Light the candle and say: "Flame so bright, healing light, fill my spirit, through the night." Gaze into the flame, letting its warm glow fill you with a sense of safety and peace, soothing your soul.

11. Rosemary Purification Bath

Add a handful of dried rosemary to your bathwater. As the herb infuses the water, say: "Rosemary bright, cleansing pure, heal my body, spirit cure." Soak in the bath, visualizing the rosemary drawing out toxins and negativity, leaving you refreshed and renewed.

12. Healing Salt Circle

Create a circle of sea salt on your altar or in a quiet space. Sit within the circle and say: "Salt so pure, circle bright, cleanse my spirit, make it light." Sit quietly, allowing the salt's energy to absorb and neutralize any emotional or spiritual pain.

13. Candle of Self-Compassion

Carve the symbol of a heart or lotus into a pink candle. Light it and say: "Flame of love, soft and kind, fill my heart, ease my mind." Focus on cultivating feelings of compassion toward yourself, letting go of self-criticism and embracing self-care.

14. Snow-Covered Pine Renewal

Find a quiet place in nature, near snow-covered pine trees if possible. Place your hands on a tree trunk and say: "Pine so strong, snow so bright, fill me with strength, bring me light." Visualize the tree's energy flowing into you, bringing a sense of strength and renewal.

15. Amethyst Healing Talisman

Hold a piece of amethyst in your hands. Close your eyes and say: "Amethyst bright, healing true, ease my pain, make me new." Carry the amethyst with you to promote emotional balance and spiritual healing throughout the day.

16. Candle Flame Release

Hold a small white candle and carve symbols representing what you need to release (such as chains, knots, or waves). Light the candle and say: "Flame so bright, burn away, cleanse my spirit, clear the way." Visualize the flame burning away negativity and clearing space for positive energy.

17. Healing Tree of Life Visualization

Close your eyes and imagine a large, strong tree. Visualize its roots extending deep into the earth and its branches reaching high into the sky. Say: "Tree of life, old and true, bring me healing, renew me too." Imagine the tree's energy flowing into you, grounding and revitalizing your body and soul.

18. Lavender Sleep Sachet

Fill a small pouch with dried lavender and place it under your pillow. Hold the pouch and say: "Lavender bright, scent so clear, bring me rest, draw me near." Sleep with the sachet to promote restful sleep and gentle healing through dreams.

19. Moonlit Healing Water

Fill a bowl with water and place it under the moonlight for an hour. Hold the bowl and say: "Moon's soft light, water clear, cleanse my body, draw it near." Use the moon-charged water to wash your hands, face, or feet, allowing its energy to cleanse and heal you.

20. Pine Cone Healing Focus

Hold a pine cone in your hands and focus on your intention for healing. Say: "Pine cone strong, nature's might, bring me healing, through the night." Place the pine cone on your altar as a symbol of your healing journey.

21. Candle of Inner Peace

Carve the symbol of a dove or wave into a blue candle. Light it and say: "Flame of calm, burn so clear, fill my soul, draw peace near." Sit with the candle's flame, letting its soothing light wash over you, bringing inner peace and calm.

22. Snow Bath for Renewal

Collect fresh snow in a bowl and let it melt. Pour the water into your bath, saying: "Snow so pure, water clear, cleanse my spirit, bring me near." Soak in the bath, feeling the winter energy renewing your body and spirit.

23. Healing Smoke Ritual

Light a bundle of dried sage and waft the smoke around your body, saying: "Smoke of sage, healing so bright, cleanse my aura, with your light." The smoke clears away negative energy, leaving you feeling lighter and more at peace.

24. Winter Herb Tea

Brew a tea using dried rosemary, thyme, and mint. Hold the cup and say: "Herbs of green, warmth so clear, bring me strength, draw me near." Drink the tea to boost your physical and spiritual vitality, allowing the herbs' properties to cleanse and rejuvenate you.

25. Snow Quartz Crystal Healing

Hold a piece of snow quartz in your hands. Close your eyes and say: "Quartz of snow, pure and bright, bring me healing, with your light." Keep the quartz on your person or near your bed to promote healing and clarity.

26. Candle of Calm

Carve the symbol of a wave or lotus into a lavender candle. Light it and say: "Flame of calm, burn so clear, ease my spirit, draw me near." Allow the candle to burn while you focus on its light, letting it draw in serenity and release stress.

27. Healing Yule Tree Ritual

Stand before your Yule tree with your hands on your heart. Close your eyes and say: "Tree of Yule, evergreen bright, heal my spirit, with your light." Visualize the tree's energy flowing into you, bringing a sense of renewal and strength.

28. Rosemary Healing Amulet

Place a sprig of dried rosemary in a small pouch. Hold the pouch and say: "Rosemary bright, healing true, grant me strength, make me new." Carry the pouch with you to promote physical healing and protect your spirit.

29. Snowflake Candle Meditation

Place a white candle on your altar. Light it and hold a snowflake crystal in your hand. Say: "Flame and snow, pure and bright, bring me healing, through the night." Gaze into the flame, letting its light blend with the crystal's energy to bring you clarity and peace.

30. Herbal Healing Circle

Create a circle on your altar using dried herbs such as lavender, rosemary, and sage. Sit within the circle, holding your hands over your heart. Say: "Circle of herbs, healing true, bring me peace, make me new." Meditate within the circle, drawing on the herbs' energy for emotional and spiritual healing.

31. Winter Healing Blanket

Hold a cozy blanket and say: "Blanket warm, shield so near, wrap me in peace, bring me clear." Wrap the blanket around you as you sleep or rest, allowing it to absorb and transform any physical or emotional pain.

32. Yule Log Healing Candle

Carve symbols of healing (such as stars, hearts, or trees) into a green candle. Light it on your altar, saying: "Yule log bright, candle of cheer, bring me healing, throughout the year." Let the candle burn as you meditate on its light, filling you with the warmth of renewal.

33. Snow-Covered Pine Meditation

Visualize a snow-covered pine forest. Say: "Forest of white, pine so strong, bring me peace, where I belong." Imagine walking through the forest, breathing in the crisp air, and letting the tranquility of the scene wash over you, promoting inner peace and healing.

34. Candle Flame for Inner Healing

Hold a white candle and focus on an area of your life that needs healing. Light the candle and say: "Flame so pure, light so clear, heal my spirit, bring it near." Visualize the flame illuminating and healing the area of your life you have chosen.

35. Yule Tree Blessing for Healing

Hold your hands over your Yule tree and close your eyes. Say: "Tree of green, life so bright, bring me healing, with your light." Visualize the tree's energy flowing into you, filling you with hope, strength, and the promise of renewal.

Chapter 22: Weather and Season Control Spells

In ancient traditions, practitioners of magic have sought to harness the forces of nature to influence weather conditions for protection, travel, and agriculture. Yule, with its deep connection to the cycles of nature, is a particularly potent time to work with winter's elements. This chapter presents 20 detailed spells aimed at respectfully influencing winter weather conditions. These spells call upon the power of the elements, nature spirits, and seasonal energies to bring about safety in travel, protection from severe weather, and support for agricultural needs.

1. Gentle Snowfall Invocation

On a calm winter's day, take a small bowl of water and place it outside. Sprinkle a pinch of salt into the water, saying: "Water of life, salt so clear, call forth snowflakes, draw them near." Close your eyes and visualize a gentle snowfall. This spell encourages a calm and light snow to grace the land, particularly useful for a festive Yule atmosphere.

2. Storm-Soothing Candle Spell

If a winter storm threatens your safety, light a blue candle and sprinkle sea salt around its base. Say: "Wind and snow, calm your might, bring us peace, through this night." As the candle burns, visualize the storm's intensity lessening, transforming into a gentle, steady snow.

3. Safe Travel Charm

Before embarking on a winter journey, hold a piece of carnelian or clear quartz in your hands. Close your eyes and say: "Stone of guard, stone of light, guide my path, through snow and night." Carry the stone with you during travel to invoke protection and safe passage through inclement weather.

4. Clear Skies Request

When you need a break in the clouds for travel or outdoor activities, hold a small piece of sunstone in your hand. Stand outside, look up at the sky, and say: "Sunstone bright, guide the way, part these clouds, bring the day." Visualize the clouds parting, allowing the sun to shine through. This spell is particularly useful when you need a brief respite from winter's gloom.

5. Snow and Ice Protection Circle

Draw a circle in the snow around your home or vehicle using a small branch or stick. As you draw, say: "Circle of snow, shield so bright, guard this space, through winter's night." This circle acts as a protective barrier, warding off heavy snow or ice accumulation.

6. Early Thaw Petition

When an early thaw is needed for agricultural purposes, light a green candle and place a small bowl of warm water in front of it. Sprinkle in dried rosemary and basil, saying: "Winter's grip, loosen now, bring the thaw, bless the plow." Visualize the warmth spreading across the fields, gently melting the snow and ice.

7. Wind Calming Ritual

If strong winds threaten safety or crops, step outside and hold a small piece of lavender in your hand. Close your eyes and say: "Wind of might, calm and still, bring us peace, bend to will." Release the lavender into the wind, visualizing it carrying your request to the elements, calming the winds to a manageable level.

8. Snowmelt for Growth

Gather a bowl of snow and bring it inside to melt. As it melts, sprinkle dried thyme into the water, saying: "Snow to water, life to earth, bring forth growth, new green's birth." Pour the melted water around the base of indoor plants or into garden soil to infuse it with the energy of growth and renewal.

9. Fog Dispersal Spell

On foggy days when visibility is needed, light a white candle and hold a piece of clear quartz in your hand. Say: "Mist so thick, veil of white, part and fade, bring us sight." Visualize the fog lifting, revealing a clear path. This spell is particularly helpful for travelers navigating through dense fog.

10. Frost Shield for Crops

To protect plants from frost damage, hold a handful of sea salt and lavender. Sprinkle the mixture around the plants, saying: "Frost of night, heed my plea, guard these crops, let them be." This spell creates an energetic shield, reducing the risk of frost harming sensitive plants.

11. Ice Pathway Safety

Before walking or driving on icy paths, take a pinch of salt and sprinkle it in front of you, saying: "Ice so slick, melt away, clear this path, safe I stay." Visualize the salt working its magic, melting ice and creating a safer surface to travel on.

12. Snowfall Encouragement for Crops

If crops need additional moisture from snowfall, place a bowl of water on your altar and surround it with pinecones. Sprinkle dried sage into the water, saying: "Snow so pure, fall so light, bless this earth, through the night." Leave the bowl on your altar until the next snowfall, then pour the water into the soil as an offering to the land.

13. Hailstorm Ward

In the event of an impending hailstorm, light a black candle and place a small piece of iron (such as a nail) at its base. Say: "Hail of ice, cease your flight, calm your wrath, through this night." Visualize the hail dissolving into rain or snow, lessening its impact on the land.

14. Snow Wall of Protection

For severe winter storms, create a snow wall by building a small snowbank around your property's perimeter. As you form the snowbank, say: "Wall of snow, strong and high, guard this space, till storms pass by." This physical and energetic barrier protects against heavy snowdrifts.

15. Blizzard Soothing Ritual

If a blizzard is raging outside, light a blue and a white candle side by side. Hold a piece of clear quartz and say: "Blizzard fierce, wind and snow, calm your fury, let peace flow." Visualize the storm losing its intensity, transforming into a peaceful, gentle snowfall.

16. Rain and Snow Balance Spell

To achieve a balance between rain and snow for optimal agricultural growth, fill a bowl halfway with snow and halfway with rainwater. Hold the bowl and say: "Water of sky, snow of land, blend in peace, by nature's hand." Pour the mixture into the soil, asking the elements to provide balanced weather for the season.

17. Winter Fog Protection

Before entering a foggy area, light a silver candle and hold a piece of moonstone. Say: "Fog of night, veil so thick, guard my steps, quick and slick." Visualize a path clearing before you, illuminated by the moonstone's light.

18. Frost and Ice Banishment

For icy conditions that pose a risk, mix salt and rosemary in a small dish. Sprinkle a pinch on your doorstep, saying: "Ice so cold, frost so clear, melt away, leave me near." This spell creates a protective barrier, preventing frost and ice from forming near the entrance.

19. Safe Passage Snow Ritual

If you must travel in heavy snow, gather a handful of snow and hold it in your hands. Say: "Snow so deep, guide my way, grant me safe passage, through the day." Release the snow back to the ground, asking it to provide a clear path as you journey.

20. Snow-Covered Harvest Spell

To encourage a nourishing snow cover for next year's crops, fill a bowl with snow and sprinkle dried thyme and lavender on top. Hold the bowl and say: "Snow of light, blanket earth, bring forth growth, new life's birth." Leave the bowl outside overnight, then pour the melted water into your garden soil as a blessing for future abundance.

Chapter 23: Spells of Unity and Togetherness

Yule is a time of gathering, a season where families and communities come together to celebrate the return of light amidst winter's darkness. It is an opportunity to foster unity, deepen bonds, and create peace within our circles. This chapter provides 30 detailed spells aimed at strengthening relationships, promoting cooperation, and cultivating harmony among loved ones. Through these rituals, you will use candles, herbs, crystals, and symbols of unity to foster a spirit of togetherness that endures well beyond the winter season.

1. Unity Candle Circle

Gather your family or community members and sit in a circle. Place a white candle in the center. Each person holds hands and focuses on the candle's flame. Say together: "Candle bright, flame of light, bind us now, hearts unite." Visualize the flame connecting everyone in the circle, fostering warmth and unity.

2. Hearth of Harmony

Light your fireplace or a large candle in your home. Sprinkle dried lavender and rosemary around the hearth, saying: "Hearth of warmth, fire so bright, bring us peace, through the night." Let the fire's light fill the room with a sense of calm, inviting cooperation and harmony among family members.

3. Yule Family Blessing Ritual

Before a family gathering, carve symbols of unity (such as hearts or circles) into a green candle. Light the candle, saying: "Candle of green, light so clear, bless this family, draw us near." Place the candle in the center of the table during the gathering, allowing its energy to promote love and togetherness.

4. Circle of Trust Spell

Create a circle using clear quartz crystals. Place the crystals on your altar or in a central room of your home. Hold your hands over the crystals and say: "Circle of trust, strong and bright, guard our hearts, bring us light." This crystal circle strengthens the bond of trust within the family, fostering open communication and cooperation.

5. Lavender Peace Sachet

Fill small pouches with dried lavender and rosemary. Give one to each family member, saying: "Herbs of peace, scent so clear, bring us calm, draw us near." Keep the sachets in bedrooms or carry them as a reminder to approach each other with patience and understanding.

6. Candle of Forgiveness

Carve the word "Forgiveness" into a pink candle. Light it and say: "Flame of love, burn so bright, melt away pain, heal our fight." Sit quietly, focusing on the flame, and allow any feelings of resentment or anger to dissolve. This spell encourages forgiveness within families and communities, opening the way for renewed unity.

7. Heart Harmony Stones

Collect small stones and draw a heart symbol on each one. Place the stones in a bowl and hold your hands over them, saying: "Stones of earth, hearts so true, bring us peace, old and new." Give a stone to each family or community member, asking them to keep it as a token of shared love and harmony.

8. Peaceful Gatherings Spell

Before hosting a gathering, light a white candle and sprinkle a circle of salt around its base. Say: "Candle bright, salt so clear, bring us peace, draw us near." Let the candle burn for a while, filling the space with calm energy, ensuring a harmonious and joyful gathering.

9. Lavender Tea for Unity

Brew a pot of lavender tea and pour a cup for each person present. Hold your cup and say: "Tea of peace, warmth so clear, bring us love, draw us near." Drink the tea together, allowing its calming properties to promote understanding and connection.

10. Knot of Togetherness

Take a piece of ribbon or yarn and tie three knots, focusing on unity and cooperation. As you tie each knot, say: "Knot of love, knot of light, bind us together, day and night." Hang the knotted ribbon in a shared space to remind everyone of their connection and commitment to each other.

11. Yule Wreath of Unity

Create a wreath using evergreen branches, holly, and pinecones. As you weave the materials together, say: "Wreath of green, circle true, bind our hearts, old and new." Hang the wreath on your front door to invite the energy of unity and warmth into your home.

12. Circle of Understanding

Sit in a circle with family or community members. Place a blue candle in the center and light it, saying: "Flame of calm, light so clear, bring us peace, draw us near." Take turns sharing thoughts or feelings, allowing the candle's light to foster a space of understanding and support.

13. Family Protection Charm

Create a charm using a small pouch filled with rosemary, sage, and a piece of clear quartz. Hold the pouch and say: "Charm of light, herbs so clear, guard our hearts, keep us near." Hang the pouch in a central room to protect family unity and promote harmony.

14. Crystal Circle of Friendship

Arrange rose quartz crystals in a circle on your altar. Hold your hands over the crystals and say: "Crystals bright, circle true, strengthen our bonds, renew and glue." The crystals radiate love and positivity, deepening the bonds within your community.

15. Candle of Shared Joy

Carve the word "Joy" into a yellow candle. Light it during family meals or gatherings, saying: "Flame of joy, burn so bright, bring us laughter, day and night." The candle's energy enhances the mood, filling the space with warmth and shared happiness.

16. Altar of Unity

Create a unity altar in a shared space. Place symbols of family (such as photos, heirlooms, or objects representing each member) on the altar. Light a white candle in the center and say: "Altar of love, light so clear, bind us together, keep us near." Visit the altar regularly to renew the bond of unity.

17. Salt and Rosemary Circle

Sprinkle a circle of salt mixed with dried rosemary around a room where family gatherings take place. As you sprinkle, say: "Circle of calm, herbs so bright, bring us peace, keep us tight." This circle creates an atmosphere of peace, reducing tensions and promoting cooperation.

18. Candle of Compassion

Carve the word "Compassion" into a light blue candle. Light the candle and say: "Flame of calm, burn so clear, open our hearts, draw us near." Sit quietly, focusing on cultivating compassion for each other. This spell encourages understanding and patience within families.

19. Yule Tree Unity Spell

Stand together around your Yule tree. Hold hands and say: "Tree of Yule, evergreen bright, bind our hearts, with love's light." Visualize the tree's energy connecting each person, filling the space with warmth and unity.

20. Peace Offering Ritual

Create a small offering bowl and fill it with lavender, rose petals, and salt. Place the bowl on your altar, saying: "Offering of peace, scents so clear, bring us calm, draw us near." Invite family members to take a pinch of the mixture whenever they need to feel connected and at peace.

21. Knot of Love and Support

Hold a piece of red thread and tie a knot for each family member, saying their name as you do so. Say: "Knot of love, tie so true, bind us close, me and you." Keep the knotted thread on your altar as a reminder of your love and support for one another.

22. Candle of Open Communication

Carve the symbol of a spiral into a purple candle. Light it during discussions, saying: "Flame of light, guide our words, open our hearts, let us be heard." The candle creates a space for honest and open communication, promoting understanding and connection.

23. Yule Feast Blessing

Before sharing a meal, hold hands around the table. Say together: "Feast of Yule, food so bright, bless this family, with love and light." This blessing infuses the meal with positive energy, fostering a sense of unity and joy.

24. Family Crystal Charm

Select a clear quartz crystal and hold it in your hands. Close your eyes and say: "Crystal bright, light so clear, guard our family, draw us near." Place the crystal in a central room to radiate positive energy and protect the unity of the household.

25. Circle of Patience

Gather in a circle and hold hands. Place a lavender candle in the center and light it, saying: "Circle of calm, light so pure, bring us patience, make us sure." Allow the candle to burn as a reminder to approach each other with patience and understanding.

26. Candle of Reconciliation

Carve symbols of peace (such as a dove or olive branch) into a white candle. Light it, saying: "Flame of peace, burn so bright, heal our hearts, through the night." Focus on letting go of past disagreements, opening the way for reconciliation and unity.

27. Yule Tree Ornament of Unity

Create or select an ornament that represents unity (such as a heart, star, or circle). Before hanging it on the Yule tree, hold it in your hands and say: "Ornament bright, symbol so clear, bring us together, keep us near." This ornament serves as a reminder of the family's bond.

28. Family Circle Candle Ritual

Sit in a circle with a green candle at the center. Light the candle and say: "Flame of green, light so true, bring us together, old and new." Each person takes turns sharing their feelings or thoughts, allowing the candle to create a space of unity and openness.

29. Rosemary Door Blessing

Hang a bundle of dried rosemary above the main entrance to your home. As you hang it, say: "Rosemary bright, guard this door, bring us peace, forevermore." The rosemary's energy encourages a peaceful and cooperative atmosphere within the household.

30. Candle of Family Protection

Carve protective symbols (such as circles or pentacles) into a black candle. Light it and say: "Flame of guard, burn so clear, protect our hearts, keep us near." Allow the candle to burn, creating a shield of protection around the family, fostering an environment of safety and unity.

Chapter 24: Solstice Night Rituals

The Winter Solstice, also known as Yule, marks the longest night of the year. It is a time of deep magic, introspection, and the turning point when the days begin to grow longer, welcoming the return of the sun. This chapter contains 45 rituals specifically designed for the magic of Solstice Night, harnessing its potent energy for healing, protection, transformation, and renewal. Through these rituals, you will work with the elements of the night—fire, darkness, light, and nature—to embrace the profound changes and hopes the Solstice brings.

1. Candle of Light's Return

On Solstice Night, carve the sun symbol into a gold or yellow candle. Light it at dusk, saying: "Longest night, darkness deep, bring the light, from winter's sleep." Allow the candle to burn throughout the night to symbolize the return of the sun and the promise of brighter days.

2. Night's Reflection Meditation

Sit in a darkened room with a single white candle. Light the candle and say: "Flame so bright, through the night, guide my thoughts, in purest light." Gaze into the flame, reflecting on the past year's experiences. Allow any lessons or insights to come to you, using the Solstice's energy to gain clarity.

3. Yule Log Lighting

Prepare a Yule log using a piece of wood, carved with symbols of renewal and protection. Decorate it with pine branches, holly, and ribbons. On Solstice Night, light the log in your fireplace, saying: "Log of Yule, fire bright, bring us warmth, through this night." Let the fire burn, filling your space with warmth and hope.

4. Evergreen Blessing

Collect sprigs of evergreen (such as pine, fir, or cedar) and place them on your altar. Light a green candle and say: "Evergreen bright, life so true, bless this space, renew it too." Leave the candle burning for an hour, allowing the energy of the evergreen to infuse your home with protection and renewal.

5. Moonlit Crystal Charge

Place moonstone, clear quartz, or snowflake obsidian on a windowsill where moonlight can reach them. As you set them down, say: "Moon so high, on this night, charge these stones, with your light." Let the crystals charge overnight to enhance their power for future spells.

6. Solstice Night Healing Bath

Draw a warm bath and add sea salt, dried lavender, and a few drops of pine essential oil. As the bath fills, say: "Water pure, herbs so bright, cleanse my spirit, through this night." Soak in the bath, allowing the energy of the Solstice to cleanse and renew you.

7. Star Wish Ritual

On Solstice Night, write a wish for the coming year on a piece of paper. Fold it into the shape of a star and hold it up to the night sky. Say: "Stars so bright, in the night, grant my wish, with your light." Place the star on your altar until your wish is fulfilled.

8. Candle Circle of Protection

Arrange nine candles in a circle on your altar—three white, three blue, and three green. Light each candle clockwise, saying: "Circle of light, on Solstice Night, guard this space, with all your might." Sit within the circle to feel its protective energy surrounding you.

9. Yule Tree Blessing

Stand before your Yule tree with hands over your heart. Close your eyes and say: "Tree of Yule, evergreen bright, bless this home, with your light." Visualize the tree's energy filling your home with warmth, protection, and joy.

10. Solstice Night Shadow Work

Light a black candle and place a mirror in front of you. Gaze into the mirror, saying: "Shadow deep, darkness bright, show me truths, on this night." Reflect on any hidden fears or emotions, using the Solstice's transformative energy to bring them to light and release them.

11. Candle of Gratitude

Carve the word "Gratitude" into a green candle. Light it and say: "Flame of thanks, burning bright, fill my heart, on this night." Reflect on what you are grateful for, allowing the flame's light to magnify your feelings of appreciation.

12. Pine Cone Offering

Collect pine cones and place them on your altar. Hold your hands over them and say: "Pine of earth, evergreen true, accept my thanks, for life renewed." Leave the pine cones on the altar overnight as an offering to nature spirits, inviting their blessings for the year ahead.

13. Candle of Inner Light

Carve the symbol of the sun into a white candle. Light it, saying: "Flame so pure, light of mine, shine within, through wintertime." Sit quietly, focusing on the flame and visualizing your inner light growing stronger.

14. Winter Night's Breath Meditation

Go outside and take a deep breath of the crisp, cold air. As you exhale, say: "Breath of night, cold and clear, fill my lungs, banish fear." Repeat this several times, allowing the winter air to clear your mind and renew your spirit.

15. Circle of Harmony

Gather family or friends in a circle. Light a blue candle in the center and say: "Circle of peace, on this night, bring us calm, guide our light." Hold hands and share wishes for harmony and unity, letting the candle's light strengthen your bond.

16. Yule Night Incense Ritual

Burn incense made of pine, frankincense, and myrrh on your altar. As the smoke rises, say: "Smoke of Yule, scent so bright, cleanse this space, on this night." Waft the smoke around your home, inviting the Solstice's energy to purify and bless each room.

17. Candle of Letting Go

Carve symbols representing what you wish to release (such as chains or waves) into a black candle. Light it, saying: "Flame of dark, burn away, cleanse my soul, clear the way." As the candle burns, visualize it consuming your burdens, leaving you free and renewed.

18. Solstice Night's Fire Scrying

Build a small fire in a fireplace or light a large candle. Gaze into the flames, saying: "Fire so bright, on this night, show me visions, of future light." Observe the flames, allowing images or messages to appear that may offer guidance for the coming year.

19. Candle of Future Hopes

Carve symbols of hope (such as stars or hearts) into a yellow candle. Light it, saying: "Flame of hope, burn so clear, bring forth dreams, through the year." Meditate on your hopes and desires for the future, letting the candle's light empower them.

20. Midnight Reflection Spell

At midnight on Solstice Night, light a single white candle and sit quietly. Say: "Midnight's hush, still and clear, bring me peace, draw me near." Reflect on the past year's journey, embracing the lessons and letting go of any regrets.

21. Candle of Friendship

Carve the word "Friendship" into a blue candle. Light it during a gathering, saying: "Flame of joy, warmth so bright, bind our hearts, through this night." Allow the candle's energy to strengthen the bond between friends, fostering a sense of togetherness.

22. Moonstone Water Blessing

Place a moonstone in a bowl of water and set it under the moonlight for an hour. Hold the bowl and say: "Moon's soft light, water clear, cleanse my spirit, draw it near." Use the water to wash your hands, face, or feet, inviting the Solstice's energy to renew you.

23. Candle of Past Release

Carve the year's numbers into a black candle. Light it and say: "Flame of time, burn so bright, release the past, on this night." Visualize the candle burning away the past year's challenges, making room for new beginnings.

24. Evergreen Circle of Protection

Arrange a circle of evergreen branches around your altar. Light a white candle in the center, saying: "Circle of green, life so bright, guard this space, through the night." This circle protects your home and invites the Solstice's energy of renewal.

25. Candle of Peace

Carve the word "Peace" into a lavender candle. Light it, saying: "Flame of calm, light so pure, bring me peace, long and sure." Sit quietly, allowing the candle's light to fill you with a sense of deep tranquility.

26. Yule Night Tree Meditation

Sit quietly before your Yule tree. Close your eyes and say: "Tree of light, evergreen true, bring me calm, make me new." Breathe deeply, absorbing the tree's peaceful energy and renewing your spirit.

27. Candle of Strength

Carve symbols of strength (such as mountains or trees) into a red candle. Light it, saying: "Flame of might, burn so clear, fill my heart, bring me near." Focus on the flame, feeling its warmth infusing you with courage and resolve for the coming year.

28. Candle of the Dark Moon

On the Solstice night's dark moon, light a black candle. Say: "Moon of dark, night so deep, reveal the truths, as I sleep." Allow the candle to burn down completely as you sleep, inviting dreams that reveal hidden truths.

29. Yule Blessing Pouch

Fill a small pouch with dried rosemary, lavender, and a piece of pine. Hold it in your hands and say: "Herbs of peace, scents so clear, bless this space, keep harm near." Hang the pouch near your bed to invite the Solstice's blessings into your life.

30. Candle of Transformation

Carve symbols of change (such as spirals or butterflies) into a purple candle. Light it, saying: "Flame of change, burn so bright, transform my life, through the night." Sit with the candle, focusing on how you wish to transform in the coming year.

31. Solstice Night Prayer Circle

Gather with family or friends in a circle. Hold hands and say: "Longest night, stars so bright, bring us peace, through this night." Take turns sharing prayers or wishes, letting the circle's energy amplify your intentions.

32. Candle of Guidance

Carve the symbol of a star into a white candle. Light it, saying: "Flame of light, star so clear, guide my path, through the year." Let the candle burn as you meditate on the guidance you seek for the future.

33. Yule Night's Gift Ritual

Hold a small, wrapped gift for yourself. Close your eyes and say: "Gift of love, small and bright, bring me joy, through this night." Open the gift, allowing its energy to fill you with self-love and joy.

34. Pine Needle Protection Spell

Place pine needles around the edges of your windowsills and doorways. As you place each needle, say: "Needles sharp, green and bright, guard this home, through the night." The pine creates a natural barrier, protecting your space during the Solstice.

35. Yule Night Crystal Grid

Create a crystal grid using clear quartz, amethyst, and rose quartz on your altar. Place a candle in the center, saying: "Crystals bright, grid so true, charge this space, renew it too." This grid amplifies the Solstice's energy, filling your home with light and love.

36. Candle of Inner Peace

Carve the symbol of a dove into a light blue candle. Light it, saying: "Flame of calm, burn so clear, fill my soul, draw me near." Sit quietly, focusing on the candle's light to find peace within.

37. Evergreen Garland Blessing

Create a garland using pine, cedar, and holly. As you weave it, say: "Garland bright, nature's might, bless this home, through the night." Hang the garland to invite nature's blessings into your space.

38. Solstice Night Chant

Hold a piece of clear quartz and chant: "Night of longest, stars so bright, guide my soul, through the light." Repeat until you feel a sense of calm and connection to the Solstice's energy.

39. Candle of Love

Carve the symbol of a heart into a pink candle. Light it, saying: "Flame of love, burn so clear, fill my heart, draw me near." Allow the candle's light to fill you with love and compassion for yourself and others.

40. Solstice Night's Water Blessing

Fill a bowl with water and place it under the night sky. Hold your hands over it and say: "Water of night, so pure and bright, cleanse and bless, bring us light." Use this water to sprinkle around your home, blessing and purifying it.

41. Solstice Night's Candle Meditation

Light a green candle and sit before it, saying: "Flame of Yule, light so true, bring me peace, make me new." Close your eyes and focus on your breathing, allowing the candle's energy to center and calm you.

42. Solstice Night's Silence

Sit in total silence for a few minutes, holding a piece of snowflake obsidian. Say: "Night of stillness, silence deep, guide my soul, in this sleep." This ritual connects you to the profound quiet of the Solstice, offering insight and renewal.

43. Candle of Dreams

Carve the symbol of a moon into a purple candle. Light it, saying: "Flame of dream, burn so bright, guide my sleep, through the night." Allow the candle to burn while you sleep, inviting prophetic dreams.

44. Pine Cone Circle Ritual

Create a circle using pine cones around a white candle. Light the candle, saying: "Circle of pine, strong and clear, guard this space, draw us near." Sit within the circle, feeling its protective energy surrounding you.

45. Solstice Night Candle of Renewal

Carve symbols of renewal (such as spirals or leaves) into a green candle. Light it, saying: "Flame of life, burn so bright, renew my spirit, through this night." Allow the candle to burn as you meditate on its light, feeling its energy fill you with hope for the coming year.

Chapter 25: Divination and Fortune-Telling Spells

Yule, the time of the Winter Solstice, is steeped in the mystery of the longest night of the year. This time of stillness and introspection is ideal for divination and seeking insights into the year ahead. During Yule, the veil between the worlds is thin, making it easier to connect with the spiritual realm and gain guidance. This chapter provides 40 detailed spells involving various forms of divination, such as tarot, runes, scrying, and other mystical methods, to help you uncover the secrets that the season holds and to gain clarity on your path.

1. Yule Tarot Spread for the New Year

Sit quietly before your altar with your tarot deck. Light a white candle and shuffle the deck while focusing on the upcoming year. Say: "Cards of wisdom, cards of light, show me truths, guide my sight." Draw five cards and lay them in a pentagram pattern, representing the areas of life that will be influenced in the year ahead. Interpret each card, allowing their message to guide you.

2. Pinecone Pendulum Divination

Select a small pinecone and tie it to a piece of string to create a pendulum. Hold the pendulum over a piece of paper with "Yes" and "No" written on it. Say: "Pinecone of earth, wisdom so true, answer my question, guide me through." Ask your question and watch the pendulum's movement for an answer.

3. Snow Scrying Ritual

On a night with fresh snow, go outside and find a quiet place. Hold a piece of clear quartz and say: "Snow so pure, veil of night, show me visions, guide my sight." Gaze into the snow's surface, allowing patterns or images to form. Let these shapes offer guidance or answers to your questions.

4. Yule Rune Casting

Light a green candle and place it on your altar. Take your set of runes and hold them in your hands. Say: "Runes of old, symbols so bright, reveal the truths, on this Yule night." Draw three runes and lay them out. Interpret each rune, considering its significance for the coming year.

5. Candle Flame Scrying

Sit in a dark room with a single candle. Light the candle and say: "Flame of light, burn so clear, reveal the visions, bring them near." Gaze into the candle's flame, observing how it flickers, dances, or changes shape. Allow any symbols or images that appear to provide you with insight.

6. Tarot for Family Harmony

Gather with family members and light a blue candle. Say: "Cards of truth, cards of peace, show us ways, our love to release." Draw one card for each family member, interpreting how it relates to their role in fostering family harmony and unity.

7. Scrying Mirror of Yule

Place a black scrying mirror on your altar and light a white candle beside it. Say: "Mirror of night, black and bright, reveal to me, Yule's insight." Gaze into the mirror's surface, allowing it to become cloudy or reflective. Notice any shapes, symbols, or messages that appear, interpreting them for guidance.

8. Rune Protection Spell

Select three protective runes (such as Algiz, Thurisaz, and Sowilo) and place them on your windowsill. Hold your hands over the runes and say: "Runes of guard, symbols so bright, shield this space, through Yule's night." Leave the runes in place to create a protective barrier during the season.

9. Candle Wax Divination

Light a white candle and hold a bowl of cold water in front of you. Say: "Candle of light, burn so true, show me visions, clear and new." Drip wax into the water and observe the shapes it forms. Interpret the symbols to gain insights into upcoming events or guidance on a specific situation.

10. Yule Star Tarot Spread

Use your tarot deck to create a five-card star spread. Say: "Cards of stars, cards so wise, reveal my path, through the skies." The points of the star represent guidance on love, career, health, spiritual growth, and challenges. Interpret each card to uncover the influences of the upcoming year.

11. Pine Branch Rune Reading

Collect a small pine branch and place it on your altar. Scatter runes over the branch, saying: "Pine so green, runes so bright, show me visions, on this night." Interpret the runes that fall closest to the branch's center as key messages for the coming year.

12. Crystal Ball Yule Scrying

Sit in a dimly lit room with a crystal ball. Place your hands on either side of the ball and say: "Crystal clear, orb of light, reveal my path, on this Yule night." Gaze into the ball, allowing any swirling mists or images to come forth. Note any symbols or visions that appear for later interpretation.

13. Candle Shadow Divination

Light a candle and place it near a blank wall. Say: "Flame of light, cast your shade, show me truths, that do not fade." Observe the shadows the candle creates on the wall. Interpret any shapes or movements as messages from the unseen realms.

14. Snowflake Crystal Casting

Collect small snowflake-shaped crystals or stones. Hold them in your hands and say: "Snowflakes bright, crystals so true, reveal my future, guide me through." Scatter them on your altar and interpret the pattern they form for guidance and insight.

15. Yule Ogham Stick Divination

Select a few sticks or twigs representing the ancient Ogham symbols. Hold them in your hands and say: "Sticks of wood, symbols so clear, show me answers, bring them near." Drop the sticks and observe their arrangement, interpreting the patterns and symbols for insight.

16. Tarot of the Sun's Return

Light a yellow candle and shuffle your tarot deck. Say: "Cards of light, cards of sun, show me paths, new begun." Draw one card to represent the energy that will guide you as the days grow longer. Interpret its message for the return of the sun's influence in your life.

17. Rune Circle of Guidance

Lay out a circle of small stones and place your rune set in the center. Close your eyes and draw three runes, saying: "Runes of circle, runes so true, guide my steps, show me through." Interpret the drawn runes as guidance for navigating the upcoming year.

18. Candle Drip Scrying

Hold a lit candle over a bowl of snow. Let the wax drip onto the snow, saying: "Flame of night, wax so bright, show me visions, through this night." Observe the shapes formed by the wax on the snow's surface, interpreting them for messages or guidance.

19. Pine Cone Casting

Hold a pine cone in your hands and say: "Pine of earth, seed so true, show me signs, guide me through." Throw the pine cone onto the ground and observe the direction it points to reveal answers to your questions.

20. Yule Rune Bind Spell

Select runes that represent your wishes for the new year (such as Fehu for prosperity or Gebo for love). Arrange them on your altar and say: "Runes of Yule, symbols of might, bind my wishes, through this night." Leave the runes on your altar to bind their energy into your intentions.

21. Scrying Bowl of Water

Fill a dark bowl with water and set it on your altar. Light a candle beside it and say: "Water deep, mirror of night, show me visions, clear and bright." Gaze into the water's surface, allowing images or symbols to appear, offering you insight and guidance.

22. Tarot for Personal Growth

Shuffle your tarot deck and draw three cards, saying: "Cards of change, cards so true, show my path, guide me through." Interpret each card as it relates to your personal growth in the coming year, focusing on strengths, challenges, and advice.

23. Evergreen Rune Pouch

Fill a small pouch with evergreen needles and your rune set. Hold the pouch in your hands and say: "Pouch of green, runes so bright, reveal my path, on this Yule night." Draw one rune from the pouch for guidance on an important decision.

24. Crystal Wheel Divination

Create a wheel on your altar using crystals such as clear quartz, amethyst, and citrine. Spin the wheel, saying: "Crystals bright, spin so true, show me insight, guide me through." Observe which crystal lands closest to you and interpret its meaning for the coming year.

25. Candle Wax Rune Reading

Light a candle and let it drip onto a piece of parchment. Say: "Wax so bright, fall so true, show me runes, guide me through." Observe the shapes the wax forms, interpreting any that resemble runic symbols as messages for guidance.

26. Yule Tarot Tree Spread

Place your tarot cards in the shape of a tree on your altar. Say: "Cards of tree, cards of light, reveal my path, through the night." Interpret each card as representing different aspects of your life's growth in the coming year.

27. Pine Needle Fortune Telling

Collect a handful of pine needles. Hold them in your hands and say: "Needles sharp, green and bright, show me truths, on this night." Scatter them onto a flat surface and interpret the pattern they form for insights into your future.

28. Candle Circle Tarot Ritual

Arrange your tarot cards in a circle around a lit candle. Say: "Circle of cards, light so bright, guide my steps, through this night." Draw one card and interpret it as the central influence in your life for the upcoming year.

29. Solstice Night Rune Stone

Hold a single rune stone in your hands, focusing on a specific question. Say: "Rune of stone, old and wise, reveal the truth, no disguise." Look at the rune and interpret its message as guidance for your question.

30. Candle and Mirror Scrying

Place a small mirror on your altar and light a white candle in front of it. Say: "Mirror of night, candle bright, show me visions, in your light." Gaze into the mirror, focusing on the candle's reflection, and note any images or symbols that appear.

31. Yule Night Pendulum Reading

Hold a pendulum over your tarot deck and say: "Pendulum bright, swing so true, guide my hand, show me through." Allow the pendulum to hover over the cards, selecting one to draw for guidance.

32. Crystal Casting for Love

Hold a rose quartz crystal in your hands and say: "Crystal of love, pure and true, show me insights, guide me through." Toss the crystal onto a flat surface and observe its placement relative to other objects for messages about love and relationships.

33. Rune Candle Circle

Light a candle for each rune in your set and arrange them in a circle. Draw one rune and say: "Rune of light, flame so clear, show me truth, bring it near." Interpret the rune's message in the context of the candle's energy.

34. Moonlit Tarot Spread

Place your tarot cards on a windowsill under the moonlight. Draw three cards, saying: "Moon so high, cards so bright, reveal my path, through this night." Interpret the cards as they relate to your journey under the moon's influence.

35. Candle Drip Rune Casting

Light a candle and let wax drip onto a sheet of parchment. Say: "Wax of light, fall so true, show me runes, guide me through." Observe the shapes the wax forms, interpreting any runic symbols as messages for guidance.

36. Crystal Grid for Insight

Create a crystal grid on your altar using clear quartz, amethyst, and rose quartz. Place a candle in the center and say: "Crystals bright, grid so true, show me wisdom, guide me through." Meditate with the grid to gain clarity and insight.

37. Pine Branch Tarot Reading

Place a small pine branch beside your tarot deck. Draw three cards and say: "Pine so green, cards so bright, reveal my truths, on this night." Interpret the cards, using the pine's energy to enhance their meaning.

38. Yule Pendulum Reading

Hold your pendulum over a piece of paper with "Yes," "No," and "Maybe" written on it. Say: "Pendulum true, swing with might, show me answers, on this night." Ask your question and observe the pendulum's movement for guidance.

39. Snowflake Candle Scrying

Place a snowflake-shaped candle on your altar and light it. Say: "Snowflake bright, candle clear, show me visions, bring them near." Gaze into the flame, allowing images or symbols to appear.

40. Evergreen Rune Casting

Place evergreen branches around your rune set. Hold the runes and say: "Evergreen bright, runes so true, reveal my path, guide me through." Scatter the runes on your altar and interpret their messages for the year ahead.

Chapter 26: Elemental Magic for Winter

Winter is a season where the elements express their unique and powerful aspects. Earth becomes hard and cold, embracing dormancy and stillness. Water freezes into ice and snow, symbolizing purity and quiet strength. Fire, though scarce, offers warmth and light in the darkness. Air turns crisp and sharp, carrying the chill of the season. This chapter explores how to work with the elemental forces of Earth, Water, Fire, and Air in winter, providing 35 detailed spells to harness their energy for protection, transformation, healing, and renewal during this magical time.

Earth Element Spells

1. Winter Earth Protection Spell

Gather a small bowl of soil and pine needles. On your altar, mix them together, saying: "Earth of frost, firm and still, guard this home, bend to will." Place the bowl near your front door to create a protective barrier, utilizing the winter earth's energy to keep negative forces at bay.

2. Stone Circle for Grounding

Collect small winter stones (such as snow quartz or granite) and arrange them in a circle on your altar. Sit within the circle and say: "Stones of Earth, cold and bright, ground my spirit, through this night." Allow the stones' energy to anchor and stabilize you, providing balance during the winter season.

3. Evergreen Earth Renewal

Place a sprig of pine or fir on your altar. Hold it in your hands and say: "Earth of green, life so strong, renew my spirit, where I belong." Breathe deeply, visualizing the evergreen's strength filling you with the grounded energy of the Earth.

4. Salt and Rosemary Circle of Protection

Mix sea salt and dried rosemary in a bowl. Sprinkle this mixture in a circle around your home, saying: "Earth of salt, herb so true, guard this space, see me through." This protective spell calls upon the Earth's stabilizing properties to create a shield around your living space.

5. Crystal Earth Connection

Hold a piece of snowflake obsidian in your hands and say: "Stone of Earth, cold and deep, grant me strength, in winter's sleep." Visualize the crystal's energy rooting you to the Earth's core, offering support and resilience during the season.

6. Winter Soil Healing

Collect a small amount of winter soil and place it in a pouch. Hold it to your heart and say: "Earth so cold, ground so true, heal my heart, make it new." Keep the pouch near your bed to draw on the Earth's healing power while you sleep.

7. Evergreen Blessing of Stability

Gather evergreen branches and create a small wreath. Hang the wreath on your door, saying: "Earth of green, circle so bright, bring me balance, through the night." This wreath invites the stabilizing energy of the Earth into your home, providing emotional and spiritual grounding.

Water Element Spells

8. Snow Cleansing Ritual

Collect fresh snow in a bowl and let it melt. Dip your hands into the water and say: "Water of snow, pure and bright, cleanse my soul, through this night." Wash your hands, allowing the melted snow to purify and refresh your energy.

9. Winter Ice Protection Spell

Fill a small container with water and place it outside to freeze. As it solidifies, say: "Ice so clear, frozen tight, guard this space, through the night." Place the container on your windowsill to create an icy barrier that protects your home from negativity.

10. Candle Snow Scrying

Fill a bowl with snow and place a lit candle beside it. Drip candle wax onto the snow, saying: "Water of ice, flame of light, show me truths, through this night." Observe the shapes formed by the melting wax on the snow's surface for messages or insights.

11. Winter Stream Meditation

If near a stream or river, stand beside it and close your eyes. Say: "Water of winter, flowing free, wash away burdens, set me free." Listen to the sound of the water, visualizing it carrying away your worries and refreshing your spirit.

12. Icicle Blessing for Clarity

Select an icicle and hold it in your hands. Say: "Water of ice, clear and bright, grant me clarity, bring me light." Place the icicle in a bowl and let it melt, then use the water to wash your face, inviting mental clarity and insight.

13. Snowflake Crystal Spell

Collect snowflakes in a small jar. Hold the jar and say: "Flakes of snow, pure and bright, bring me peace, through this night." Keep the jar on your altar to draw upon the calming energy of winter water.

14. Ice Bath Renewal

Add ice cubes and sea salt to your bathwater. As you immerse yourself, say: "Water of ice, cold and clear, cleanse my spirit, draw me near." Soak in the water, visualizing it drawing out negativity and leaving you refreshed and revitalized.

15. Moonlit Water Purification

Leave a bowl of water outside under the full moon on a clear winter night. Say: "Moon of night, water so clear, cleanse my spirit, bring me near." Use this moon-charged water to wash your hands or sprinkle around your home for purification.

Fire Element Spells

16. Candle of Winter Warmth

Carve the symbol of the sun into a red or gold candle. Light it and say: "Flame of fire, warm and bright, bring me comfort, through this night." Sit before the candle, allowing its warmth to fill you with a sense of safety and hope.

17. Hearth Blessing Ritual

Light your fireplace or a candle on your hearth. Sprinkle dried rosemary around the base and say: "Fire of hearth, flame so true, guard this home, bring us through." Let the fire burn, filling your space with warmth and protection.

18. Candle of Inner Strength

Carve a mountain symbol into a white candle. Light it and say: "Flame of strength, burn so clear, fill my heart, bring me near." Focus on the flame, feeling its warmth ignite your inner courage and resilience.

19. Yule Fire Release

Write down something you wish to release on a piece of paper. Light a candle and hold the paper above the flame, saying: "Flame of Yule, burn away, cleanse my spirit, clear the way." Allow the paper to catch fire and burn safely, visualizing your burdens being released.

20. Candle Flame Protection

Light a black candle and hold a piece of iron near the flame. Say: "Flame of night, guard so true, protect my space, see me through." Let the candle burn, creating a barrier of protection in your home.

21. Winter Solstice Fire Scrying

Light a large candle on the Winter Solstice. Gaze into the flame and say: "Flame of light, reveal my path, guide my steps, through winter's wrath." Observe how the flame moves, using its dance to gain insight into your future journey.

22. Candle of Transformation

Carve symbols of change into a purple candle. Light it, saying: "Flame of change, burn so bright, transform my life, through this night." Focus on the candle's light, letting it burn away old patterns and create space for new growth.

23. Hearth Stone Protection

Heat a small stone by the fire. Once warm, hold it and say: "Stone of fire, warmth so bright, guard my spirit, through the night." Keep the stone near your bed or carry it with you as a charm for protection and courage.

Air Element Spells
24. Winter Wind Cleansing
Stand outside on a windy winter day. Close your eyes and say: "Wind of winter, cold and clear, cleanse my soul, draw me near." Feel the wind blowing around you, visualizing it sweeping away negativity and filling you with fresh energy.

25. Breath of Clarity
Sit in a quiet place and take a deep breath of cold winter air. Exhale slowly, saying: "Air of frost, breath so clear, grant me vision, bring it near." Repeat several times, allowing the crisp air to sharpen your mind and bring clarity.

26. Candle Smoke Divination
Light a blue candle and hold a feather in your hand. Pass the feather through the smoke, saying: "Air of night, smoke so clear, show me visions, bring them near." Observe how the smoke moves around the feather, interpreting its patterns for messages.

27. Snowflake Incense Ritual
Light a stick of pine or cedar incense. Say: "Air of snow, scent so bright, cleanse this space, through the night." Waft the smoke around your home, inviting the purifying energy of winter air to clear your space.

28. Breath of Warmth
Hold your hands over your heart and breathe in deeply, saying: "Breath of life, air so warm, fill my spirit, transform." Visualize your breath spreading warmth through your body, igniting inner strength and comfort.

29. Winter Air Blessing
Hold a small bell and stand outside. Ring the bell, saying: "Air of winter, sharp and clear, bless this space, draw me near." The sound of the bell carries on the wind, spreading blessings and inviting positive energy into your surroundings.

30. Feather of Insight

Hold a feather in your hand and close your eyes. Say: "Feather of air, light and true, bring me wisdom, guide me through." Blow gently on the feather, asking for insights into a question or situation. Listen to the air's whisper for guidance.

31. Snowstorm Air Protection

In the face of an approaching storm, light a blue candle and hold a piece of moonstone. Say: "Air of storm, fierce and true, guard this space, bring us through." Visualize the storm's winds bending around your home, protecting it from harm.

Combined Element Spells

32. Winter Element Circle

Create a circle on your altar using symbols of each element: a stone (Earth), a bowl of water (Water), a candle (Fire), and incense (Air). Light the candle and incense, saying: "Earth, Water, Fire, Air, circle bright, guard this space, through the night." This circle calls upon all elements to protect and bless your space.

33. Candle Water Scrying

Fill a bowl with water and place a candle beside it. Light the candle and say: "Water and fire, blend so bright, reveal my truths, through this night." Gaze into the water, observing the candle's reflection and any images that form for guidance.

34. Snow Salt Protection

Mix snow and salt in a bowl. Sprinkle the mixture around your home, saying: "Earth and water, blend so clear, guard this space, keep harm near." This spell creates a protective barrier using the grounding properties of Earth and the purifying power of Water.

35. Hearth Air Renewal

Light incense near your fireplace or heater. As the warmth fills the room, say: "Fire and air, blend so true, cleanse my spirit, make it new." Let the smoke carry away negativity, while the warmth brings comfort and renewal.

Chapter 27: Moon Phases and Yule Spells

The moon's phases hold powerful energy, each phase influencing the world around us in different ways. During the Yule season, the moon's magic is intertwined with the energies of the longest night, renewal, and the return of light. By aligning your spellwork with the moon's phases, you can amplify your intentions and embrace the unique gifts of each phase. This chapter presents 30 spells tailored to the moon phases occurring during Yule—New Moon, Waxing Crescent, First Quarter, Waxing Gibbous, Full Moon, Waning Gibbous, Last Quarter, and Waning Crescent—providing you with rituals for release, manifestation, and transformation during the season.

New Moon Spells (Beginnings and Intention Setting)

1. New Moon Wish Jar

On the Yule New Moon, fill a small jar with salt, rosemary, and a piece of moonstone. Hold the jar in your hands and say: "New moon bright, darkened sky, grant my wishes, let them fly." Whisper your intentions into the jar and seal it with wax. Place it on your altar to absorb the moon's energy for manifesting your desires.

2. New Moon Cleansing Bath

Prepare a bath with sea salt, lavender, and a few drops of pine essential oil. As the bath fills, say: "New moon's night, water clear, cleanse my spirit, draw me near." Soak in the bath, visualizing the water washing away old energy and preparing you for new beginnings.

3. Candle of New Intentions

Carve symbols of what you wish to manifest (such as stars, hearts, or runes) into a white candle. Light it, saying: "New moon's light, flame so true, set my path, bright and new." Focus on your intentions as the candle burns, allowing the moon's energy to empower your goals.

4. New Moon Reflection Spell

Sit quietly under the dark sky. Light a single white candle and say: "Moon so new, dark and bright, reveal my truths, through this night." Reflect on what you want to release and what you wish to invite into your life during the Yule season.

Waxing Crescent Moon Spells (Growth and Attraction)
5. Waxing Moon Growth Spell

Hold a small green candle in your hands. Carve a leaf symbol into the candle and say: "Crescent moon, growing bright, bring me growth, day and night." Light the candle and visualize your intentions growing like a plant reaching for the light.

6. Crystal Charging Ritual

Place a clear quartz crystal under the moonlight during the Waxing Crescent phase. Hold it up to the moon and say: "Crescent moon, light so clear, charge this stone, draw it near." Use this charged crystal in future rituals to amplify the energy of growth and attraction.

7. Candle of Confidence

Carve the word "Confidence" into a yellow candle. Light it during the Waxing Crescent moon, saying: "Crescent moon, waxing light, fill my heart, with courage bright." Allow the candle's energy to build your self-assurance as you pursue your goals.

8. Attraction Mirror Spell

Sit before a mirror under the Waxing Crescent moon. Hold a rose quartz crystal and say: "Moon of growth, draw it near, reflect my charm, pure and clear." Visualize your desired outcome, letting the moon's energy attract it to you.

First Quarter Moon Spells (Action and Decision-Making)

9. First Quarter Moon Candle Ritual

Carve a spiral symbol into a red candle. Light it, saying: "Quarter moon, half so bright, guide my actions, through the night." Focus on the actions you need to take to manifest your intentions, allowing the candle's energy to strengthen your resolve.

10. Decision-Making Rune Casting

Light a white candle and hold your rune set in your hands. Say: "Quarter moon, light so clear, show me choices, guide me near." Draw three runes and interpret them for guidance on an important decision you are facing during the Yule season.

11. Crystal Grid for Motivation

Create a crystal grid on your altar using citrine, carnelian, and clear quartz. Place a lit candle in the center and say: "Quarter moon, waxing light, fill me with drive, day and night." Sit before the grid, drawing in its energy to boost your motivation and drive.

12. Candle of Determination

Carve a mountain symbol into a blue candle. Light it during the First Quarter moon, saying: "Quarter moon, growing high, strengthen my will, reach the sky." Allow the candle to burn while you focus on over-coming obstacles in your path.

Waxing Gibbous Moon Spells (Refinement and Progress)

13. Waxing Gibbous Blessing Spell

Hold a small sprig of pine and a clear quartz crystal in your hands. Stand under the moon and say: "Gibbous moon, nearly full, bless my work, let it pull." Visualize the moon's energy blessing your progress, refining your efforts to bring them closer to fruition.

14. Candle of Focus

Carve an eye symbol into a purple candle. Light it during the Waxing Gibbous moon, saying: "Moon so full, waxing bright, sharpen my mind, guide my sight." Allow the candle's flame to focus your thoughts and intentions, clearing away distractions.

15. Crystal Water for Clarity

Place a piece of amethyst in a bowl of water and leave it under the Waxing Gibbous moon. Say: "Gibbous moon, light so clear, cleanse this water, draw it near." Use this water to wash your hands or face, inviting clarity and focus into your life.

16. Candle of Refinement

Carve symbols of refinement (such as a diamond or spiral) into a white candle. Light it, saying: "Gibbous moon, shine so true, refine my path, clear my view." Meditate on how you can fine-tune your actions to bring your goals closer.

Full Moon Spells (Manifestation and Celebration)

17. Yule Full Moon Ritual

On the night of the Yule Full Moon, light a silver or white candle. Stand outside and say: "Moon so bright, full of might, bring my wishes, into sight." Visualize the moon's light filling you with energy, amplifying your intentions and manifesting them into reality.

18. Full Moon Water Blessing

Fill a bowl with water and place it under the Full Moon's light. Hold your hands over it and say: "Moon so full, light so clear, bless this water, draw it near." Use the water to sprinkle around your home, purifying and blessing the space with the moon's energy.

19. Full Moon Crystal Charging

Place moonstone, clear quartz, and amethyst on a windowsill under the Full Moon. Say: "Moon so bright, stones so clear, charge with power, draw it near." Use these charged crystals in your future spellwork to enhance their potency.

20. Full Moon Circle of Protection

Stand in a circle of white candles under the Full Moon. Light each candle clockwise, saying: "Circle of light, full moon bright, guard this space, through the night." Visualize the circle creating a protective barrier around you, using the moon's energy to shield against negativity.

Waning Gibbous Moon Spells (Release and Reflection)
21. Candle of Release

Carve symbols representing what you wish to release (such as chains or knots) into a black candle. Light it during the Waning Gibbous moon, saying: "Moon so full, waning bright, release my burdens, clear my sight." Focus on letting go of negativity, allowing the candle's flame to consume and transform it.

22. Cleansing Smoke Ritual

Burn sage or cedar incense during the Waning Gibbous moon. Waft the smoke around your space, saying: "Moon of release, smoke so clear, cleanse this home, draw it near." Let the incense purify your environment, removing residual negative energy.

23. Crystal Purge Spell

Hold a piece of smoky quartz in your hands. Stand under the Waning Gibbous moon and say: "Moon so bright, shadows clear, cleanse this stone, bring it near." Visualize the quartz absorbing and transforming any lingering negative energy within you.

24. Wax Seal Release

Write down a habit or belief you wish to release on a piece of parchment. Drip wax from a black candle onto the paper, saying: "Moon of release, seal so clear, bind this burden, draw it near." Burn the parchment in a safe place, releasing the burden into the moon's light.

Last Quarter Moon Spells (Reflection and Letting Go)
25. Candle of Reflection

Carve the symbol of a crescent moon into a blue candle. Light it during the Last Quarter moon, saying: "Quarter moon, waning bright, guide my thoughts, through the night." Reflect on what you have learned over the Yule season, letting go of what no longer serves you.

26. Winter Wind Releasing Ritual

Stand outside on a windy night during the Last Quarter moon. Hold a piece of paper with what you wish to release written on it. Say: "Moon of wind, waning free, take this burden, away from me." Release the paper into the wind, letting it carry away your troubles.

27. Crystal Cleanse for Renewal

Place a piece of snowflake obsidian in a bowl of salt. Leave it under the moonlight, saying: "Moon so clear, waning bright, cleanse this stone, through the night." Use the cleansed crystal for grounding and protection in future spellwork.

28. Salt Water Purification

Mix sea salt and water in a bowl. Stand under the Last Quarter moon and say: "Moon so clear, waning light, cleanse this water, bring it right." Use the water to wash your hands, purifying your energy as you let go of the past.

Waning Crescent Moon Spells (Rest and Preparation)
29. Candle of Rest

Carve a crescent moon symbol into a lavender candle. Light it during the Waning Crescent moon, saying: "Crescent moon, waning bright, bring me peace, through this night." Allow the candle's light to fill you with calm, preparing you for the new cycle ahead.

30. Winter Dream Spell

Place a piece of amethyst under your pillow on the Waning Crescent moon. Say: "Moon of sleep, dream so near, bring me peace, draw me clear." Let the stone invite restful sleep and insightful dreams, preparing your mind and spirit for the coming New Moon.

Chapter 28: Aromatherapy and Incense Spells

The Yule season is rich with scents that evoke warmth, comfort, and the magic of winter. Aromatherapy and incense have long been used in magical practices to alter the atmosphere, uplift the spirit, and channel specific energies. Essential oils, herbs, and incense sticks can enhance your rituals, helping you connect more deeply with the magic of Yule. This chapter presents 25 detailed spells using classic Yule scents like pine, cinnamon, frankincense, cloves, cedarwood, and others to create a magical atmosphere for protection, healing, abundance, and joy.

1. Pine Purification Ritual

Burn a bundle of pine needles on your altar to purify your space. As the smoke rises, say: "Pine so green, scent so pure, cleanse this home, bring peace for sure." Walk around each room, wafting the smoke with your hand to clear out negative energy and invite peace into your home.

2. Cinnamon Abundance Spell

Light a cinnamon-scented candle or burn cinnamon incense. Hold a small bowl of coins or seeds and say: "Cinnamon warm, spice so sweet, draw abundance, make it meet." Allow the scent to fill the space, envisioning it attracting prosperity and abundance into your life.

3. Frankincense Protection Ritual

Burn frankincense resin or light frankincense incense sticks. Stand in the center of the room and say: "Frankincense pure, scent of old, shield this home, with light so bold." Waft the smoke toward each corner, creating a protective barrier around your space.

4. Cedarwood Grounding Spell

Add a few drops of cedarwood essential oil to a diffuser or simmering pot. As the scent spreads, say: "Cedarwood scent, grounding and true, anchor my spirit, renew me too." Sit quietly, breathing in the aroma to ground yourself and find balance amidst winter's stillness.

5. Yule Spice Infusion

Mix dried cloves, cinnamon sticks, and orange peels in a pot of simmering water. As the steam fills the room, say: "Spices of Yule, warm and bright, fill this space, with joy and light." Allow the warm, spicy scent to infuse your home with the essence of Yule, bringing comfort and cheer.

6. Rosemary Smoke Cleansing

Burn a bundle of dried rosemary to cleanse and protect your space. As the smoke rises, say: "Rosemary bright, smoke so clear, cleanse this space, draw good near." Walk through each room, wafting the smoke to clear out negativity and invite positive energy.

7. Myrrh Meditation Ritual

Place a few drops of myrrh essential oil on a cloth or in a diffuser. Sit quietly, breathing in the scent, and say: "Myrrh so deep, scent so true, calm my mind, bring me through." Let the aroma deepen your meditation, enhancing inner peace and clarity.

8. Clove Harmony Spell

Light clove incense and place a piece of garnet on your altar. Say: "Clove so warm, spice of cheer, bring us harmony, draw us near." Allow the scent to fill the space, fostering a peaceful and loving atmosphere within your home.

9. Fir Needle Peace Infusion

Add fir needle essential oil to a diffuser and let its fresh, woodsy scent fill the room. As the fragrance spreads, say: "Fir so green, scent so light, bring me peace, through this night." Breathe in the aroma, allowing it to calm your mind and ease tension.

10. Pine Cone Blessing

Hold a pine cone and place a few drops of pine essential oil on it. Say: "Pine of Yule, scent so clear, bless this home, throughout the year." Place the pine cone on your altar or in a central location in your home to invite the blessings of nature into your space.

11. Cinnamon and Orange Abundance Simmer Pot

Place cinnamon sticks, dried orange peels, and cloves in a simmering pot of water. As the steam rises, say: "Spices and citrus, warm and bright, draw abundance, day and night." Visualize the scent attracting prosperity and joy into your life.

12. Frankincense and Myrrh New Year's Purification

On Yule Eve, burn a mixture of frankincense and myrrh resin on a charcoal disc. As the smoke fills the room, say: "Resins of old, sacred and clear, cleanse this space, for the new year." Allow the smoke to purify your space, preparing it for the new beginnings Yule brings.

13. Wintergreen Renewal Ritual

Add a few drops of wintergreen essential oil to a diffuser. Stand in the center of the room and say: "Wintergreen bright, fresh and true, cleanse this space, make it new." Breathe in the invigorating scent, letting it refresh your mind and spirit.

14. Cedar Incense for Strength

Light a stick of cedar incense and hold a piece of tiger's eye stone. Say: "Cedarwood scent, strength so bold, fill me with courage, as days grow cold." Allow the scent to bolster your inner strength, filling you with the energy to face the challenges of winter.

15. Cinnamon and Clove Protection Circle

Burn a cinnamon incense stick and place cloves in a circle on your altar. As the scent spreads, say: "Cinnamon and clove, circle so clear, guard this space, keep harm near." Visualize the scent forming a protective barrier around you and your space.

16. Yule Candle Anointing

Add a few drops of frankincense and pine essential oils to a carrier oil. Anoint a white candle with the mixture, saying: "Scent of Yule, blend so bright, fill this space, with peace and light." Light the candle to invite the essence of Yule into your rituals.

17. Lavender and Pine Peace Spell

Mix a few drops of lavender and pine essential oils in a diffuser. As the scent fills the room, say: "Lavender calm, pine so bright, bring us peace, through Yule's night." Sit quietly, letting the aroma soothe your spirit and invite tranquility into your space.

18. Cinnamon Oil Abundance Charm

Place a cinnamon stick in a small vial with a few drops of cinnamon essential oil. Seal the vial and say: "Cinnamon strong, scent so sweet, draw abundance, make it meet." Keep the vial on your altar or carry it with you to attract prosperity.

19. Pine and Sage Smoke Cleanse

Combine dried pine needles and sage in a fire-safe bowl. Light them and say: "Pine and sage, smoke so true, cleanse this space, make it new." Walk through each room, wafting the smoke to purify and protect your home.

20. Cedarwood Bath for Grounding

Add a few drops of cedarwood essential oil to a warm bath. As you soak, say: "Cedarwood scent, grounding and clear, center my spirit, bring me near." Close your eyes and breathe in the woodsy aroma, allowing it to ground and stabilize you.

21. Frankincense Dream Ritual

Place a few drops of frankincense essential oil on a cloth and tuck it under your pillow. Say: "Frankincense bright, scent of dreams, bring me visions, clear as streams." Let the aroma guide you into a restful sleep, inviting insightful dreams.

22. Clove and Orange Incense for Joy

Burn clove and orange-scented incense sticks on your altar. Say: "Clove and orange, scent so light, bring us joy, through this night." Allow the aroma to fill your home, lifting the spirits of everyone within.

23. Pine Room Spray for Energy

Mix a few drops of pine essential oil with water in a spray bottle. Walk through your home, spritzing the mixture, and say: "Pine so fresh, scent so clear, bring me energy, draw it near." Use this spray to invigorate and energize your space during the winter months.

24. Cinnamon Candle Ritual for Love

Anoint a pink candle with a few drops of cinnamon essential oil. Light the candle and say: "Cinnamon warm, scent of love, fill this space, with blessings from above." Let the scent invite warmth, love, and affection into your home.

25. Yule Spice Smudge

Create a smudge bundle using cinnamon sticks, dried orange peels, cloves, and pine needles. Light the bundle and say: "Spices of Yule, blend so bright, cleanse this space, bring warmth and light." Use the smudge to purify your space, filling it with the vibrant energy of Yule.

Chapter 29: Blessings for the New Year

As Yule marks the turning point from darkness to light, it is the ideal time to welcome and bless the coming year. These blessings help set the tone for the months ahead, inviting prosperity, joy, health, protection, and harmony for oneself, loved ones, and the world. This chapter presents 40 detailed spells to bless yourself, your family, and the world, harnessing the powerful energies of Yule to create a positive and abundant new year. Each ritual uses candles, herbs, crystals, and symbols of Yule to magnify your intentions for a joyful year filled with new possibilities.

1. Candle of New Beginnings

Carve the symbol of the sun into a yellow candle. Light it at dawn on New Year's Day, saying: "Flame of light, sun so bright, bless this year, with new delight." Allow the candle to burn completely, filling your home with the energy of fresh starts and new opportunities.

2. Family Harmony Jar

Fill a small jar with lavender, rosemary, and a piece of rose quartz. Seal it with a ribbon, saying: "Herbs of peace, stone of love, bless this family, from above." Place the jar in a central room of your home to promote harmony and unity throughout the year.

3. New Year's Salt Circle

Create a circle of sea salt around a white candle. Light the candle and say: "Circle of salt, pure and true, bless this space, make it new." Sit quietly within the circle, allowing its protective energy to shield you and bring blessings for the year ahead.

4. Pinecone Prosperity Charm

Hold a pinecone in your hands and place a drop of cinnamon oil on it. Say: "Pine of Yule, scent so sweet, bring prosperity, make it meet." Place the pinecone on your altar or a central space to invite abundance into your home.

5. Candle of Good Health

Carve symbols of health (such as a heart or a spiral) into a green candle. Light it and say: "Flame of green, light so clear, bless this body, through the year." Allow the candle to burn for a few minutes each day, filling your space with healing energy.

6. Evergreen House Blessing

Tie sprigs of pine, cedar, and holly with a green ribbon. Hang the bundle above your front door, saying: "Evergreens bright, life so true, bless this home, make it new." This bundle invites nature's blessings into your home, fostering prosperity and protection.

7. Full Moon Abundance Ritual

On the first full moon of the new year, light a gold candle and place a bowl of coins nearby. Say: "Moon so full, shining bright, bring us fortune, day and night." Let the candle burn completely, visualizing its light attracting prosperity and success.

8. Candle of Family Protection

Carve protective symbols (such as a pentacle or a circle) into a black candle. Light it in the main room of your home, saying: "Flame of guard, burn so clear, protect this family, through the year." Allow the candle's energy to create a shield of protection around your loved ones.

9. Cinnamon and Orange New Year's Simmer Pot

Place cinnamon sticks, dried orange peels, and cloves in a simmering pot of water. As the steam rises, say: "Spices of warmth, scent so bright, bless this space, bring joy and light." Let the warm fragrance infuse your home, filling it with the energy of abundance and joy.

10. Crystal Grid for Prosperity

Create a crystal grid on your altar using citrine, green aventurine, and clear quartz. Place a small gold candle in the center, saying: "Crystals bright, grid so clear, draw abundance, through the year." Leave the grid up for a month to attract prosperity and opportunities.

11. Peaceful Home Ritual

Place a blue candle in a bowl of water. Light the candle, saying: "Water of calm, flame of peace, bless this home, let love increase." Let the candle burn for a while, creating a peaceful atmosphere that nurtures harmony and understanding among family members.

12. Candle of Joy

Carve the word "Joy" into a pink candle. Light it at dusk on New Year's Eve, saying: "Flame of love, bright and clear, bring us joy, through the year." Let the candle's warmth fill your home with happiness and a sense of celebration.

13. World Peace Incense Spell

Burn frankincense and myrrh incense on New Year's Eve. Hold your hands over the smoke and say: "Smoke so high, scent so bright, bring the world, peace this night." Visualize the smoke spreading peace and love around the globe, blessing all beings with harmony.

14. Rosemary Protection Charm

Fill a small pouch with dried rosemary and a piece of amethyst. Hold the pouch and say: "Herb of guard, stone so true, protect this year, make it new." Hang the pouch near your bed or carry it with you for protection throughout the year.

15. Candle of Friendship

Carve symbols of unity (such as hearts or stars) into a blue candle. Light it during a gathering of friends, saying: "Flame of bonds, burn so clear, bless this friendship, through the year." Allow the candle's energy to strengthen and nurture the relationships around you.

16. Yule Wreath Blessing

Create a wreath using pine branches, holly, and pinecones. Hang the wreath on your door, saying: "Wreath of green, circle of life, bless this home, banish strife." This wreath invites nature's blessings and protection into your home.

17. Candle of Love

Carve a heart symbol into a red candle. Light it on New Year's Day, saying: "Flame of love, burning bright, fill our hearts, with pure delight." Let the candle's energy warm your space, inviting love and compassion into your life.

18. Pine and Lavender Home Blessing

Place pine needles and dried lavender in a bowl of water. Sprinkle a few drops in each corner of your home, saying: "Pine and lavender, fresh and clear, bless this home, through the year." This spell fills your space with peace, protection, and positivity.

19. Candle of Gratitude

Carve the word "Gratitude" into a green candle. Light it and say: "Flame of thanks, bright and clear, bless this heart, throughout the year." Reflect on the blessings you have and express gratitude, allowing the candle to magnify your positive energy.

20. Family Circle of Light

Gather your family in a circle and light a white candle in the center. Hold hands and say: "Circle of love, flame so bright, bless this family, through the night." This ritual strengthens the bond between family members and fills your home with harmony and warmth.

21. Frankincense New Year's Candle

Anoint a gold candle with frankincense oil. Light it at midnight on New Year's Eve, saying: "Flame of Yule, scent so clear, bring us blessings, through the year." Let the candle burn for a while, inviting prosperity and peace into your life.

22. Wintergreen Bath for Blessings

Add a few drops of wintergreen essential oil to a warm bath. As you soak, say: "Wintergreen fresh, scent so true, bless this body, make it new." Visualize the water filling you with the energy of renewal and blessings for the coming year.

23. Crystal Candle Blessing

Place a piece of clear quartz beside a lit white candle. Hold your hands over the candle and say: "Crystal bright, flame so pure, bless this year, make it sure." Allow the candle to burn, charging the crystal with positive energy to carry with you throughout the year.

24. Yule Tree Blessing Ritual

Stand before your Yule tree with hands over your heart. Say: "Tree of green, evergreen bright, bless this home, with love and light." Visualize the tree's energy filling your home with joy, harmony, and blessings for the new year.

25. Candle of Compassion

Carve a lotus symbol into a light blue candle. Light it on the morning of New Year's Day, saying: "Flame of calm, light so clear, bring us compassion, through the year." Let the candle burn, filling your space with the energy of empathy and understanding.

26. Evergreen Circle of Abundance

Create a circle using evergreen branches and pinecones on your altar. Light a green candle in the center, saying: "Circle of green, life so true, draw abundance, make it new." Let the candle burn for an hour to attract prosperity and growth in the coming year.

27. Cinnamon and Clove Abundance Spell

Light a cinnamon-scented candle and place cloves around its base. Say: "Cinnamon warm, clove so bright, bless this year, day and night." Let the candle burn to attract prosperity and joy into your home.

28. Candle of World Healing

Carve a globe symbol into a white candle. Light it on New Year's Eve, saying: "Flame of hope, light so clear, heal this world, through the year." Visualize the candle's light spreading healing energy across the earth, blessing all beings with peace and health.

29. Rosemary and Sage Cleansing Ritual

Burn dried rosemary and sage on your altar. Waft the smoke around your space, saying: "Herbs of guard, smoke so true, cleanse this home, make it new." Allow the smoke to purify and bless your space for the new year.

30. Candle of Patience

Carve a tree symbol into a blue candle. Light it and say: "Flame of calm, light so true, fill us with patience, make us new." Allow the candle to burn, filling your home with a sense of patience and understanding for the coming year.

31. Yule Stone Blessing

Hold a piece of snowflake obsidian in your hands. Close your eyes and say: "Stone of earth, cold and clear, bless this spirit, through the year." Place the stone on your altar to invite grounding and protection into your life.

32. Candle of Success

Carve symbols of success (such as a star or mountain) into a yellow candle. Light it on New Year's Day, saying: "Flame of gold, burn so bright, bless my path, with guiding light." Let the candle's energy fill you with confidence and drive for the year ahead.

33. Crystal Grid for Love

Create a crystal grid using rose quartz, garnet, and amethyst on your altar. Place a pink candle in the center, saying: "Crystals bright, grid so true, draw love near, make it new." Let the grid radiate loving energy throughout your home.

34. Pine and Cinnamon Abundance Bath

Add pine needles and a cinnamon stick to a warm bath. As you soak, say: "Pine and spice, warm and true, draw abundance, make it new." Visualize the water filling you with the energy of prosperity and joy for the new year.

35. Candle of Inner Strength

Carve a mountain symbol into a red candle. Light it and say: "Flame of might, burn so clear, fill me with strength, through the year." Allow the candle's light to strengthen your spirit, preparing you to face the challenges of the new year.

36. Lavender Peace Ritual

Light lavender incense and hold a piece of amethyst. Say: "Lavender scent, smoke so clear, bring us peace, through the year." Let the aroma fill your home, promoting a peaceful and harmonious environment.

37. Candle of Self-Love

Carve a heart symbol into a pink candle. Light it on New Year's Day, saying: "Flame of love, light so true, fill my heart, make it new." Allow the candle to burn, surrounding you with the energy of self-love and acceptance.

38. Yule Night Meditation

Sit quietly before a lit white candle on New Year's Eve. Close your eyes and say: "Night of Yule, dark and bright, bless my soul, with guiding light." Meditate on your intentions for the new year, inviting clarity and peace into your mind.

39. Candle of Protection for the World

Carve the globe symbol into a black candle. Light it and say: "Flame of guard, burn so clear, shield this world, through the year." Visualize the candle's energy forming a protective shield around the earth.

40. Candle of Growth

Carve symbols of growth (such as leaves or spirals) into a green candle. Light it and say: "Flame of life, light so clear, bless this growth, through the year." Allow the candle to burn, inviting personal and spiritual growth into your life.

Chapter 30: Transformation and Self-Growth Spells

Yule, the Winter Solstice, is a time of transformation as the world moves from darkness toward the returning light. This powerful turning point in the year is perfect for focusing on personal transformation, inner strength, and spiritual growth. During Yule, we are invited to turn inward, reflect on our lives, and set intentions for who we wish to become in the coming year. This chapter offers 45 detailed spells designed to help you transform your inner world, build strength, and pursue spiritual growth, using the magical energies of Yule to guide your journey.

1. Candle of Inner Transformation

Carve symbols of change (such as spirals or butterflies) into a purple candle. Light it at dusk on Yule night and say: "Flame of change, burn so bright, transform my spirit, through this night." Sit quietly, focusing on the flame as you visualize shedding old patterns and embracing your true self.

2. Evergreen Branch Renewal

Hold a sprig of evergreen (pine, cedar, or fir) in your hands. Close your eyes and say: "Evergreen strong, life so pure, renew my soul, make it sure." Visualize the branch filling you with its resilient energy, aiding your journey of self-renewal.

3. Crystal of Self-Reflection

Hold a piece of snowflake obsidian in your hands and stand under the Yule moon. Say: "Stone of dark, cold and clear, reflect my truths, draw them near." Close your eyes, allowing the stone's energy to reveal insights into aspects of yourself that need growth or change.

4. Candle of Strength Ritual

Carve a mountain symbol into a red candle. Light it on Yule night, saying: "Flame of might, burn so clear, fill me with strength, draw me near." Sit quietly, absorbing the candle's energy, and let it boost your inner strength to face future challenges.

5. Pine Needle Empowerment Bath

Add pine needles and a few drops of cedarwood oil to a warm bath. As you soak, say: "Pine of strength, cedar so clear, empower my spirit, draw it near." Visualize the water washing away self-doubt, filling you with the courage to embrace change.

6. Yule Night Meditation

Sit quietly before a lit white candle and close your eyes. Say: "Night of Yule, dark and bright, guide my thoughts, through this night." Meditate on your past year, reflecting on areas for growth and setting intentions for transformation in the year ahead.

7. Waxing Moon Growth Spell

On the next waxing moon after Yule, light a green candle. Carve a leaf symbol into the candle and say: "Moon of growth, light so clear, bless my path, guide me near." Let the candle burn, focusing on its energy to nurture your personal growth.

8. Self-Discovery Mirror Spell

Sit before a mirror in a dimly lit room with a single candle. Hold a piece of clear quartz and say: "Mirror bright, light so clear, reveal my truths, bring them near." Gaze into the mirror, allowing thoughts or emotions to surface, and reflect on your journey.

9. Candle of Patience

Carve the symbol of a tree into a blue candle. Light it on Yule morning and say: "Flame of calm, burn so true, fill me with patience, make me new." Let the candle burn, filling you with the energy to approach your transformation with patience and perseverance.

10. Pine Cone Intentions

Hold a pine cone in your hands and close your eyes. Whisper your intentions for self-growth into the pine cone, then place it on your altar, saying: "Pine of Yule, life so bright, bless these intentions, through this night." Allow the pine cone to radiate your intentions, drawing the energy of transformation to you.

11. Snow Cleansing Ritual

Gather fresh snow in a bowl and hold it in your hands. Say: "Snow of Yule, pure and bright, cleanse my spirit, through this night." As the snow melts, visualize it washing away old, limiting beliefs, clearing the path for self-growth.

12. Amethyst Self-Growth Spell

Hold an amethyst crystal in your hands. Close your eyes and say: "Amethyst bright, stone of sight, guide my spirit, through the night." Keep the crystal near your bed to encourage self-awareness and growth in your dreams.

13. Wintergreen Transformation Bath

Add a few drops of wintergreen oil to a warm bath. As you soak, say: "Wintergreen fresh, scent so true, transform my spirit, make it new." Breathe in the aroma, visualizing your spirit transforming and embracing its full potential.

14. Circle of Light Ritual

Create a circle of white candles on your altar. Light each one clockwise, saying: "Circle of light, flame so bright, transform my soul, through this night." Sit within the circle, feeling the energy of the flames supporting your journey of self-transformation.

15. Candle of Self-Love

Carve the word "Love" into a pink candle. Light it on Yule night, saying: "Flame of love, burn so clear, fill my heart, draw it near." Allow the candle's warmth to surround you, building self-love and acceptance as a foundation for personal growth.

16. Rosemary Self-Cleansing

Burn a bundle of dried rosemary on your altar. As the smoke rises, say: "Herb of guard, scent so true, cleanse my spirit, make it new." Waft the smoke around you, allowing it to purify your energy and remove obstacles to your self-growth.

17. Candle of Confidence

Carve the symbol of the sun into a yellow candle. Light it at dawn on Yule morning, saying: "Flame of gold, bright and clear, fill me with confidence, draw it near." Visualize the candle's light filling you with the strength to embrace your personal power.

18. Pine and Lavender Peace Spell

Place pine needles and dried lavender in a bowl of water. Hold your hands over the bowl and say: "Pine of strength, lavender true, grant me peace, make me new." Use this water to wash your hands, inviting peace and calmness into your self-growth journey.

19. Moonstone Night Ritual

Hold a piece of moonstone in your hands and stand under the Yule moon. Say: "Moonstone bright, light of night, guide my path, through the light." Keep the moonstone by your bed to inspire clarity and intuition during your transformation.

20. Candle of Clarity

Carve the symbol of an eye into a white candle. Light it at dusk on Yule night, saying: "Flame of sight, burn so clear, bring me clarity, draw it near." Allow the candle's light to sharpen your intuition, helping you see the truth in your journey.

21. Candle of Forgiveness

Carve symbols of release (such as broken chains) into a black candle. Light it on Yule night, saying: "Flame of dark, burn away, free my heart, clear the way." Focus on letting go of past hurts, creating space for transformation and growth.

22. Crystal Grid for Inner Strength

Create a crystal grid on your altar using tiger's eye, carnelian, and citrine. Place a red candle in the center, saying: "Crystals bright, grid so clear, fill me with strength, through the year." Let the grid empower you with courage and resilience.

23. Evergreen Blessing Ritual

Place an evergreen wreath on your altar and hold your hands over it. Say: "Wreath of green, life so bright, bless my spirit, through this night." Visualize the wreath filling you with its vibrant, transformative energy.

24. Candle of Growth

Carve the symbol of a leaf into a green candle. Light it during the first crescent moon after Yule, saying: "Flame of life, burn so clear, guide my growth, through the year." Focus on the candle's energy nurturing your personal and spiritual development.

25. Pinecone Self-Reflection Charm

Hold a pinecone in your hands and whisper your thoughts and feelings into it. Place the pinecone on your altar, saying: "Pine of Yule, strong and true, guide my growth, make me new." Keep the pinecone as a reminder to reflect on your journey regularly.

26. Candle of Wisdom

Carve symbols of wisdom (such as a star or an owl) into a blue candle. Light it on Yule night, saying: "Flame of mind, burn so bright, bring me wisdom, through this night." Allow the candle to fill you with insights for personal and spiritual growth.

27. Snow Water Renewal

Collect snow in a small bowl and hold it in your hands. Say: "Water of snow, pure and bright, renew my spirit, through the night." Use the melted snow to wash your face or hands, inviting renewal into your journey.

28. Winter Wind Release Ritual

Stand outside on a windy winter night. Hold a piece of paper with what you wish to release written on it. Say: "Wind of Yule, blow so clear, take my burdens, bring me near." Let the wind carry away the paper, releasing what no longer serves you.

29. Candle of Balance

Carve the symbol of a yin-yang into a white candle. Light it on Yule night, saying: "Flame of balance, burn so true, bring me peace, make me new." Allow the candle to harmonize your inner world, balancing emotions and thoughts.

30. Pine and Sage Bath

Add pine needles and dried sage to a warm bath. As you soak, say: "Pine of strength, sage so clear, cleanse my soul, draw me near." Let the water wash away negativity, making room for your personal transformation.

31. Lavender and Cedar Meditation

Add a few drops of lavender and cedar essential oils to a diffuser. Sit before the diffuser and say: "Lavender calm, cedar clear, guide my mind, draw it near." Meditate on your intentions for self-growth, letting the aromas support your focus.

32. Candle of Self-Respect

Carve the word "Respect" into a red candle. Light it on Yule morning and say: "Flame of power, burn so true, fill my heart, make it new." Allow the candle to boost your sense of self-worth and respect.

33. Pine Cone of Gratitude

Hold a pine cone in your hands and whisper your gratitude for the year into it. Place the pine cone on your altar, saying: "Pine of Yule, bright and clear, fill my heart, through this year." Let the pine cone's energy magnify your gratitude and transform your outlook.

34. Crystal Candle Reflection

Place a piece of clear quartz beside a lit white candle. Hold your hands over the candle and say: "Crystal clear, flame so bright, guide my thoughts, through the night." Allow the crystal to amplify the candle's energy, aiding your journey of self-reflection.

35. Candle of Courage

Carve the symbol of a lion into a red candle. Light it during the waning moon after Yule, saying: "Flame of might, burn so clear, fill me with courage, draw me near." Let the candle's light fill you with bravery to embrace your transformation.

36. Wintergreen Candle for Clarity

Anoint a white candle with wintergreen oil. Light it on Yule night, saying: "Scent so pure, flame so bright, grant me clarity, through this night." Allow the scent and light to clear away mental fog, aiding your self-growth.

37. Candle of Forgiveness

Carve a wave symbol into a blue candle. Light it on Yule night, saying: "Flame of calm, burn so true, grant me forgiveness, make me new." Focus on releasing self-judgment, allowing forgiveness to be the seed of your transformation.

38. Amethyst and Pine Meditation

Hold a piece of amethyst and a pine sprig in your hands. Close your eyes and say: "Stone of sight, pine so clear, guide my thoughts, bring me near." Meditate on the changes you seek, letting the stone and pine enhance your focus and intuition.

39. Candle of Inner Peace

Carve the symbol of a dove into a lavender candle. Light it on Yule morning, saying: "Flame of peace, burn so true, calm my heart, make it new." Allow the candle's light to soothe your spirit, fostering inner peace and balance.

40. Pine and Rosemary Bath

Add pine needles and dried rosemary to a warm bath. As you soak, say: "Pine of strength, rosemary true, cleanse my spirit, make it new." Visualize the water infusing you with strength and renewal.

41. Candle of Wisdom

Carve the symbol of an owl into a blue candle. Light it on Yule night, saying: "Flame of sight, burn so bright, grant me wisdom, guide my flight." Let the candle's energy deepen your understanding of your path and choices.

42. Snow Water Reflection

Collect snow in a bowl and let it melt. Hold the bowl and say: "Water of snow, clear and true, reflect my spirit, make it new." Use the water to wash your face, inviting clarity and self-reflection into your life.

43. Yule Tree Meditation

Sit quietly before your Yule tree. Close your eyes and say: "Tree of Yule, life so bright, guide my soul, through the night." Breathe deeply, feeling the tree's energy supporting your journey of self-growth.

44. Candle of Truth

Carve the symbol of an eye into a purple candle. Light it on Yule night, saying: "Flame of sight, burn so clear, show me truths, draw them near." Allow the candle to reveal insights into your inner self, aiding your transformation.

45. Pine Cone of Hope

Hold a pine cone and whisper your hopes for the new year into it. Place it on your altar, saying: "Pine of Yule, hope so bright, guide my path, through the night." Let the pine cone's energy nurture your hopes and dreams as you transform and grow.

Chapter 31: Crafting Magical Yule Gifts

The tradition of gift-giving during Yule is a beautiful way to share love, joy, and blessings with those we care about. Handmade gifts carry a special magic, as they are infused with the time, energy, and love put into creating them. This chapter presents 30 spells for enchanting your handmade Yule gifts with additional layers of love, protection, luck, and positive energy. By incorporating simple rituals into the crafting process, you can turn your gifts into magical talismans that continue to bring warmth and blessings to the recipients throughout the year.

1. Love-Infused Candle

Carve the recipient's initials into a candle (pink for love and friendship, green for prosperity, white for peace). As you carve, say: "Candle bright, flame of love, bless this gift, with light from above." Anoint the candle with lavender oil, visualizing it radiating love and joy every time it is lit.

2. Protection Sachet

Fill a small cloth bag with rosemary, dried lavender, and a piece of amethyst. As you fill the bag, say: "Herbs of peace, stone so bright, protect this soul, day and night." Tie the bag with a ribbon, focusing on surrounding the recipient with a protective shield of calm and positive energy.

3. Luck-Boosting Charm Bracelet

String together beads of green aventurine, tiger's eye, and citrine on a bracelet. As you thread each bead, say: "Beads of luck, charm so bright, bring fortune near, day and night." Visualize the bracelet carrying luck and positive energy to the wearer with every step they take.

4. Happiness-Infused Bath Bombs

Craft bath bombs using a mixture of Epsom salts, baking soda, citric acid, and essential oils. Add dried rose petals or lavender to the mixture, saying: "Bomb of joy, scent so clear, bring happiness, draw it near." Focus on the bath bombs filling the recipient's bath with joy and relaxation.

5. Evergreen Wreath of Protection

Create a wreath using pine, cedar, and holly. As you weave each branch, say: "Wreath of green, circle so true, protect this home, bring blessings through." Enchant the wreath to bring protection, abundance, and harmony to the recipient's household.

6. Cinnamon Stick Ornament

Tie a bundle of cinnamon sticks with a red ribbon, adding a sprig of evergreen for decoration. Hold the ornament in your hands and say: "Cinnamon warm, evergreen true, bring joy and luck, the whole year through." Gift it to spread warmth, love, and prosperity throughout the year.

7. Love-Knotted Scarf

As you knit or crochet a scarf, visualize each stitch filled with warmth and love. Say: "Stitch by stitch, thread so bright, weave in love, hold it tight." Enchant the scarf to wrap the recipient in comfort, love, and protection whenever they wear it.

8. Candle of Friendship

Carve the word "Friendship" into a candle. Anoint it with rose or lavender oil, saying: "Flame of joy, light so clear, bless this bond, bring us near." Gift the candle with the intention of strengthening the friendship and bringing happiness whenever it is lit.

9. Herb-Infused Soap

Mix dried rosemary, lavender, and a few drops of frankincense oil into a homemade soap base. As you stir, say: "Herbs of light, scent so clear, cleanse and bless, bring joy near." Visualize the soap filling the recipient's baths with protective and uplifting energy.

10. Pinecone Good Fortune Charm

Hold a pinecone in your hands and whisper words of blessing into it, saying: "Pine of Yule, seed so bright, bring good fortune, through the night." Attach a ribbon to the pinecone for hanging. Gift it as a charm to invite luck and prosperity into the recipient's life.

11. Enchanted Candle Jar

Craft a candle in a glass jar, using essential oils and herbs. As you pour the melted wax, say: "Candle of light, flame so true, bring peace and joy, blessings too." Anoint the jar with a drop of frankincense oil to seal the enchantment before gifting.

12. Rose Petal Love Sachet

Fill a small cloth bag with dried rose petals, lavender, and a rose quartz crystal. As you fill the bag, say: "Petals of love, stone so bright, bring warmth and joy, day and night." Gift this sachet to bring love, warmth, and comfort into the recipient's life.

13. Cozy Spell-Infused Blanket

As you knit or crochet a blanket, focus on each stitch being filled with warmth and protection. Say: "Stitch by stitch, weave in care, warm this soul, everywhere." Enchant the blanket to offer comfort and a sense of security whenever it is used.

14. Cinnamon Luck Candle

Create a candle using cinnamon-scented wax. Hold the candle in your hands and say: "Candle of luck, scent so bright, draw fortune near, through the night." Visualize the candle's light bringing luck and positivity to the recipient every time they light it.

15. Rosemary Protection Oil

Create an oil infusion with rosemary sprigs and olive oil. Hold the bottle and say: "Oil of light, herb so clear, protect and bless, bring good cheer." Gift the oil as an anointing blend for candles, doorways, or personal use to ward off negativity.

16. Cinnamon and Clove Pomander

Stud an orange with cloves and roll it in a mixture of cinnamon and nutmeg. Hold it in your hands and say: "Spices of warmth, scent so sweet, bring joy and luck, let it meet." Gift the pomander to fill the recipient's space with the warm, joyful energy of Yule.

17. Crystal-Infused Water Bottle

Place a rose quartz crystal inside a clear water bottle. Hold the bottle in your hands and say: "Crystal of love, light so clear, bless this water, draw joy near." Gift it to fill the recipient's water with love, calmness, and positive energy.

18. Scented Bath Salts of Calm

Mix Epsom salts with dried lavender and a few drops of lavender essential oil. Stir the mixture, saying: "Salts of calm, scent so true, bless this soul, make it new." Gift the bath salts to promote relaxation and tranquility for the recipient.

19. Candle of Abundance

Carve the symbol of a star into a green candle. Anoint it with cinnamon oil, saying: "Flame of green, light so clear, bring abundance, draw it near." Gift the candle to bring prosperity and success into the recipient's life.

20. Pine and Lavender Pillow

Fill a small pillow with pine needles and dried lavender. Hold it and say: "Pine of strength, lavender so clear, bring peace and rest, draw it near." Enchant the pillow to promote restful sleep and calming energy for the recipient.

21. Protection-Infused Mug

Draw a small protection symbol (such as a pentacle) on the bottom of a mug using non-toxic, food-safe markers. Hold the mug and say: "Mug of warmth, drink of light, protect this soul, day and night." Gift the mug as a daily reminder of warmth, comfort, and protection.

22. Love-Infused Lip Balm

Mix beeswax, coconut oil, and a drop of rose oil to make a lip balm. As you stir the mixture, say: "Balm of love, smooth and clear, bless these lips, draw joy near." Gift the balm to keep the recipient's lips soft and filled with the energy of love.

23. Crystal Garden of Blessings

Plant small succulents in a pot and place a clear quartz crystal at the base of each plant. Hold your hands over the pot and say: "Plants of green, stones so bright, bless this space, with love and light." Gift the garden to bring natural blessings into the recipient's home.

24. Candle of Peace

Carve the word "Peace" into a white candle. Anoint it with lavender oil, saying: "Flame of calm, light so clear, bring peace and joy, draw it near." Gift the candle to create a peaceful atmosphere wherever it is lit.

25. Yule Spice Simmer Pot Blend

Mix dried orange peels, cinnamon sticks, cloves, and star anise in a small jar. Hold the jar and say: "Spices of Yule, warm and bright, bring joy and peace, through this night." Gift it with instructions to simmer in water, filling the recipient's home with warmth and positive energy.

26. Pine Protection Ornament

Create an ornament using pine needles, dried rosemary, and a ribbon. Hold the ornament and say: "Pine and herb, circle so bright, protect this space, day and night." Gift it as a charm for the recipient to hang in their home for year-round protection.

27. Wishing Stone

Select a small, smooth stone and draw a star symbol on it using a gold or silver pen. Hold the stone in your hands and say: "Stone of light, wish so true, grant blessings bright, bring joy through." Gift the stone as a token of hope and wishes for the recipient.

28. Amulet of Strength

Create a necklace using a piece of tiger's eye or carnelian. Hold the amulet and say: "Stone of might, strength so clear, bless this soul, bring courage near." Gift the necklace to empower the recipient with inner strength and resilience.

29. Candle of Healing

Carve the symbol of a spiral into a blue candle. Anoint it with eucalyptus oil, saying: "Flame of healing, light so true, bless this body, make it new." Gift the candle to aid in the recipient's physical and emotional healing journey.

30. Love and Luck Jar

Fill a small jar with dried rose petals, lavender, rosemary, and a piece of aventurine. Hold the jar and say: "Herbs of love, stone of luck, bless this gift, bring joy in flux." Seal the jar with a ribbon and gift it to bring love and luck to the recipient's life.

Chapter 32: Community and World Spells

Yule is a time of unity and giving, extending beyond individual well-being to include the community and the world. The turning of the year during the Winter Solstice provides an opportunity to send positive energy, healing, and blessings outward, aiming to foster peace, health, and harmony on a global scale. This chapter offers 50 detailed spells designed to generate and channel this energy for the benefit of your local community and the world. Using candles, crystals, herbs, and visualization, you can contribute to the global effort for a more peaceful, healthy, and balanced world.

1. Candle of Global Peace

Carve a globe symbol into a white candle. Light it on Yule night, saying: "Flame of peace, light so clear, spread your calm, far and near." Visualize the candle's light expanding outward, enveloping the world in peace and unity.

2. Rosemary World Healing Ritual

Burn a bundle of dried rosemary on your altar. As the smoke rises, say: "Herb of light, scent so clear, heal this world, draw us near." Visualize the smoke spreading across the globe, purifying negativity and promoting health and well-being for all.

3. Crystal Grid for Global Harmony

Create a crystal grid on your altar using clear quartz, rose quartz, and amethyst. Arrange the stones in the shape of a world map or a circle, with a white candle in the center. Light the candle and say: "Crystals bright, stones so clear, spread harmony, far and near." Visualize the grid's energy radiating out, promoting global understanding and peace.

4. Pinecone of Hope

Hold a pinecone in your hands and whisper wishes for the world into it, such as peace, health, and compassion. Place the pinecone on your altar, saying: "Pine of Yule, seed so true, spread hope and light, through and through." Let it serve as a beacon of hope for global unity and healing.

5. Full Moon World Blessing

On the first full moon after Yule, light a white candle and place a bowl of water in front of it. Say: "Moon so full, shining bright, bless this world, with purest light." Sprinkle the water around your altar, visualizing it spreading blessings of peace and well-being across the world.

6. Circle of Protection for the Earth

Arrange nine white candles in a circle on your altar. Light each candle clockwise, saying: "Circle of light, flame so clear, protect this earth, far and near." Visualize the circle creating a protective barrier around the planet, shielding it from harm and negativity.

7. Rosemary Smoke for Community Healing

Burn rosemary incense and walk around your home or neighborhood, wafting the smoke and saying: "Smoke of light, herb so clear, bless this community, draw us near." Visualize the smoke spreading blessings of health, unity, and protection to everyone within the community.

8. Candle of Compassion

Carve the word "Compassion" into a pink candle. Light it on Yule night, saying: "Flame of love, light so bright, fill each heart, with kindness's might." Visualize the candle's light touching hearts worldwide, fostering empathy and understanding among people.

9. Crystal for Global Health

Hold a piece of green aventurine in your hands and close your eyes. Say: "Stone of life, light so clear, bless this earth, draw health near." Place the crystal in a central location in your home to continuously send out energy for global health and healing.

10. Water Blessing for Rainforests

Fill a bowl with water and place it on your altar. Hold your hands over the bowl and say: "Water of life, pure and true, bless the forests, make them new." Visualize the water absorbing energy, then pour it outside near plants or trees, offering the blessing to rainforests and ecosystems around the world.

11. Candle for Environmental Healing

Carve the symbol of a tree into a green candle. Light it and say: "Flame of earth, burn so bright, heal this planet, day and night." Visualize the candle's light nourishing the earth, restoring balance to natural ecosystems.

12. World Protection Pouch

Fill a small pouch with rosemary, lavender, and a piece of snowflake obsidian. Hold it in your hands and say: "Herbs of guard, stone so clear, protect this world, far and near." Keep the pouch on your altar to continuously send out protective energy for the world.

13. Candle of Joy for the World

Carve a sun symbol into a yellow candle. Light it on Yule morning, saying: "Flame of joy, light so true, bless this earth, make it new." Allow the candle's light to spread warmth, joy, and hope across the globe.

14. Winter Wind of Change Spell

Stand outside on a windy winter night. Close your eyes and say: "Wind of Yule, blow so clear, bring us change, draw it near." Visualize the wind carrying messages of peace and positive transformation to every corner of the earth.

15. Crystal Network for Global Connection

Hold a clear quartz crystal and say: "Stone of light, connection so true, link us together, old and new." Place the crystal on your altar with the intention of creating an energetic network of unity and understanding among people worldwide.

16. Candle for Community Harmony

Carve symbols of unity (such as interlocking circles) into a blue candle. Light it, saying: "Flame of peace, burn so bright, bless our community, day and night." Visualize the candle's light promoting harmony and cooperation within your local community.

17. Salt Circle for World Protection

Create a circle of sea salt around a globe or world map on your altar. Stand before it and say: "Circle of salt, pure and true, guard this world, make it new." Visualize the salt creating a protective shield around the earth.

18. Candle of Healing Light

Carve the symbol of a spiral into a white candle. Light it on Yule night, saying: "Flame of light, burn so clear, spread healing warmth, far and near." Allow the candle's light to radiate outward, sending healing energy to all who need it.

19. Pine and Lavender World Blessing

Mix pine needles and dried lavender in a bowl. Hold the bowl and say: "Pine of strength, lavender so true, bless this world, make it new." Scatter the mixture around your altar, visualizing it spreading blessings of peace and protection worldwide.

20. Candle for the Homeless

Carve the word "Shelter" into a green candle. Light it and say: "Flame of hope, burn so clear, bring warmth and homes, draw them near." Visualize the candle's light reaching those without shelter, providing warmth, protection, and hope.

21. Crystal Grid for Wildlife Protection

Create a crystal grid using tiger's eye, smoky quartz, and jade. Arrange the stones in the shape of an animal paw or tree. Place a white candle in the center, saying: "Crystals bright, guard so true, protect the creatures, old and new." Allow the grid to continuously send out protective energy for wildlife.

22. Rosemary Community Cleansing

Burn a rosemary bundle and walk around your home or neighborhood, saying: "Smoke of light, herb so bright, cleanse this space, day and night." Visualize the smoke clearing away negativity and inviting harmony into your community.

23. Candle of Understanding

Carve the symbol of an eye into a purple candle. Light it on Yule morning, saying: "Flame of truth, burn so clear, open minds, draw us near." Visualize the candle's light spreading understanding and empathy among people worldwide.

24. Lavender Peace Sachet

Fill a small cloth bag with dried lavender and a piece of rose quartz. Hold the bag and say: "Lavender calm, stone of love, bring peace to all, from above." Keep the sachet near your bed to send out calming energy for world peace.

25. World Healing Snow Ritual

Collect fresh snow in a bowl and place it on your altar. Hold your hands over the snow and say: "Snow of Yule, pure and bright, heal this world, through the night." As the snow melts, visualize its energy spreading healing warmth across the planet.

26. Candle of Global Love

Carve a heart symbol into a pink candle. Light it and say: "Flame of love, light so bright, bless this earth, day and night." Visualize the candle's light filling the world with love, compassion, and kindness.

27. Pine Needle World Protection

Scatter pine needles around your altar in a circle. Light a white candle in the center, saying: "Pine of guard, circle so true, protect this world, old and new." Visualize the circle creating a protective barrier around the planet.

28. Crystal for Rainfall Blessings

Hold a piece of aquamarine in your hands and say: "Stone of water, blessing so clear, bring rain and life, draw it near." Place the crystal outside during a rainstorm to bless areas of the world in need of rain and renewal.

29. Candle for Refugees

Carve the word "Home" into a blue candle. Light it and say: "Flame of hope, burn so bright, guide the lost, through the night." Visualize the candle's light providing guidance, safety, and hope for refugees worldwide.

30. Sage Smoke for Global Cleansing

Burn sage incense on your altar and hold a globe or world map. Waft the smoke around it, saying: "Sage of light, smoke so true, cleanse this world, make it new." Visualize the smoke clearing negativity and filling the earth with light.

31. Candle of Inner Strength for Leaders

Carve symbols of strength (such as mountains or lions) into a gold candle. Light it, saying: "Flame of might, burn so clear, guide our leaders, year by year." Visualize the candle's light providing wisdom, compassion, and strength to global leaders.

32. Pinecone of Prosperity for the World

Hold a pinecone and whisper blessings of prosperity for all into it. Place the pinecone on your altar, saying: "Pine of Yule, seed so bright, bless this earth, with fortune's light." Let it serve as a beacon of abundance for communities in need.

33. Crystal Grid for Peaceful Protests

Create a grid using black tourmaline, rose quartz, and clear quartz. Arrange the stones in the shape of a circle. Light a white candle in the center, saying: "Crystals bright, guard and clear, bless all voices, draw them near." Visualize the grid promoting peaceful expression and unity.

34. Candle of Health

Carve a spiral into a green candle. Light it on Yule night, saying: "Flame of life, burn so clear, bless all bodies, draw health near." Allow the candle's light to radiate healing energy across the globe.

35. Wintergreen Candle for Global Awakening

Anoint a white candle with wintergreen oil. Light it on Yule morning, saying: "Scent of truth, light so bright, awaken minds, through the night." Visualize the candle's energy awakening compassion and understanding in people around the world.

36. World Blessing Jar

Fill a jar with salt, rosemary, and a clear quartz crystal. Seal the jar with wax and say: "Jar of light, bless this earth, bring us peace, joy, and worth." Place the jar on your altar to continuously send blessings to the world.

37. Candle of Education

Carve the symbol of a book into a blue candle. Light it and say: "Flame of wisdom, burn so clear, grant us knowledge, draw it near." Visualize the candle's light illuminating minds, spreading education and understanding across the globe.

38. Amethyst World Healing

Hold an amethyst crystal and say: "Stone of sight, healing so clear, bless this earth, draw peace near." Place the crystal on a globe or world map, allowing it to continuously send healing energy to areas in need.

39. Candle of Unity

Carve interlocking circles into a white candle. Light it on Yule night, saying: "Flame of unity, burn so bright, bind us together, in peace and light." Visualize the candle's light weaving a web of connection and harmony among all people.

40. Sage and Pine World Cleansing

Burn a mixture of dried sage and pine needles on your altar. As the smoke rises, say: "Smoke of guard, scent so true, cleanse this world, make it new." Visualize the smoke spreading across the earth, purifying negativity and inviting peace.

41. Candle of Warmth for the Needy
Carve the word "Warmth" into a red candle. Light it on a cold winter night, saying: "Flame of warmth, burn so bright, bless those in need, through this night." Visualize the candle's light providing warmth and comfort to those who lack it.

42. Crystal Circle for Global Connection
Arrange clear quartz crystals in a circle on your altar. Hold your hands over the circle and say: "Crystals bright, link so true, connect all hearts, make us new." Visualize the circle creating an energetic network of love and understanding worldwide.

43. World Protection Spray
Mix sea salt and water in a spray bottle, adding a few drops of lavender oil. Walk around your space, spraying the mixture, and say: "Water of guard, scent so clear, bless this world, draw us near." Visualize the mist protecting the earth from harm.

44. Candle of Forgiveness
Carve a wave symbol into a blue candle. Light it and say: "Flame of peace, burn so true, wash away hate, make it new." Visualize the candle's light spreading forgiveness and reconciliation among people worldwide.

45. Crystal of Calm for Oceans
Hold a piece of aquamarine and say: "Stone of water, calm so true, bless the oceans, make them new." Place the crystal on a map of the oceans to send calming energy to the world's waters.

46. Candle for the Hungry
Carve the word "Nourish" into a green candle. Light it and say: "Flame of hope, burn so bright, feed the hungry, through the night." Visualize the candle's light providing nourishment to those in need.

47. Amethyst Circle for Mental Health

Place an amethyst crystal in the center of a circle of lavender sprigs. Light a white candle and say: "Flame of calm, stone so bright, bless all minds, through the night." Visualize the energy of the circle promoting mental health and peace for all.

48. Pine Protection for Wildlife

Scatter pine needles around an animal figurine on your altar. Light a candle and say: "Pine of guard, circle so true, protect the creatures, old and new." Visualize the circle protecting wildlife and natural habitats worldwide.

49. World Tree Blessing

Hold an evergreen branch and say: "Tree of life, strength so true, bless this world, make it new." Place the branch on your altar to symbolize the world tree, sending its strength and blessings to all living beings.

50. Candle of Global Renewal

Carve a spiral into a green candle. Light it on Yule night, saying: "Flame of growth, burn so clear, renew this world, draw it near." Visualize the candle's light bringing renewal, hope, and harmony to every corner of the earth.

Appendix

Appendix A: Glossary: Definitions of Key Terms and Symbols

This glossary provides detailed definitions of key terms, symbols, and concepts used throughout the spell book. It serves as a reference guide to deepen your understanding of the magical practices and symbols woven into the Yule spells, rituals, and traditions. Whether you're a beginner or an experienced practitioner, this glossary will help clarify the terminology and enhance your spellcasting experience.

A

- **Abundance**: In magical terms, abundance represents an overflowing of positive energy, prosperity, wealth, or success. Spells for abundance often involve drawing in prosperity and blessings into one's life.
- **Altar**: A sacred space or surface used for magical work, meditation, and rituals. It is typically decorated with candles, crystals, herbs, tools, and symbolic items related to the spell or ritual being performed.
- **Amethyst**: A purple quartz crystal associated with spiritual growth, intuition, peace, and healing. Used in spells for clarity, wisdom, and calming the mind.
- **Anointing**: The act of applying oil to an object or body part in order to consecrate or empower it with magical properties. Anointing is often used to charge candles, talismans, and other tools with specific energies.

- **Aquamarine**: A pale blue gemstone linked with water energy. It symbolizes calmness, clarity, and communication. Used in spells for emotional healing, peace, and enhancing intuition.
- **Athame**: A ritual knife, typically double-edged, used in various magical traditions for directing energy, casting circles, and cutting through negative influences. It is not used for physical cutting but rather for spiritual or energetic work.

B

- **Bath Ritual**: A cleansing spell involving soaking in water infused with herbs, salts, oils, or crystals. Bath rituals are used for purification, relaxation, and filling oneself with positive energy.
- **Binding**: A magical act of restricting or containing energy, usually to prevent harm or unwanted influences. Binding spells are used to protect, stop negative behavior, or banish negative energy.
- **Black Candle**: Represents protection, banishing negativity, and releasing unwanted energies. Often used in spells for protection, transformation, and releasing negative influences.
- **Blessing**: A spell or ritual performed to invoke positive energies, bestow goodwill, or bring forth divine protection. Blessings can be for individuals, spaces, objects, or global peace.

C

- **Candles**: Essential tools in spellcasting, representing the element of Fire. Different candle colors symbolize various intentions, such as green for prosperity, pink for love, white for purity, and black for protection.
- **Casting**: The act of performing a spell or ritual. Casting involves focusing energy, using words of power, tools, and ingredients to bring about a desired effect.

- **Cedar**: A sacred herb used for purification, grounding, and protection. In Yule rituals, cedar brings the strength and endurance of the forest, helping to connect with Earth energy.
- **Circle**: A sacred, magical space created by casting a boundary (often with an athame or wand) for protection during spellwork. The circle serves as a container for raised energy and a shield against unwanted influences.
- **Citrine**: A yellow crystal associated with the Sun, abundance, joy, and success. Used in spells for manifesting prosperity, boosting confidence, and enhancing creativity.
- **Clarity**: The state of being clear-minded, free from confusion or mental clutter. In spellwork, clarity is sought to gain insight, make decisions, and understand truths.
- **Crystal Grid**: An arrangement of crystals on a surface in a specific geometric pattern to direct energy toward a specific goal. Each crystal is chosen for its properties to amplify the grid's intention, such as healing, protection, or abundance.

D

- **Divination**: The practice of seeking knowledge of the future, unknown information, or insight through various methods such as tarot, runes, scrying, or pendulums. Often used during Yule to reflect on the past year and set intentions for the future.
- **Drawing Down**: The process of invoking energy from a celestial source, such as the moon, stars, or sun, into oneself or an object. Common in rituals during the full moon phase.
- **Dream Spell**: A spell that influences dreams, often for the purpose of gaining insight, healing, or setting intentions during sleep. Dream spells often include herbs like lavender and crystals like amethyst.

E

- **Elemental Magic**: Magic that involves the four classical elements—Earth, Water, Fire, and Air. Each element corresponds to different aspects of nature and the human experience. For example, Earth represents grounding and abundance, Water represents emotions and intuition, Fire symbolizes transformation and passion, and Air corresponds to intellect and communication.
- **Evergreen**: Trees like pine, fir, and cedar that retain their foliage throughout the year. Symbolizes immortality, resilience, and life force. Used in Yule spells for protection, renewal, and connecting with nature's enduring energy.
- **Epsom Salt**: A mineral compound used in magical baths for cleansing, relaxation, and spiritual detoxification. It draws out negative energy and replenishes the spirit.

F

- **Full Moon**: A phase of the moon when it is fully illuminated. Represents completion, manifestation, and peak energy. Full Moon rituals are ideal for charging crystals, performing divination, and spells for abundance or release.
- **Frankincense**: A sacred resin used in incense, associated with purification, spiritual growth, and protection. Its warm, resinous aroma is often used to cleanse spaces and enhance meditation during Yule rituals.

G

- **Green Candle**: Represents growth, abundance, prosperity, and healing. Used in spells for manifesting wealth, good health, and nurturing new beginnings.
- **Grounding**: The practice of connecting one's energy to the Earth, stabilizing and balancing emotions, thoughts, and spirit. Often achieved through visualization, crystals, or contact with nature, grounding is crucial before and after spellwork.

H

- **Herbs**: Plants used in spellcraft for their magical properties. Common Yule herbs include rosemary (protection), pine (strength), cinnamon (abundance and warmth), and lavender (calm and love).
- **Healing**: In magical terms, healing refers to restoring balance and well-being on physical, emotional, mental, or spiritual levels. Healing spells can involve crystals, herbs, candles, and visualization.
- **Holly**: An evergreen plant symbolizing protection, endurance, and the cycle of life and death. Used in Yule spells and decorations to invite prosperity and ward off negative energies.

I

- **Incense**: A fragrant material that, when burned, releases aromatic smoke. Used in rituals for purification, consecration, or as an offering to deities and spirits. Incense can also enhance the energy of spellwork.
- **Intention**: The focused desire or purpose behind a spell. Setting a clear intention is the first step in successful spellwork, directing energy toward the desired outcome.

J

- **Jar Spell**: A type of spell where ingredients are sealed in a jar to concentrate and continuously radiate magical energy. Jar spells are used for protection, abundance, love, and more.

L

- **Lavender**: A herb used for its calming, protective, and healing properties. Incorporated into Yule rituals to promote peace, relaxation, and love.
- **Luck**: A favorable outcome or fortune, often invoked in spells to attract good opportunities, positive events, and success.

M

- **Meditation**: A practice of focused contemplation or mindfulness to connect with one's inner self, higher consciousness, or the energies around them. Used in spellwork to prepare the mind, set intentions, and receive guidance.
- **Moon Phases**: The cyclical changes of the moon, each phase carrying specific energies for magical work. Common phases used in Yule spellwork include the New Moon (beginnings and intention-setting), Full Moon (manifestation and completion), and Waning Moon (release and letting go).

N

- **New Moon**: The dark phase of the moon cycle, representing new beginnings, rebirth, and potential. Ideal for spells that involve setting intentions, starting new projects, or planting seeds for the future.

O

- **Obsidian**: A black volcanic glass used for protection, grounding, and uncovering hidden truths. Snowflake obsidian, with its white inclusions, represents purity and the light within darkness, making it fitting for Yule rituals.
- **Offering**: A gift presented to spirits, deities, or nature as an act of gratitude or to request their blessings. Offerings can include food, drink, incense, flowers, or other items.

P

- **Pentacle**: A five-pointed star enclosed in a circle, representing the elements (Earth, Water, Fire, Air, and Spirit) in harmony. Used for protection, balance, and as a symbol of the interconnectedness of all things.
- **Protection**: The act of shielding oneself, others, or spaces from negative influences, energies, or harm. Protection spells often involve herbs, crystals, candles, or symbols like circles and pentacles.
- **Purification**: The process of cleansing oneself, an object, or space of negative energy. Methods include smoke cleansing, salt, water, herbs, and crystals.

Q

- **Quartz**: A versatile crystal that comes in many forms, each with different properties. Clear quartz amplifies energy, rose quartz attracts love, and smoky quartz grounds and protects.

R

- **Rosemary**: An herb associated with protection, cleansing, and mental clarity. Often burned as incense or used in sachets to ward off negativity and purify spaces.
- **Runes**: An ancient alphabetic script used in divination and magical workings. Each rune carries a specific meaning and energy, often used for guidance and setting intentions.

S

- **Sachet**: A small cloth bag filled with herbs, crystals, or other magical ingredients, used as a charm for protection, love, abundance, or healing.
- **Scrying**: The practice of looking into a reflective surface (such as a mirror, water, or crystal) to receive visions, messages, or insights. Commonly used during Yule to gain wisdom for the coming year.
- **Snow**: Represents purity, transformation, and stillness. Used in Yule spells for cleansing, renewal, and preserving wishes.

T

- **Talismans**: Objects imbued with magical energy to serve a specific purpose, such as protection, luck, or health. Talismans can be jewelry, stones, or other items consecrated during rituals.
- **Transformation**: The process of change, growth, or becoming something new. Transformation spells focus on inner growth, releasing old patterns, and welcoming new possibilities.

W

- **Wand**: A ritual tool used for directing energy during spellcasting, often made from wood, crystal, or metal. The wand represents the element of Air or Fire, depending on tradition.
- **White Candle**: Symbolizes purity, peace, protection, and spiritual strength. Used in Yule spells for cleansing, blessings, and invoking light.
- **Winter Solstice**: Also known as Yule, it marks the longest night of the year and the return of the sun. A time of celebration, renewal, reflection, and the welcoming of light.

Y

- **Yule**: The Winter Solstice celebration, honoring the rebirth of the sun, the cycle of nature, and the return of light. It is a time for gathering with loved ones, introspection, and spellwork for the coming year.
- **Yule Log**: A traditional piece of wood burned during Yule rituals, symbolizing warmth, light, and the promise of spring. Modern versions may be decorated and kept as a centerpiece on the altar.

This glossary is meant to provide clarity and insight into the language of Yule magic. Use it as a guide to deepen your understanding of the terms and symbols found throughout this spell book, enhancing your connection to the rituals and their meanings.

Appendix B: Yule Correspondences: A Reference Guide to Herbs, Crystals, Colors, and Symbols Associated with Yule Magic

Yule, the Winter Solstice, is a time of profound energy shifts and magic. In celebrating the return of the light, practitioners draw upon a range of natural elements, symbols, and colors to enhance their spellwork. This appendix serves as a comprehensive reference guide to the herbs, crystals, colors, and symbols most commonly associated with Yule magic. By understanding and using these correspondences, you can align your spells with the powerful energies of the season and deepen your connection to the spirit of Yule.

Herbs and Plants

Yule herbs and plants are chosen for their connection to winter, protection, renewal, and the welcoming of light. Here are some of the most common Yule herbs:

1. Pine

- **Attributes**: Strength, resilience, protection, prosperity, purification
- **Uses**: Pine needles and cones are often used in spells for protection, renewal, and attracting prosperity. Pine branches are popular in Yule wreaths and altar decorations, symbolizing eternal life and the resilience of nature.

2. Holly

- **Attributes**: Protection, luck, courage, endurance
- **Uses**: Holly leaves and berries are used for protection spells, often hung in homes to ward off negative energies. Holly wreaths symbolize the cycle of life, death, and rebirth, and are used to invite luck and courage during Yule.

3. Cedar

- **Attributes**: Purification, healing, protection, grounding
- **Uses**: Cedar is burned as incense for purification and protection. Cedarwood essential oil is used in grounding rituals, providing a connection to the earth's energy and fostering emotional balance.

4. Rosemary

- **Attributes**: Protection, purification, love, memory
- **Uses**: Often burned as incense to cleanse spaces, rosemary is also added to sachets for protection. Its associations with memory make it a powerful herb for Yule rituals focused on reflection and setting intentions.

5. Cinnamon

- **Attributes**: Warmth, prosperity, protection, love
- **Uses**: Cinnamon sticks are used in spells to attract prosperity and protection. Its warm, spicy scent makes it a popular addition to Yule candles, incense, and potpourri, invoking the warmth and joy of the season.

6. Ivy

- **Attributes**: Endurance, fidelity, protection, growth
- **Uses**: Ivy is used in Yule wreaths and garlands as a symbol of enduring life and spiritual growth. It also serves as a protective charm when woven into wreaths or worn as a talisman.

7. Frankincense

- **Attributes**: Purification, spiritual growth, protection, healing
- **Uses**: Burned as incense during Yule rituals to purify the space and invite spiritual awareness. Frankincense essential oil is also used to anoint candles and talismans for added protection and divine connection.

8. Myrrh

- **Attributes**: Healing, protection, transformation, spiritual connection
- **Uses**: Burned alongside frankincense, myrrh enhances spiritual growth and healing. It is often used in Yule rituals to transform negative energy and invite divine guidance.

9. Lavender

- **Attributes**: Peace, love, purification, relaxation
- **Uses**: Used in spells to promote peace, love, and calm. Lavender is commonly added to Yule sachets and incense to encourage relaxation and emotional healing.

10. Cloves

- **Attributes**: Protection, prosperity, courage, purification
- **Uses**: Cloves are added to Yule pomanders, incense, and spells to bring warmth, courage, and protection. They are also used in abundance rituals to attract prosperity.

Crystals

Yule crystals resonate with the energies of protection, renewal, strength, and the returning light. They amplify the intentions set during the Winter Solstice, aiding in spiritual growth and healing.

1. Clear Quartz

- **Attributes**: Amplification, clarity, energy, protection
- **Uses**: Clear quartz is a master healer and amplifier of intentions, making it a versatile crystal in Yule rituals. It can be placed on altars to enhance spellwork and cleanse the space of negativity.

2. Amethyst

- **Attributes**: Spiritual growth, intuition, peace, healing
- **Uses**: Used for meditation and dream spells during Yule to enhance intuition and spiritual growth. Amethyst aids in calming the mind and promotes clarity during times of introspection.

3. Rose Quartz

- **Attributes**: Love, compassion, emotional healing, harmony
- **Uses**: Incorporated into Yule spells for love and friendship, rose quartz fosters self-love and compassion. It can be placed in the home or on the altar to promote a harmonious and loving atmosphere.

4. Snowflake Obsidian

- **Attributes**: Balance, grounding, protection, transformation
- **Uses**: Used in Yule rituals for grounding and releasing negative patterns. Snowflake obsidian helps to find the light within the darkness and balance the spirit during winter's introspective period.

5. Garnet

- **Attributes**: Strength, passion, vitality, protection
- **Uses**: Garnet is a stone of strength and regeneration, often used in Yule rituals to reignite passion and energy for the new year. It can be worn as jewelry or placed on the altar to foster courage and drive.

6. Green Aventurine

- **Attributes**: Abundance, prosperity, luck, growth
- **Uses**: Placed on Yule altars or carried as a charm to attract prosperity and encourage personal growth. Green aventurine resonates with the energy of the returning light, bringing luck and positive opportunities.

7. Citrine

- **Attributes**: Abundance, joy, success, energy
- **Uses**: Used in Yule spells to attract abundance, success, and happiness. Citrine's bright, sunny energy is ideal for rituals celebrating the return of the sun and new beginnings.

8. Tiger's Eye

- **Attributes**: Courage, strength, protection, grounding
- **Uses**: Used in Yule rituals to enhance inner strength, courage, and stability. Tiger's eye is worn or carried as a talisman to ground energy and protect against negativity.

Colors

The colors associated with Yule reflect the natural world during the Winter Solstice and the themes of light, renewal, and warmth.

1. Green

- **Attributes**: Renewal, growth, prosperity, fertility
- **Uses**: Representing the evergreens, green is used in Yule decorations, candles, and talismans to symbolize renewal, abundance, and the promise of spring.

2. Red

- **Attributes**: Passion, vitality, strength, love
- **Uses**: Symbolizing warmth and life force, red candles are used in Yule rituals to invoke strength, courage, and love. It also represents the berries of holly, a traditional Yule plant.

3. White

- **Attributes**: Purity, peace, protection, spiritual strength
- **Uses**: White candles and crystals are used to represent the snow-covered landscape, purity, and the light of the returning sun. White is also used in spells for protection and cleansing.

4. Gold

- **Attributes**: Sun energy, success, abundance, vitality
- **Uses**: Gold symbolizes the return of the sun's light at Yule. Gold candles and decorations are used to attract abundance, success, and joy in the coming year.

5. Silver

- **Attributes**: Moon energy, reflection, intuition, protection
- **Uses**: Silver represents the moon's light and the quiet reflection of winter. It is used in Yule rituals to enhance intuition, promote inner peace, and invoke the energies of the moon.

6. Blue

- **Attributes**: Calm, healing, peace, clarity
- **Uses**: Blue candles and decorations are used to invoke tranquility and promote healing. Blue is also associated with water and ice, representing the quiet, contemplative aspect of winter.

Symbols

Symbols are powerful tools in Yule magic, representing deeper meanings and energies. They can be incorporated into spells, altar decorations, and ritual tools.

1. Evergreen Wreath

- **Attributes**: Eternal life, strength, protection, the cycle of the seasons
- **Uses**: Hung on doors or placed on altars, the wreath represents the eternal cycle of life, death, and rebirth. It invites protection, luck, and prosperity into the home.

2. Yule Log

- **Attributes**: Light, warmth, rebirth, family unity
- **Uses**: Traditionally burned on the hearth during Yule, the Yule log symbolizes the return of the sun and the warmth of family gatherings. It is often decorated with symbols of the season, such as holly, pine cones, and candles.

3. Pentacle

- **Attributes**: Balance, protection, harmony, the elements
- **Uses**: A five-pointed star enclosed in a circle, the pentacle represents the harmony of the elements (Earth, Air, Fire, Water, and Spirit). Used in Yule rituals to invoke balance, protection, and connection with nature.

4. Sun

- **Attributes**: Light, life force, vitality, renewal
- **Uses**: The sun is a central symbol of Yule, representing the rebirth of light and the warmth that will return to the earth. Sun symbols are used in spells for energy, abundance, and positive transformations.

5. Stars

- **Attributes**: Guidance, hope, inspiration, light in darkness
- **Uses**: Stars symbolize the light of hope and inspiration in the winter darkness. Used in Yule spells to guide intentions, inspire dreams, and remind us of the light within ourselves.

6. Snowflakes

- **Attributes**: Purity, transformation, uniqueness, stillness
- **Uses**: Representing the purity and stillness of winter, snowflakes are used in Yule spells for cleansing, inner reflection, and embracing change.

Conclusion

This reference guide to Yule correspondences provides insight into the herbs, crystals, colors, and symbols that embody the spirit of the Winter Solstice. By incorporating these correspondences into your spellwork, you align yourself with the energies of Yule, enhancing your magic and deepening your connection to the season's transformative power.

Appendix C: Moon Phase Calendar: A Calendar of Moon Phases Relevant to Yule and Spellcasting

The moon phases hold a central role in magical practices, influencing the energy that we draw upon for spellcasting. During Yule, the moon's influence can enhance our rituals, intentions, and meditative practices, aligning our magic with the natural ebb and flow of energy. This appendix provides a detailed calendar of moon phases relevant to Yule, offering insight into the types of spells that are best suited for each phase during the winter season. Understanding and timing your spellwork with the moon's cycles can significantly amplify its power and effectiveness.

Overview of Moon Phases

Before diving into the calendar, it's important to understand the basic moon phases and how they influence spellcasting:

- **New Moon**: A time for new beginnings, setting intentions, and planting the seeds for future growth.
- **Waxing Crescent**: Ideal for spells that focus on growth, attraction, and bringing in new opportunities.
- **First Quarter**: Best for taking action, overcoming obstacles, and decision-making.
- **Waxing Gibbous**: A phase for refining intentions, making final adjustments, and building momentum.
- **Full Moon**: A time of manifestation, celebration, peak energy, and completing goals.
- **Waning Gibbous**: Suitable for gratitude, sharing results, and beginning to release what is no longer needed.
- **Last Quarter**: Ideal for letting go, banishing negativity, and making room for new beginnings.
- **Waning Crescent**: A time for rest, reflection, and inner work in preparation for the next cycle.

Yule Moon Phase Calendar
December (Yule Season)

Yule typically falls on December 21st or 22nd, the Winter Solstice, which marks the longest night of the year and the return of the light. The moon phases around this date provide a magical backdrop for spell-casting that aligns with the themes of rebirth, introspection, and renewal.

December 1-4: Last Quarter Moon

- **Energy**: Release, banishing, letting go
- **Best Spells**: Spells for letting go of negativity, releasing bad habits, and clearing obstacles.
- **Yule Connection**: As you prepare for Yule, use this time to clear away what no longer serves you. This creates a clean slate, allowing for the new light and energy of the solstice to fill your life. Use banishing rituals with herbs like rosemary or cedar to cleanse your space and spirit.

December 5-10: Waning Crescent Moon

- **Energy**: Rest, reflection, preparation
- **Best Spells**: Meditation, introspection, rest, and quiet inner work.
- **Yule Connection**: The waning crescent before Yule is perfect for slowing down, reflecting on the past year, and contemplating your intentions for the new year. Use this phase to perform inner peace spells and dream rituals to gain insight and clarity about your path forward.

December 11: New Moon

- **Energy**: New beginnings, intention-setting, planting seeds
- **Best Spells**: New beginnings, goal-setting, manifestation.
- **Yule Connection**: The New Moon in December is powerful for setting intentions for the upcoming Yule season. This is the time to plant the seeds of change and renewal you wish to manifest with the return of the sun. Perform candle rituals to set your intentions, using white or silver candles to symbolize the moon's energy.

December 12-18: Waxing Crescent Moon

- **Energy**: Growth, attraction, building energy
- **Best Spells**: Spells for growth, prosperity, attracting new opportunities, and strengthening intentions.
- **Yule Connection**: As the moon begins to grow, focus on spells that attract prosperity, health, and positivity into your life in preparation for Yule. Use crystals like citrine or green aventurine during this phase to enhance spells for abundance and personal growth.

December 19: First Quarter Moon

- **Energy**: Action, overcoming obstacles, decision-making
- **Best Spells**: Spells for courage, making decisions, taking action, and problem-solving.
- **Yule Connection**: The first quarter moon is an excellent time to take tangible steps toward the goals you set during the New Moon. Use this energy to solidify your Yule preparations, creating protective charms or setting up your Yule altar. Perform

spells with herbs like cedar and rosemary to invoke strength and courage.

December 20-24: Waxing Gibbous Moon

- **Energy**: Refinement, progress, preparation
- **Best Spells**: Spells for refining intentions, building momentum, and finalizing plans.
- **Yule Connection**: This phase is all about refining your intentions and preparations as you approach Yule. Use the waxing gibbous energy to create blessing jars, bake enchanted Yule treats, or prepare gifts infused with positive energy. Focus on spells that amplify joy, warmth, and love in your life.

December 21-22: Yule (Winter Solstice)

- **Energy**: Rebirth, renewal, return of light
- **Best Spells**: Spells for rebirth, renewal, celebration, manifestation, and invoking the return of the sun.
- **Yule Connection**: On the night of Yule, regardless of the moon phase, perform rituals to honor the return of the light. Light candles to symbolize the sun's rebirth, and cast spells for personal transformation and new beginnings. Create Yule talismans with symbols of the sun, evergreen wreaths, and gold candles.

December 25-27: Full Moon

- **Energy**: Manifestation, peak energy, celebration, completion
- **Best Spells**: Spells for manifestation, gratitude, celebration, and completing goals.
- **Yule Connection**: The Full Moon's energy is especially potent during this time. Use it to manifest your Yule wishes, amplifying the power of spells for abundance, health, and peace. This is also

an ideal phase for divination rituals to gain insight into the new year. Perform gratitude rituals with crystals like amethyst and rose quartz to celebrate the light returning to the earth.

December 28-31: Waning Gibbous Moon

- **Energy**: Gratitude, sharing results, releasing excess
- **Best Spells**: Spells for giving thanks, releasing what is not needed, and preparing for future growth.
- **Yule Connection**: As the moon begins to wane after its fullness, focus on gratitude and reflection. Perform spells to release any lingering negativity, creating space for the new year's light and blessings. Incorporate herbs like sage and lavender into your rituals to promote peace and cleansing.

January (Post-Yule Period)

After Yule, the energy of the moon continues to influence the transition into the new year. Use these phases to solidify your intentions and continue your journey of transformation.

January 1-4: Last Quarter Moon

- **Energy**: Release, letting go, banishing
- **Best Spells**: Spells for releasing negativity, breaking bad habits, and clearing obstacles.
- **Post-Yule Connection**: Begin the new year by releasing the past. Perform cleansing rituals using salt, rosemary, and snowflake obsidian to rid yourself of old patterns. This sets a clear path for embracing the light and new opportunities.

January 5-9: Waning Crescent Moon

- **Energy**: Rest, reflection, preparation
- **Best Spells**: Meditation, rest, inner work, and preparing for new cycles.
- **Post-Yule Connection**: Use this phase to reflect on your Yule intentions and goals for the year. This is a quiet time for introspection, allowing you to rest and recharge before the next New Moon.

January 10: New Moon

- **Energy**: New beginnings, intention-setting, planting seeds
- **Best Spells**: Spells for fresh starts, new goals, and setting intentions.
- **Post-Yule Connection**: The first New Moon of the year is a powerful time to set new intentions. Use it to reinforce the resolutions and transformations you began during Yule, planting the seeds for growth and abundance throughout the coming months.

Tips for Yule Moon Magic

- **Align Your Spells**: Use the moon phase that aligns with your intention to enhance the power of your spellwork. For example, start manifestation spells on the New Moon, and work on release or cleansing during the Waning Moon.
- **Use Lunar Correspondences**: Incorporate colors (silver, white), crystals (moonstone, amethyst), and herbs (mugwort, lavender) associated with the moon in your rituals for added strength.
- **Charge Your Tools**: Place crystals, candles, and other magical tools under the moonlight during the appropriate phase to charge them with lunar energy.

This Moon Phase Calendar is designed to help you connect with the natural rhythms of the moon during the Yule season. By aligning your spellcasting with these phases, you can amplify your intentions and embrace the transformative energy of the Winter Solstice.

Appendix D: Seasonal Incantations: A Collection of Short Incantations for Quick Spell Work During Yule

Yule, the Winter Solstice, is a time when the magic of the season is especially potent. As the world embraces the returning light, even the simplest of incantations can carry powerful energy. This appendix offers a collection of short, potent incantations designed for quick spell work during the Yule season. Each incantation is crafted to focus intent and draw on the energies of Yule, allowing you to quickly weave magic into daily activities, rituals, or moments of need. Whether used for protection, love, healing, or prosperity, these incantations can enhance your magical practice in alignment with the season.

Protection Incantations

1. Winter Shield Incantation

"Winter winds, cold and clear,
Shield this home, hold us near.
In this place, harm shall cease,
Bring us warmth, guard with peace."

Use this incantation while sprinkling salt or laying down protective herbs at doorways or windows to create a protective barrier around your home.

2. Evergreen Ward

"Evergreen, bold and true,
Guard this space, old and new.
Roots of strength, leaves of might,
Protect this home, day and night."

Recite this incantation as you hang an evergreen wreath or garland on your door, invoking the tree's protective qualities.

3. Candle of Protection

"Flame of Yule, burning bright,
Guard this home through the night.
By this light, keep us whole,
Shield us now, protect each soul."

Chant this while lighting a white or black candle to invoke its protective power, allowing the flame to act as a ward against negative energies.

4. Snow-Cleansing Spell

"Snow so pure, cold and bright,
Cleanse this space with winter's light.
Wash away all dark and fear,
Leave but peace and warmth held near."

Use this incantation when sprinkling snow or snow water around your space to cleanse it of negativity.

5. Holly Guard Incantation

"Holly bright, with berries red,
Guard this place, keep harm in dread.
Spikes of green, nature's shield,
From all evil, this space is sealed."

Chant this as you place holly sprigs around your home for a natural protective barrier.

Love and Friendship Incantations

6. Yule Love Light

"Flame of warmth, heart so true,
Bring me love, old and new.
Light the way, shine so clear,
Fill my life with love sincere."

Recite this as you light a pink or red candle to attract love, whether self-love or romantic, into your life.

7. Friendship Bonding Spell

"Friendship's spark, strong and bright,
May it grow through Yule's night.
With this spell, hearts entwine,
Bless this bond with love divine."

Use this incantation when giving a handmade gift to a friend, infusing it with your intention to strengthen your bond.

8. Pinecone of Affection

"Pine of green, seed so small,
Bring love and joy to one and all.
May hearts grow close, warm and kind,
In this spell, let love we find."

Whisper this incantation into a pinecone before placing it on your altar or gifting it to a loved one.

9. Winter's Embrace

"Winter winds, soft and light,
Wrap me in love, through this night.
Tender warmth, hearts align,
Blessed be this love divine."

Recite this while holding a piece of rose quartz to invite love, warmth, and affection into your life or relationship.

10. Evergreen Love Charm

"Evergreen bright, standing tall,
Love and joy to those who call.
Bless this space, hearts entwine,
In this season, love be mine."

Use this incantation while tying a ribbon around an evergreen branch to create a love charm for your space.

Healing and Peace Incantations
11. Snowflake Healing
"Snowflake pure, cold and white,
Heal this soul through Yule's night.
Mend and soothe, bring to rest,
Peaceful heart, may I be blessed."

Chant this while holding a piece of snowflake obsidian to promote emotional healing and inner peace.

12. Candle of Peace
"Flame of peace, burn so bright,
Calm this heart, through the night.
Still the mind, ease all woe,
Bring me peace, let it flow."

Recite this as you light a blue or lavender candle to invoke a sense of calm and tranquility.

13. Wintergreen Healing
"Wintergreen, cool and clear,
Heal my body, bring peace near.
In this stillness, I find light,
Restore my health, day and night."

Use this incantation while anointing your hands with wintergreen oil for a spell of physical and emotional healing.

14. Yule Bath of Calm
"Water warm, herbs of peace,
Cleanse this body, bring release.
Wash away stress and pain,
In this bath, health regain."

Whisper this incantation over a bath infused with lavender and rosemary to soothe the body and mind.

15. Pine of Renewal
"Pine so green, life so strong,
Bring me strength, where I belong.
Heal and renew, like the tree,
Grant me peace, so mote it be."
Chant this as you place pine branches or cones on your altar to invoke their renewing energy.

Abundance and Prosperity Incantations

16. Yule Prosperity Spell
"Gold and green, Yule's bright cheer,
Bring me wealth through this year.
Open paths, clear the way,
Prosperity grows, day by day."
Use this incantation while lighting a green or gold candle to attract abundance and prosperity into your life.

17. Cinnamon Luck
"Cinnamon warm, spice so sweet,
Bring me luck, swift and fleet.
Fortune's wheel, turn my way,
Blessings bright, come today."
Recite this while burning cinnamon incense or placing a cinnamon stick on your altar to draw in luck and good fortune.

18. Pinecone Wealth Charm

"Pinecone small, seed so bright,
Bring me wealth, day and night.
Grow my fortune, steady and true,
Abundance comes, old and new."

Whisper this incantation into a pinecone before using it as a charm for attracting financial prosperity.

19. Snow Prosperity

"Snow of white, pure and clear,
Draw in wealth, bring it near.
From the earth, gold and grain,
Fill my life, abundance reign."

Use this incantation while sprinkling snow or snow water around your space to invite prosperity and blessings.

20. Herb of Abundance

"Rosemary bright, herb of old,
Bring to me, wealth untold.
By your power, luck be mine,
Prosperity flows, gift divine."

Chant this while hanging a sprig of rosemary above your door to attract abundance into your home.

Inner Strength and Transformation Incantations

21. Yule Strength

"Winter's cold, strong and clear,
Grant me strength, hold it near.
Courage bright, in heart reside,
Through this change, be my guide."

Recite this while holding a piece of tiger's eye crystal to draw on its strength and courage during times of transformation.

22. Candle of Transformation
"Flame of change, burn so bright,
Transform my soul through this night.
Old to new, let me grow,
Guide my path, let light flow."
Use this incantation when lighting a purple or white candle to invoke personal transformation and growth.

23. Crystal of Courage
"Stone of earth, strong and true,
Grant me courage, make me new.
Hold me firm, keep me whole,
Guide my steps, free my soul."
Chant this as you hold a piece of garnet or carnelian, infusing yourself with the crystal's transformative power.

24. Moonlight of Renewal
"Moonlight bright, silver hue,
Renew my strength, make me true.
Wash away what's old and worn,
Let me rise, reborn, reborn."
Use this incantation when standing under the moonlight to renew your spirit and set intentions for transformation.

25. Snow Reflection
"Snow of light, pure and still,
Reflect my truth, guide my will.
In your silence, I find me,
Strength and peace, so mote it be."
Recite this while gazing at freshly fallen snow, using its purity as a mirror for self-reflection and inner strength.

Quick Blessings and Gratitude Incantations

26. Gratitude Offering

"Yule's bright light, blessings near,
I give thanks, pure and clear.
For this day, for love and cheer,
Grateful heart, I hold dear."

Whisper this incantation when placing an offering on your altar to express gratitude during the Yule season.

27. Pine of Blessings

"Pine so green, life's delight,
Bless this space, with love's light.
Joy and warmth, here shall grow,
Blessings bright, ever flow."

Chant this as you place pine branches or wreaths around your home to invite blessings and positive energy.

28. Yule Feast Blessing

"Food of earth, gift so fine,
Bless this meal, may it shine.
Health and joy, love's embrace,
Fill our hearts, bless this space."

Recite this short blessing before sharing a Yule meal to invoke love, warmth, and togetherness.

29. Candle of Joy

"Flame of joy, light so clear,
Fill this space with warmth and cheer.
Happiness bright, love's embrace,
Bless this home, bless this place."

Use this incantation when lighting a yellow or gold candle to invite joy and celebration into your space.

30. Morning Blessing
"Sun of Yule, rising bright,
Fill my day with love and light.
Guide my steps, show the way,
Bless my path, this winter's day."

Whisper this incantation upon waking to bless your day with positivity and light during the Yule season.

These seasonal incantations are crafted to align with the magical energies of Yule. They are short yet potent, designed for quick spell work that you can easily integrate into your daily routine or rituals. Whether you are casting for protection, love, healing, prosperity, or transformation, these incantations provide a simple way to harness the season's magic and draw it into your life.

Appendix E: Further Reading: Recommended Books, Articles, and Websites for In-Depth Study of Yule and Magical Practices

The magic of Yule is steeped in rich traditions, folklore, and rituals that have been passed down through centuries. For those seeking to deepen their understanding of Yule, its practices, and the magical arts in general, this appendix provides a comprehensive list of further reading. From books that explore the historical and spiritual aspects of Yule to resources on spellcraft, herbs, crystals, and the cycles of the moon, these recommendations will offer valuable insights and guidance. This curated selection includes books, articles, and websites for practitioners at all levels, whether you are a beginner or an advanced practitioner.

Books

The following books are chosen for their depth of knowledge on Yule, the Winter Solstice, and various aspects of magical practice. Each offers a unique perspective, providing both historical context and practical guides to enhance your spellwork during Yule and beyond.

1. "The Winter Solstice: The Sacred Traditions of Christmas" by John Matthews

- **Overview**: This book explores the origins and traditions of the Winter Solstice, highlighting the customs and spiritual significance of Yule. Matthews delves into the rituals, myths, and lore surrounding the season, including Yule's connection to ancient pagan festivals.
- **Why Read**: A fantastic starting point for understanding the historical roots of Yule and its influence on modern celebrations. It provides inspiration for incorporating traditional Yule elements into your magical practices.

2. "Yule: Rituals, Recipes & Lore for the Winter Solstice" by Susan Pesznecker

- **Overview**: Part of the "Llewellyn's Sabbat Essentials" series, this book provides an accessible and comprehensive guide to Yule. It covers the history of Yule, modern practices, crafts, rituals, and magical workings related to the season.
- **Why Read**: Offers practical suggestions for celebrating Yule, including spells, recipes, and crafts. Perfect for anyone looking to integrate seasonal rituals into their magical practice.

3. "The Wicca Bible: The Definitive Guide to Magic and the Craft" by Ann-Marie Gallagher

- **Overview**: This comprehensive guide covers Wiccan beliefs, practices, spells, and rituals, providing insight into the craft as a whole. The section on seasonal celebrations includes information on Yule, with suggestions for rituals and correspondences.
- **Why Read**: A valuable resource for understanding how Yule fits into the broader Wheel of the Year in Wiccan tradition. It's an excellent guide for beginners exploring seasonal magic.

4. "A Year of Ritual: Sabbats & Esbats for Solitaries & Covens" by Sandra Kynes

- **Overview**: Kynes offers rituals and celebrations for all eight sabbats, including Yule, as well as esbat (moon) rituals. This book provides both solitary and group rituals, making it adaptable for different practitioners.
- **Why Read**: The detailed Yule rituals and seasonal spells make this an essential addition to your magical library, offering inspiration for crafting personalized ceremonies.

5. "Earth Power: Techniques of Natural Magic" by Scott Cunningham

- **Overview**: This classic guide explores the use of natural elements in magic, including earth, air, fire, and water. While not specifically focused on Yule, it offers a wealth of information on using herbs, stones, candles, and natural forces in spellwork.
- **Why Read**: Provides foundational knowledge on using natural correspondences, which is crucial for enhancing your Yule spellwork. Cunningham's straightforward approach makes this a must-read for beginners.

6. "Llewellyn's Complete Book of Correspondences: A Comprehensive & Cross-Referenced Resource for Pagans & Wiccans" by Sandra Kynes

- **Overview**: This extensive reference book provides correspondences for every aspect of magical practice, including herbs, crystals, colors, moon phases, and seasonal celebrations like Yule.
- **Why Read**: An indispensable resource for creating your own Yule spells, rituals, and incantations. It allows you to quickly find the appropriate correspondences for any magical working.

7. "Crystals for Healing: The Complete Reference Guide with Over 200 Remedies for Mind, Heart & Soul" by Karen Frazier

- **Overview**: This guide details how to use crystals for healing, energy work, and magical practice. It covers over 200 crystals, their properties, and their uses in various spells and rituals.
- **Why Read**: Offers detailed information on Yule-relevant crystals like garnet, snowflake obsidian, and clear quartz, providing inspiration for incorporating them into your winter rituals.

8. "Cunningham's Encyclopedia of Magical Herbs" by Scott Cunningham

- **Overview**: A comprehensive guide to the magical properties of herbs, including correspondences and practical uses in spells, charms, and rituals.
- **Why Read**: An essential reference for using herbs in Yule spells, such as rosemary, pine, cinnamon, and holly. Provides detailed instructions for creating herbal charms, incense, and more.

9. "The Modern Witchcraft Guide to the Wheel of the Year: From Samhain to Yule, Your Guide to the Wiccan Holidays" by Judy Ann Nock

- **Overview**: Nock provides an in-depth exploration of each sabbat in the Wheel of the Year, with an entire chapter dedicated to Yule. This book includes rituals, crafts, and spells tailored to each season.
- **Why Read**: It provides a modern take on celebrating Yule, offering practical suggestions for enhancing your solstice magic.

Articles

Articles provide quick, focused insights into specific aspects of Yule magic. Here are some recommended articles for deepening your understanding of Yule practices.

1. "Yule: The Winter Solstice" on The White Goddess

- **Overview**: This online article explores the history, folklore, and modern-day practices associated with Yule. It includes information on traditional Yule symbols, herbs, and crystals.
- **Why Read**: Offers a quick, yet comprehensive overview of Yule, ideal for those seeking inspiration for their celebrations and spellwork.

2. "Yule Traditions: Bringing Light to the Darkest Night" on Learn Religions

- **Overview**: A detailed article covering various Yule traditions, including the Yule log, greenery, and symbolic foods. It also provides suggestions for family-friendly Yule activities and rituals.
- **Why Read**: This article is helpful for understanding the cultural and symbolic aspects of Yule, which you can incorporate into your seasonal spellwork.

3. "Moon Phases and Their Magic" on Llewellyn Worldwide

- **Overview**: An article that explains the magical energies of each moon phase and how to align spellwork with the lunar cycle.
- **Why Read**: A valuable reference when using the moon phase calendar in your Yule rituals, helping you choose the right timing for your magical workings.

Websites

The internet is full of valuable resources for learning about Yule and other magical practices. The following websites offer articles, guides, and forums for continued study.

1. Llewellyn Worldwide (www.llewellyn.com)

- **Overview**: Llewellyn Worldwide is a leading publisher of books on magic, witchcraft, and paganism. Their website offers a vast library of articles, seasonal rituals, and guides to various magical practices, including Yule.
- **Why Visit**: A trusted source for quality content on Yule and other aspects of the magical arts. Their annual "Llewellyn's Sabbats Almanac" is also a valuable tool for planning your seasonal spellwork.

2. The White Goddess (www.thewhitegoddess.co.uk)

- **Overview**: A comprehensive online resource covering pagan festivals, mythology, magical correspondences, and rituals. The Yule section offers detailed information on traditions, symbols, and spellwork associated with the season.
- **Why Visit**: A treasure trove of information for both beginner and advanced practitioners, with correspondences and practical guides tailored to each sabbat.

3. Learn Religions: Paganism/Wicca (www.learnreligions.com/paganism-wicca-4684809)

- **Overview**: Learn Religions provides a wealth of articles on various aspects of paganism, Wicca, and witchcraft. The Yule section offers detailed guides on Yule traditions, rituals, and correspondences.

- **Why Visit**: Offers well-researched and easily digestible articles that cater to all levels of practitioners, making it a go-to resource for exploring the lore and practices of Yule.

4. Witchvox (www.witchvox.com)

- **Overview**: An online community and resource hub for pagans, witches, and Wiccans. The site offers articles, essays, and guides on a wide range of topics, including Yule celebrations and magical practices.
- **Why Visit**: A valuable platform for connecting with the global pagan community and exploring diverse perspectives on Yule and spellwork.

5. Patheos Pagan (www.patheos.com/pagan)

- **Overview**: Patheos Pagan features blogs, articles, and resources written by various authors within the pagan community. It includes content on sabbats, rituals, and personal experiences with Yule.
- **Why Visit**: Provides a diverse array of viewpoints and insights into modern Yule practices, allowing you to explore different ways to incorporate the season's magic into your life.

Conclusion

This collection of recommended books, articles, and websites provides a wealth of knowledge for those looking to deepen their understanding of Yule and enhance their magical practice. By exploring these resources, you can gain a richer appreciation of the season's traditions, expand your spellcraft repertoire, and connect with the global community of magical practitioners.

Message from the Author:

I hope you enjoyed this book, I love astrology and knew there was not a book such as this out on the shelf. I love metaphysical items as well. Please check out my other books:

-Life of Government Benefits

-My life of Hell

-My life with Hydrocephalus

-Red Sky

-World Domination:Woman's rule

-World Domination:Woman's Rule 2: The War

-Life and Banishment of Apophis: book 1

-The Kidney Friendly Diet

-The Ultimate Hemp Cookbook

-Creating a Dispensary(legally)

-Cleanliness throughout life: the importance of showering from childhood to adulthood.

-Strong Roots: The Risks of Overcoddling children

-Hemp Horoscopes: Cosmic Insights and Earthly Healing

- Celestial Hemp Navigating the Zodiac: Through the Green Cosmos

-Astrological Hemp: Aligning The Stars with Earth's Ancient Herb

-The Astrological Guide to Hemp: Stars, Signs, and Sacred Leaves

-Green Growth: Innovative Marketing Strategies for your Hemp Products and Dispensary

-Cosmic Cannabis

-Astrological Munchies

-Henry The Hemp

-Zodiacal Roots: The Astrological Soul Of Hemp

- **Green Constellations: Intersection of Hemp and Zodiac**

-Hemp in The Houses: An astrological Adventure Through The Cannabis Galaxy

-Galactic Ganja Guide

Heavenly Hemp

Zodiac Leaves

Doctor Who Astrology

Cannastrology

Stellar Satvias and Cosmic Indicas

Celestial Cannabis: A Zodiac Journey

AstroHerbology: The Sky and The Soil: Volume 1

AstroHerbology:Celestial Cannabis:Volume 2

Cosmic Cannabis Cultivation

The Starry Guide to Herbal Harmony: Volume 1

The Starry Guide to Herbal Harmony: Cannabis Universe: Volume 2

Yugioh Astrology: Astrological Guide to Deck, Duels and more

Nightmare Mansion: Echoes of The Abyss

Nightmare Mansion 2: Legacy of Shadows

Nightmare Mansion 3: Shadows of the Forgotten

Nightmare Mansion 4: Echoes of the Damned

The Life and Banishment of Apophis: Book 2

Nightmare Mansion: Halls of Despair

Healing with Herb: Cannabis and Hydrocephalus

Planetary Pot: Aligning with Astrological Herbs: Volume 1

Fast Track to Freedom: 30 Days to Financial Independence Using AI, Assets, and Agile Hustles

Cosmic Hemp Pathways

How to Become Financially Free in 30 Days: 10,000 Paths to Prosperity

Zodiacal Herbage: Astrological Insights: Volume 1

Nightmare Mansion: Whispers in the Walls

The Daleks Invade Atlantis

Henry the hemp and Hydrocephalus

10X The Kidney Friendly Diet

Cannabis Universe: Adult coloring book

Hemp Astrology: The Healing Power of the Stars

Zodiacal Herbage: Astrological Insights: Cannabis Universe: Volume 2

Planetary Pot: Aligning with Astrological Herbs: Cannabis Universes: Volume 2

Doctor Who Meets the Replicators and SG-1: The Ultimate Battle for Survival

Nightmare Mansion: Curse of the Blood Moon

The Celestial Stoner: A Guide to the Zodiac

Cosmic Pleasures: Sex Toy Astrology for Every Sign

Hydrocephalus Astrology: Navigating the Stars and Healing Waters

Lapis and the Mischievous Chocolate Bar

Celestial Positions: Sexual Astrology for Every Sign

Apophis's Shadow Work Journal: : A Journey of Self-Discovery and Healing

Kinky Cosmos: Sexual Kink Astrology for Every Sign

Digital Cosmos: The Astrological Digimon Compendium

Stellar Seeds: The Cosmic Guide to Growing with Astrology

Apophis's Daily Gratitude Journal

Cat Astrology: Feline Mysteries of the Cosmos

The Cosmic Kama Sutra: An Astrological Guide to Sexual Positions

Unleash Your Potential: A Guided Journal Powered by AI Insights

Whispers of the Enchanted Grove

Cosmic Pleasures: An Astrological Guide to Sexual Kinks

369, 12 Manifestation Journal

Whisper of the nocturne journal(blank journal for writing or drawing)

The Boogey Book

Locked In Reflection: A Chastity Journey Through Locktober

Generating Wealth Quickly:

How to Generate $100,000 in 24 Hours

Star Magic: Harness the Power of the Universe

The Flatulence Chronicles: A Fart Journal for Self-Discovery

The Doctor and The Death Moth

Seize the Day: A Personal Seizure Tracking Journal

The Ultimate Boogeyman Safari: A Journey into the Boogie World and Beyond

Whispers of Samhain: 1,000 Spells of Love, Luck, and Lunar Magic: Samhain Spell Book

Apophis's guides:

Witch's Spellbook Crafting Guide for Halloween

If you want solar for your home go here: https://www.harborso-lar.live/apophisenterprises/

Get Some Tarot cards: https://www.makeplayingcards.com/sell/
apophis-occult-shop

<u>Get some shirts: https://www.bonfire.com/store/apophis-shirt-emporium/</u>

Instagrams:
@apophis_enterprises,
@apophisbookemporium,
@apophisscardshop
Twitter: @apophisenterpr1
 Tiktok:@apophisenterprise
Youtube: @sg1fan23477, @FiresideRetreatKingdom

Podcast: Apophis Chat Zone: https://open.spotify.com/show/
5zXbrCLEV2xzCp8ybrfHsk?si=fb4d4fdbdce44dec

Newsletter: https://apophiss-newsletter-27c897.beehiiv.com/